On Aggression and Violence

On Aggression and Violence

An Analytic Perspective

Richard Mizen
and
Mark Morris

First published 2007 by
PALGRAVE MACMILLAN
Houndmills, Basingstoke, Hampshire RG21 6XS and
175 Fifth Avenue, New York, N.Y. 10010
Companies and representatives throughout the world

PALGRAVE MACMILLAN is the global academic imprint of the Palgrave
Macmillan division of St. Martin's Press, LLC and of Palgrave Macmillan Ltd.
Macmillan® is a registered trademark in the United States, United Kingdom
and other countries. Palgrave is a registered trademark in the European
Union and other countries.

ISBN-13: 978-1-4039-0218-4
ISBN-10: 1-4039-0218-6

This book is printed on paper suitable for recycling and
made from fully managed and sustained forest sources.

A catalogue record for this book is available from the British Library.

Library of Congress Cataloging-in-Publication Data

A catalog record for this book is available from the Library of Congress

10   9   8   7   6   5   4   3   2   1
16   15   14   13   12   11   10   09   08   07

Printed and bound in China

Contents

Acknowledgements

Some passages in Chapters 1 and 4 have previously been included in a paper published in the *Journal of Analytic Psychology*. The authors are grateful to the editors of the above journal for giving their permission for this material to be included in this book.

The authors would also like to thank Richard Carvalho for kindly commenting upon an earlier draft of Chapters 6 and 7, but the views expressed herein are entirely the responsibility of Richard Mizen and Mark Morris.

Authors' Note

Before we proceed, some initial clarification regarding our use of words and concepts may be helpful when reading this book.

We have found it useful to make a distinction, both clinically and theoretically between imaginative activity, which is conscious and imaginative activity that is unconscious. To distinguish these we have adopted Susan Isaacs' alternative spellings; 'fantasy' to refer to conscious imaginative activity, and 'phantasy' to refer to unconscious imaginative activity (Isaacs 1952). We have not addressed the way in which Isaacs uses the latter spelling to imply organized and perhaps innate patterns of mentation and our usage is limited to the descriptive.

What we mean by imaginative activity and especially the extent to which it involves maps generated at differing levels of neurological functioning will be gone into in due course, especially in Chapters 6 and 7. Suffice to say here that the generation of images is an important component part of mentation; neurological maps or images both structure mentation and constitute mental contents. These images include visio-spatial images but are not confined to them. This is important because human beings privilege visio-spatial imagery and visual perception within a particular part of the light spectrum. In consequence of this our mental constructions are both directly and indirectly dependent upon the sensory apparatus available and the ways in which we favour vision over other sensory media. We can imagine that Martians perhaps privilege some other sensory medium and live in a world that is differently constructed; certainly animals other than humans do so to a greater or lesser extent.

Thus many but not all of the mental concepts that we use for thinking, in an analogous way are based upon this. Concepts such as 'projection/introjection', 'empathy', 'seeing another's point of view', 'consideration' (literally 'with the stars') all appeal to subtle and not so subtle visio-spatial analogies. As Bion has noted, this constitutes a hidden prejudice, which may distort our capacity to formulate concepts. Auditory analogies such as harmony and dissonance may have some currency but these are few compared to the visio-spatial ones.

We also wish to comment upon our use of the words 'feeling', 'emotions' and 'affects'. To take the last first, our use of 'affect' is intended as an umbrella term which includes emotions and feelings. Damasio has located the physiological, and perhaps evolutionary, origin of these in the body's self-regulatory mechanisms including the autoimmune system. It is to be doubted whether or not one can usefully consider immune responses, say to invasive organisms as an affective experience, so perhaps 'affects' might reasonably be limited to those areas of experience, which are *capable* of being made conscious even if they are not necessarily. Nearly a century ago, Jung (1921) distinguished emotion and feeling, proposing that the latter is a more psychologically differentiated version of the former. Emotion is more likely to involve a visceral experience compared to feeling. It might be said, for example, that we have feelings, but emotions have us. Jung proposed that emotion resided more thoroughly in the physiological realm and feeling in the psychological. This is a distinction, which more recent theorists have come to quite independently (Damasio 1999; Panksepp 1998) and it is one that we in consequence have adopted.

Some clarification of the use of the word 'psychotic' may be helpful also. Contemporary psychiatry has emphasized form over content and so psychiatric practice and theory has tended to describe phenomenologically, the patterns of delusion, morbid ideas and functional impairment that characterize what are believed to constitute psychiatric syndromes such as schizophrenia, manic depression and so on. Various psychiatric theories have been proposed, mostly of a static mechanistic kind, to account for these phenomena. This may be contrasted with analytic theory, which has emphasized content. From this perspective, 'psychosis' refers not to visible signs and symptoms, but to underlying dynamic mental states. Thus the psychotic state of mind in its simplest form is one in thrall, to a greater or lesser extent, to an overwhelming fear of annihilation (as opposed to neurosis where the fear is 'only' of being badly hurt). Discernible symptoms are the consequence of the various ways in which the mind seeks to protect itself from this over-whelming anxiety although it is true that these distorting meas-ures (which may also commonly be described as 'psychotic' but in reality are psychotic *defences* and involve the denial of real-ity, especially psychic reality), while protecting in the short term, often have the consequence of exacerbating anxiety in the longer term. A body analogy here might be the inflammatory response.

Finally, we wish briefly to mention the subject of confiden-tiality. For anyone writing about matters, which pertain to passionate, hot feelings such as aggression or sexuality, the pub-lication of case material can be extraordinarily exposing even where attempts have been made to disguise material and preserve anonymity. Certainly the transference implications of an analyst or therapist using a patient's material cannot be over-looked even after the successful termination of a completed analysis or therapy. With more disturbed or incarcerated patients, there is also the question of informed consent and of course in many of the situations to which we will here refer not much in the way of hopeful or remedial outcome to treatment is either expected or likely. Publication is inevitably an intrusive and affecting matter, even after an analysis or therapy is over and the material has been thoroughly worked through. The difficulties that arise from this are not to be underestimated, there-fore. One solution might be to eschew clinical material, but this seems to us to leave something so abstract and divested of ordi-nary clinical experience as to seriously undermine its usefulness. The difficulties in publication especially of horrifying, shocking and painful material may thus actively discourage discussion within this area. But Britton has written sensitively not only about problems of publication but also of analysts' responsibil-ity to publish and share ideas and we believe that aggression and violence are areas that badly need consideration from an ana-lytic perspective (Britton 1998).

While aware that it is not an entirely satisfactory solution we have therefore adopted the following strategy. We have used some actual cases, albeit presented in an anonymous form to protect patients' identities, and would like to thank the patients who have generously given permission for us to use their material. We have, however, also created fictional cases for the purposes of illustration, which we believe accurately, represent typical clinical situations with which we are familiar. As an added measure to protect the confidentiality of patients, we have not indicated which cases are real and which are fictional.

Preface

The late Donald Meltzer wrote an important paper called 'The problem of violence' (Meltzer 1986); had he not already used that title we would have done so. It perhaps more accurately than our own, acknowledges violence as difficult to understand, even mysterious and as presenting immediate and pressing difficulties for individuals and for society as well as clinically and for theoretical conceptualization.

Our attempt to explore this subject is predicated upon the idea that violence needs to be differentiated from aggression, both theoretically and clinically and our theorizing is useful only insofar as it helps us to make this distinction clinically; as we shall see it is in the nature of violence and aggression that this is no easy task. We have also attempted to locate aggression in a developmental progression, in particular emphasizing the development of mind, separation, individuation, the capacity for thinking and especially thinking about feeling.

The function of affects, including those that fall within the category of 'aggression', has been variously defined but from at least the time of the Enlightenment, the emphasis has been upon the extent to which they are felt to be unfortunate vestiges of either a primitive, fallen or animal past which distort human perception and subvert rationality; anxiety generated by and about aggression has played no small part in this. The tendency has been to divide affects into legitimate and illegitimate categories. The 'legitimate' have been seen as evidence of man's uniquely elevated position in a hierarchy of creation (regardless of whether this is defined in religious or purely secular terms), while 'illegitimate' affects, evidence of humankind's irredeemably base nature. From the perspective of 'rational' thought, both have been treated with suspicion and emotions, for the most part, have been seen as needing mastering, eradicating or as unworthy of or inaccessible to scientific investigation.

More recently, however, researchers and theoreticians in the human sciences have begun to consider the extent to which affects may be considered as functional. To give a recent example, the neurologist Damasio has characterized the function of affects as in the service of promoting homeostasis both physiological and psychological (Damasio 2004). He suggests that at the same time as allowing evaluation of objects in an organism's environment based on a multiplicity of factors which could not be processed quickly, cognitively, affects alert living beings to threats or deficits which affect internal and external homeostasis organized around optimal levels of functioning or conditions which are optimal for the functioning of the organism. By means of their aversive and appetitive, unpleasurable and pleasurable qualities, affects motivate organisms to behaviours and activities which are likely to restore homeostasis; at the simplest level feeding, drinking, seeking shelter or safety are examples of this.

In our view there is much to be said for this conception but we feel that it lacks an important dimension that one might call mental or at least proto-mental, if contrasted with the more mechanistic cause and effect processes described by Damasio. We think that one might more accurately say that affects orientate the organism, say the self, to its environment and in particular to objects in its environment (and we will see in Chapter 6 that these objects include aspects internal to the organism or to the self, including internal objects). Trying to avoid being anthropomorphic or imply a capacity for mentation which does not exist, one might say that affects enable a sense to arise, in all living things in which they can be shown to be present of 'what is this object for me?'. To claim this as a conscious sense or even a matter that requires any sort of self-awareness is to claim far too much. Nonetheless it may be possible to begin to understand how mentation, consciousness and meaning derived from a capacity for self-reflection may have at their base, primitive physiological systems which function to orientate an organism to its world both internal and external (Panksepp 1998).

From this perspective aggression, we suggest, is neutral; it is merely a component part of the affective repertoire with which all human beings are endowed, for use, misuse or abuse according to circumstance. This may be complicated by other affective elements and involve the qualification and balancing of competing affective responses; 'there are similarities between us but we are different', 'I want it, but not at any price', 'love the sinner, hate the sin' and so on. This becomes increasingly complex and nuanced even when it involves fixed behavioural responses contingent upon affects and more complex still where impulses towards behavioural patterns are of a kind that are available to psychological modification. Finally there is affective experience that is confined to a predominantly psychological, imaginal realm. We will consider some of the mechanisms for these in Chapter 6.

Only lately has it become possible to propose models that link bodily functioning to truly psychological processes without depriving affects of their motivational force in the way that, for example, the James-Lange theory did. The tendency has always been to either treat psychological processes as though they are epiphenomenal physical processes or construct variations on the Cartesian, mind/body split, 'homunculus' theme. As we will also see in Chapter 6, this has had consequences for the development of mind and self-consciousness.

These matters are important in understanding violence, because while aggression is capable of integration and indeed plays a necessary part in the processes of integration and the development of self-consciousness, it is also, in the absence or removal of the necessary provision required for integration, subject to disintegration. It is in this, and especially the violating subjective experience that it engenders that we have located the phenomenon of violence. In our view while one can speak of aggressive behaviour that is mindless, violence is a psychological phenomenon, with behavioural consequences, not behaviour with psychological consequences. Despite the currency afforded the cliché 'mindless violence' we contend that violence is not mindless; on the contrary it represents the evacuation or ablation of mind and in this way provides useful evidence for understanding the nature and qualities, which constitute 'mind'. What is more, violence is neither inevitable nor innate and no more a part of the human condition than, say starvation, even if the problems of eradication seem at times to be as insuperable, if not more so.

Aggression, on the other hand, is innate even if its appearance and form are dictated by circumstance, internal and external, the combination of these and the extent to which the categories internal and external are not absolute. It is the disavowal of aggression, in one form or another, that gives rise to violence which is paradoxically a testament to the possession of a mind, albeit a mind or part of a mind that has been 'got rid of' because it felt to be too painful to bear.

1 The Semiotics of Aggression and Violence

The Concepts of Violence and Aggression in Context

A 22-year-old football supporter, out with friends, jeers at fans of an opposing team in a pub. A scuffle ensues, the two groups are ejected from the pub and there is a fist-fight on the pavement. The 22-year-old violently attacks the largest member of the opposing group, breaking his jaw and kicking and punching him as he falls. As police sirens are heard, both groups combine to pull him away. The man is arrested, and following conviction, he reports that every week he goes looking for a fight; the football is secondary.

A 35-year-old woman with two young children, who has been married for seven years, is regularly being beaten up by her husband during their arguments, often requiring hospital treatment. One evening, several weeks after a further severe assault, she learns of yet another infidelity, and instead of staying, she bundles the sleeping children into the car and tries to drive away. Her husband stands in the way, jeering and taunting her; she accelerates, hits him with the car and drives over him.

    During a bank robbery by terrorists raising funds, police arrive, preventing their planned escape; hostages are taken and threatened with death if the terrorists are not allowed to leave. There is a standoff that ends when soldiers assault the bank, release the hostages and kill all of the terrorists who do not immediately surrender.

1

Aggression and violence are ubiquitous, generating fervent debate concerning their legitimacy or illegitimacy, and the extent to which they constitute a threat either to society or the individual. Unremarked upon, however, is the assumption that there is agreement about their nature, albeit some disagreement about their origins, so their actual qualities are rarely considered. It is our intention to try to do this, albeit from the limited perspective of psychoanalysis, its derivatives and some of the associated disciplines upon which it draws. Analysis does not offer a comprehensive or fully formed treatment of the subject, but it does have important insights to contribute to a fuller understanding, and we will try to place these in context. Although it is not our intention to produce a critique of the analytic literature and we make no claims to comprehensiveness, we hope to consider the literature critically and do justice to the main analytic arguments.

The analytic literature on the subject is vast and also somewhat inaccessible because violence and aggression have most often been addressed as matters associated with some other topic. This commenced with Freud, who only considered aggression in passing and at first unwillingly. Only reluctantly was he later forced to more fully consider aggression as the limitations of his first metapsychological model became clear and needed revising in order to accommodate his developing clinical experience.

Freud's reluctance to relinquish the unique place he accorded sexuality led to the downplaying of the genetic role of aggression in his theorizing, and this has only partly been remedied since. So the first problem has been the absence of a coherent and systematic analytic examination of aggression comparable, for example, with his analysis of sexuality in *Three Essays on Sexuality* (1905).

A further problem perhaps arising from the first is the confusion that reigns in relation to matters of definition, although of course this is a problem in analytic writing, thinking and communication generally. Not only does there exist a Tower of Babel in the profusion of analytical models and technical languages used by various analytic 'schools', but even more confusingly there is often a profusion and diversity of *meaning* attributed to particular words.

So one of our main tasks is to consider definition: what do we mean when we use, the words 'aggression' and 'violence' and what are the implications thereby entailed? Just to take the words 'aggression' and 'violence'; frequently they are erroneously treated as though they are synonymous or inter-changeable. If they are not, then how are they related?

A third problem relates to aggression and violence as concrete acts or bodily action compared with phenomena occupying the mental realm, the world of imagination. What is the relation between murderous imaginings and a murderous assault? In due course we will consider the extent to which violent behaviours can be linked to particular states of mind and the relationships between these, but at this juncture we want to draw attention to the ease with which aggression and violence may be confused in different experiential worlds.

A further cautionary note concerns the fact that it is impossible to have a purely psychological theory of aggression or violence. A comprehensive understanding must include psychological, physiological, affective and cognitive contributing elements. Then there is the question of context. In practice, aggression and violence may only be understood in their social and cultural milieu so that economic, political, ethical, moral and religious factors play their part even where these are obscure or ambiguous in terms of cause and effect. Any understanding, which does not acknowledge these, is flawed and inadequate; where we are not explicitly addressing these factors their importance is nonetheless not to be disregarded.

The Analytic Debate on the Origins of Aggression and Violence

The so-called 'Controversial Discussions' of the British Psychoanalytic Society (King & Steiner 1991), took as one of their central issues for debate the question of whether aggression, destructiveness and violence are instinctual or acquired. Is the aggression observed in infants a response to failures in the environment, for example, the frustration of a baby's wish for a feed, or does aggression have an innate origin, which precedes, amplifies or even produces a sense of environmental insult? Put slightly differently, does the baby make attacks upon the mother associated with rage at frustration or is there an inbuilt drive to separateness and individuality, which is nonetheless capable of distortion and expression in pathological ways?

Since the time of the original debate there has been a tendency for these positions to become polarized, not least because of their internal political significance. Theoretical positions about the nature of aggression, destructiveness and violence have become defining characteristics of the identity of the analytic schools and as a result, ideas about the nature, origins and vicissitudes of aggression, destructiveness and violence have become difficult to discuss as issues in their own right. The debate has been conducted as though it is about which account is true, and this has had a tendency to paralyse further thinking even if, because the two broad positions on the nature of aggression are pretty much irreducible and encapsulate radically different attitudes to human nature, they have been developed to a high degree.

These political aspects have dogged and continue to dog analytic discourse. The division of psychoanalysis into rivalrous schools and traditions, which are contemptuous of their analytic confreres, have their own history and gather about themselves their own acolytes, disciples and protagonists. In analytic circles, Whitehead's axiom that any science that cannot forget its founding fathers is moribund, is notable only to the extent that it is ignored and much of the criticism which has often been unfairly levelled at analytic theories has been based on analysis' apparent incapacity not to develop quasi-religious traditions and articles of faith. To many outsiders these factors undermine any claims that it may have to scientific or intellectual rigour.

The development of a coherent account has thus been difficult for 'political' reasons but this has been compounded by the paradoxical and fragmentary nature of the literature. Fragmentary because analytic researchers working with manifestly aggressive and violent people have tended to be practitioners in rather isolated or unusual settings, for example, Hyatt-Williams's work with murderers at Wormwood Scrubbs Prison (Hyatt-Williams 1998); paradoxical because at the same time, Kleinian practitioners, have placed aggression, destructiveness and violence at the centre of their understanding of even their most timid patients. The imaginal world of the murderousness of ordinary men and women able to afford private psychoanalysis has been extensively explored both clinically and in the literature. The same cannot be said for the murderousness of actual murderers and perpetrators of violence, with consequent neglect of the avenues of enquiry which might weave together these two divergent areas of study.

The Semantics of Aggression and Violence

A 30-year-old child psychotherapist trainee in analysis is conscientious in paying her monthly analytic bills on time, but the analyst becomes aware of a sense of personal guilt at charging this woman who after all has small children. Reflecting on this, she notices that while there is no explicit protest about the level of fee, in the days following paying the bill the patient makes a seemingly unrelated comment about money; a car bill that is stretching the family, a boiler in the house that is on the blink and will need to be replaced. The analyst concludes that her own feeling of guilt is a projective identificatory communication from the patient that she resents the level of analytic fee. The analyst further wonders whether the patient might be challenging the value for money that she is getting or whether she is being critical of her technique or the progress of the analysis. Currently, the patient would be mortified to think that she was being so disrespectful to her analyst, so the hypothesis cannot yet be formulated, but the analyst makes a mental note.

If uninformed criticism of Freud contends that his theories and speculations are 'castles in the air', serious study shows the extent to which in reality they are firmly rooted in clinical experience. Historically his primary preoccupation was with disease and its cure and it was from this perspective that he developed his theories of general psychology. This has had far-reaching consequences because it placed him in the position where he tended to extrapolate from the pathological to the normal, rather than the other way around. To take the concept of projection, for example; over time projection came to be seen not only as defensive, as originally conceived, but also as an ordinary mental process in the service of development and normal functioning. In the same way, the related concept of projective identification accrued qualifying notations such as 'excessive' or 'normal' in order to differentiate pathological and evacuatory processes of projection and identification on the one hand and a normal means of unconscious communication on the other.

Subsequent analysts have tended to follow Freud's lead, and for this historical reason, analytic metapsychological theoretical frames in large part extrapolate from the pathological to the normal. When we come to consider aggression it is pathological manifestations such as violence that serve as the touchstone for theorizing about it, and accounts of aggression and normal development tend to be constructed as back-formations, from theories of the pathological.

In order to reconsider this, we think that it is necessary to explicitly decouple the words 'aggression' and 'violence' and consider the ways in which they are essentially different, if related, phenomena.

Consider the word 'violence': common conceptions of violence include both the mental and the physical – that which is 'internal' and imaginary and that which is 'concrete' and exists in the external world. This provides fertile ground for muddle to arise. In addition, confusions arise because of the conflation and confusion of meaning that can come to exist between associated words. Consulting a thesaurus about the word 'violent', we are offered as alternatives 'aggressive', 'brutal', 'cruel', 'sadistic', 'vicious' and so on. In the analytic literature, as elsewhere, these words may be used interchangeably or as though they are synonymous even though such assumptions are misleading and mask important differences. There are many examples of this; to cite two, Perelberg (1999) uses 'violence' interchangeably with 'aggression' as does de Zulueta (1993), even though in the latter case she notes the problem but then goes on to repeat it.

If we take the word 'brutal', for example, literally 'animal like' and compare it with say 'sadism' we can see that although the words are related and may share a degree of overlap of meaning there are also important differences. Allowing for variations in personal understanding of the meaning of these words we can, for example, make an argument that sadism requires a different quality of active splitting, projection and identification on the part of a perpetrator in relation to the victim, from brutality. In sadism the perpetrator actively invests, in phantasy (or indeed in fantasy), an unwanted, pained or terrified part of him or her self in the victim.

By contrast, in brutality the splitting may be more a matter of cutting off from the plight of the person who is subject to the violence, cruelty or pain. This seems to be the case, for example, in those societies caught up in political conflict or civil war, where one part of a population attacks another weaker part.

No doubt some people are drawn to perpetrating acts of violence out of the opportunity it affords them to gain sexualized satisfaction by divesting themselves of unwanted parts of themselves and projecting them into the powerless and vulnerable other. Fighting against 'the enemy' 'justifies' and rationalizes this. More widespread must be the extent to which people collaborate or participate in acts of violence out of anxiety about the consequences of not participating, of then becoming identified with the 'enemy' and finding themselves cast into the position of powerless victim. Rationalizations may then be secondary. Such a position does not involve the same kind of splitting and projective identification but rather the ability to split off from the capacity to comprehend and identify with the people attacked, as fellow human beings.

Presumably it is an intuitive understanding of the apparent passivity and unselfconsciousness of the actions, which is drawn upon for the purposes of the analogy implicit in the word 'brutality'. From this point of view the semiotic significance of the word is more likely to be associated with animals such as cattle, rather than with predatory animals such as lions and tigers even if it is the latter which are in many ways more obviously aggressive; the 'brutality' involves then a quality of mindlessness too.

By extension it is only a matter of quantity and degree that differentiates the brutality of the concentration camp guard, who is 'only' indifferent to the plight of the inmates or treats their plight, as it impacts on him or her, merely as an irritant, from the rest of us, who turn away from the scenes of death or unbearable suffering which appear in our newspapers or on our television screens and seek relief in mundane chores.

Tellingly there is a greater implicit awareness of these distinctions than might at first be thought. No predatory animal, or non-predatory animal defending itself aggressively, is likely to have even its most distressing, aggressive actions described as 'violent'. Even where banal anthropomorphism leads to the characterization of a cat playing (if we understanding play as 'learning work') with its prey as being called 'cruel', moral opprobrium is unlikely to be evoked.

The 80-year-old retired baker who has shocked his grand-children by recounting a near execution situation in his wartime memories is discussing the situation later with his son. He had been disturbed by the reaction of his grandchildren, and is reflecting that he had never thought of it before, but it had been terrible. Perhaps that was why he tried not to think about it. He tried to explain to his son that while a soldier in combat, killing people was his job, and if he did not do his job well, he or his friends might be killed. You had to think about the best, most efficient and safest way of doing it, but beyond that you did not think about it at all.

Problems of Definition and Conceptualization

As we have noted, a problem in both conceptualizing and defining aggression and violence is the semantic confusion that the words generate. At a simple level the word 'violence', for example, has become so saturated with pejorative connotations that it now borders upon being used as a swear word or term of abuse; certainly it is most often used to convey implicit disapproval of whatever it is being described as violent. This prejudices and poses an obstacle to any consideration of the matter. Often, analytic usage is not exempt from this so that the word 'violence' may be of no more use analytically than any other expression of preference or prejudice, undermining the attempt to understand the nature or meaning of violence.

Such problems are compounded where confusion arises out of the conflation of psychological theories with theories about behaviour. Often, theories and models of violence (and of aggression), which purport to be psychological, have very little psychology in them, but are in fact descriptions of, or theories about, behaviour. Psychological theories, theories assuming at least a significant place for mentation and mental experience, inevitably draw upon behavioural phenomena as a source of data. A hazard, however, is to confuse the two which brings with it the risk of treating disparate matters as though they are identical so that important differences between associated phenomena are lost. The risk is that the relation between behaviour and mental states are treated as though they were self-evident, when they are not and in reality may be obscure.

An example of this is the way that sexual legal offences are violent. Threat or coercion may be employed although little or no physical force is used; in strictly physical terms it is possible that a violent act of rape may be indistinguishable from consensual intercourse. Nonetheless the emotional tone of the interaction may make it quite clear that it is violent. In English law, for example, the threat to strike somebody constitutes an offence of assault as much as an actual blow. Alternatively the ambiguity of an act can either generate misunderstanding or is capable of misinterpretation or distortion in order to avoid its psychological, social or legal consequences. Examples here might be the way in which questions of consent might be a central issue of proof in determining whether or not a given act of vaginal penetration is rape, or, in a medico-legal arena, how in one context what might be treatment, in another is assault.

Two elements related to violence produce particular difficulties; the involvement or otherwise of action and questions of motivation. In a 1998 paper, Glasser, for example, adopts a definition of violence provided by Walker in 1972:

> Violence involves the bodies of both perpetrator and victim and it may thus be defined as a bodily response with the intended infliction of bodily harm on another person   (Glasser 1998, p. 887).

Glasser emphasizes bodily activity, and it will be noted that this definition circumscribes distinctions in relation to the motivation of a perpetrator, invariably linking intention to bodily action. Glasser attempts to compensate for this by subdividing violence into 'sadistic violence' on the one hand and 'self-preservative violence' on the other. The former he considers pathological, the latter non-pathological patterns of behaviour; the fight/flight response identified by ethologists (Lorenz 1967). Unfortunately this then fails to distinguish any essential characteristic of violence *per se*. Walker's definition also limits violence to action, here defined as motor activity, which is itself a problematical definition, and this excludes the possibility of violence as an exclusively psychological phenomenon and has a tendency to obscure consideration of essential psychological factors.

In 'Towards Understanding Violence: The Use of the Body and the Role of the Father' (1999), Fonagy and Target make a causal link between violence (which they define as an attack on the body) in patients and violence that the patients themselves received as children. By way of definition they state '... that violence, [is] aggression directed at the body ...' (p. 53).

However, they later go on to note that not all people who are violent have themselves been the recipients of violence. In the light of their previous contention that violence is related to the violence (which is defined as directed at the *body*) that the violent person previously experienced, they seem rather stumped and leave the matter hanging in the air. Their definition, it should be noted, is one that has an attack upon the body as a defining characteristic.

The limitation of behavioural definitions emanates from the fact that the external appearance of behaviour may be deceptive or ambiguous, relative to the psychological state of the perpetrator or the recipient of the violence and especially to what the perpetrator imagines to be the mental state of the recipient, which, as we will show, is an essential aspect of violence. It also confines violence to (or identification with) an act and divorces it from (or even treats as non-existent) any underlying psychological state and disallows the possibility of violence confined to the mental sphere. It also sets aside the possibility of non-violent (that is, non-violent in the terms that we will describe) acts of aggression, which while behaviourally similar or even identical, may in reality have very different meanings.

Despite the discipline of Psychology, including the psychodynamic varieties, tending to privilege action and behaviour when attempting at definitions, in the ordinary course of things distinctions between aggression and violence are commonly drawn and intuitively understood. Lynn MacDonald in her book *1915: The Death of Innocence* reports the recollections of a soldier in the trenches:

> ... a man was hit ... by a sniper's bullet, and died ... The new second in command ... made both platoons file past the dead man, saying to each 'you must avenge this. You must kill two Germans for every one of our dead'. I said nothing, but felt outraged. The men evidently thought he was mad. The object of war, the aim of a battle, is not primarily to kill numbers of the enemy, but to defeat his forces in battle. The men resented the Major's tactless tactics. It was the mistaken psychology

of fire-eating blimps and it made the bloodshed of war evilly bloodier   (MacDonald 1997, p. 591).

In any case definitions which relate only to bodily action and set aside emotional and psychological aspects are little relied upon. In the case, for example, of somebody killing somebody else in a situation in which they had believed themselves threatened with death by the other person, treatment of the situation by the law is likely to be highly dependent both on the circumstances in which the event took place and also upon what is understood to be the states of mind of both the person who was killed and the person doing the killing. In law, such a situation would open a defence of 'self-defence' and so might not end in a conviction for murder or indeed any conviction at all. As we will argue it may make more sense to talk about the would-be killer's attack as being violent and paradoxically, the person who kills in self-defence, not violent but aggressive. A variation on this would be that the would-be killer's attack could be thought of as being murderous, but given the difference in the psychological motivation of the man who actually does the killing, that his attack is not murderous. Here it is the meaning of the act that is central rather than the act itself. The reasonableness of the fear of death would be important as would the reasonableness of the force used against the person offering the original threat.

Such equivocations have led to complex laws and the development of an extensive system of precedents in case law. So the killing (or indeed any other kind of hurting) of another person may be judged according to a range of criteria, which will determine both the seriousness of an offence and also the way in which an individual who has killed is dealt with by the judicial and penal system. Killing another person may not be considered culpable at all if there is only an *actus reus* (guilty act) but no *mens rea* (guilty mind), because both have to be proven for an individual to be found guilty of a crime. Equally if a killing is considered justified, for example, in self-defence or in some circumstances where it is held to be involuntary, such as in an accident, no criminal conviction can take place. It may be culpable, however, and open to a lesser charge of 'manslaughter' if the person did not intend the death, but was 'reckless' and it is considered that the death might reasonably have been predicted as a possible outcome of a particular action. If the person for some reason does not understand that the killing they have committed is 'wrong', by virtue of insanity or some other disability of mind, then again, there is no *mens rea* and they are not culpable, even if in such circumstances the state reserves the right, by other means to curtail the liberty of the person who has killed, for example, by incarcerating them in a mental hospital of one sort or another. Other considerations may enter in: for example, the intentional killing of an infant by its mother may result not in a charge of murder but one of 'infanticide', which reflects the Legislature's belief that *post partum*, a mother's mental equilibrium may be for a period disturbed by the birth (say post-natal depression) and that she cannot be held responsible in the normal way for her actions.

One could go on, but the point is that even in the relatively crude sphere of legal process there is a more or less complex framework within which questions of culpability, intentionality and guilt are measured against each other and these are essentially, psychological matters. Despite this, purportedly psychological theories often lack a truly psychological perspective, emphasizing instead behaviour. As we will see, therapists and analysts may also display this tendency, and this abjuring of the patient's mind is a common countertransference or even defensive reaction on the part of practitioners. It is also true, however, as already noted that this complexity and the potential for confusion and conflation is something that readily lends itself to dissembling and deceits, conscious or unconscious and including self-deception; in practice, this is a matter which will be of considerable importance to clinicians in the therapeutic or analytic situation when considering their patients' material.

This leads us on to definitions, which are essentially psychological and motivational ones. Here the opposite problem pertains so that it becomes easy to underplay the consequences of violence or even to overlook them altogether; explanations may become banal or even *apologiae*. This is a common criticism levelled at people engaged in academic and clinical work in this field.

The difficulty in this case, is of holding together the mind of both subject and object of, for example, perpetrator and victim. This is especially difficult if the same person has been a 'perpetrator' at one time or in one frame of mind, and a 'victim' at another. Anne Alvarez attributes this to:

> ... such a split countertransference ..., such a split reaction ..., that at one moment you are upset on their behalf and sympathetic because they have been terribly abused as children themselves, and the next minute you are loathing them for what they are doing ...   (Alvarez 1997, p. 431).

This experience is likely to be a familiar one to those who have worked with people who are violent (including the abusers of children, to whom she is referring here), and Alvarez's attribution of splitting may be accurate, presumably as a defence against the painful feelings generated in the observer; or, as we will argue, it may be that the construct 'splitting' is over-extended in this case; we will return to this below. Ideally what is required is something like a 'cubist' picture, presenting manifest and obscure aspects on a single plane. Unfortunately the extent to which this may be damaging to ordinary appearances may be fatal.

The problems with these definitions are essentially qualitative in nature. One writer who has attempted to get around this is Meltzer, who proposes a concept of violence as violation (Meltzer 1986), which spans (but may not necessarily include) both the physical and the psychic by means of its appeal to subjective experience. Whatever the advantages of this approach from a qualitative point of view, it may throw up problems related to quantity, particularly in valuing the 'seriousness' of a given example of violence.

We will turn in due course to if and how much these matters may be reconciled. What we propose, however, is that the *ad hoc* development of analytic thinking on the subject of aggression and violence, subsidiary to its primary preoccupation with, for example, Eros, has led to an inadequate and rather piecemeal theorizing about aggression and violence. We will seek to disentangle the various strands of this and propose a model which understands aggression as a basic instinctual and affective component of the psyche/soma. We will consider the various related aggressive phenomena as varieties of aggression, which may or may not be capable of psychic integration, and failures of integration as the origin of pathology.

We have noted the problems that are involved not least the inexact not to say mercurial qualities of much of the language that is available to us to consider and conceptualize these matters. We have also noted the tendency towards polarization within the debate, which has led to the dichotomization of nature/nurture and environment/innate while at the same time implying the homogeneity of aggression/violence/destructiveness/sadism, despite the reality that they are heterogeneous, even if related, matters.

2 The Metapsychology of Aggression and Violence; Instinct, Development and Trauma

If it is true that analytic theory lacks comprehensive models of aggression and violence it is also true that analysts have created numerous partial accounts. To describe these would require several books and for this reason, if for no other, we are limiting ourselves to looking at two streams in relative detail: the development of Freud's ideas about aggression and the Kleinian development. We will touch on other models but have selected these two for fuller consideration because of their relative completeness, and the tensions that exist between them in their broad location of the origins of aggression in 'the environment' and in 'innate' factors, respectively. Of course we understand that this polarized attribution is in reality something of a caricature; nonetheless it contains enough truth for us to be able to use these approaches for our own purpose, which is to consider the contributions of these respective sources and how they interact. As we will see, the location of the source of aggression is important not only in the construction of theoretical models, but more importantly for how aggression and related phenomena are treated clinically.

Freud

Such has been the influence of psychoanalysis that it would be very difficult to understand contemporary concepts of aggression and violence, both analytic and non-analytic without reference to Freud. It is impossible, however, to talk about these influences as a heterogeneous whole because Freud's ideas are not themselves heterogeneous but changed and developed over time reflecting his changing emphases.

Two obvious examples of this are the way that his emphasis on sexuality colours analytic ideas about aggression and violence and how his extrapolation from the perspective of pathology colours psychoanalytic metapsychological concepts of general human psychology. Freud's great discovery was of the central place of sexuality in human psychological development and to place this in a dynamic, developmental schema. Pivotal in his understanding was the role of 'libido' and the infantile origins of mental structures growing out of the operations of the instincts, *ego* and *self-preservative*. Initially Freud thought about instinct as broadly analogous to 'drive' or 'urge', with the psychosomatic, biologically grounded connotations that contemporary usage implies, explicitly relegated to the background (1915). Only later was a more developed concept of instinct introduced, to include psychological, environmental and internal dimensions. In its original formulation instincts as components of 'libido' were conceived of as being fundamentally 'sexual' in character. Although divided into 'component instincts', and later 'ego instincts' and 'self-preservative instincts', the central, sexual character of the instincts was emphasized. This came to be something of an article of faith for Freud with important implications for the way in which Freud and subsequent analysts thought about aggression.

The fundamental dynamic in Freud's early model concerned psychic conflict between one group comprising of drives towards appetitive gratification on the one hand and self-preservative instincts on the other. Conflict was conceived to arise out of the clash between an instinctual drive towards pleasure and away from unpleasure and the need to accept the limitations imposed by reality; untrammelled hedonism, blind to external hazard threatens survival.

One implication of this is that if sexuality is *the* instinctual basis for the psyche, aggression must be merely an aspect of sexuality and a subordinate component part of it. Thus Freud's earliest references to aggression (1905) in *Three Essays on Sexuality* relate to aggression stirred up by the infant's attempts to control the object of his or her desire, and the conflict that this engenders; between the wish to achieve the object of desire and the anxiety engendered by the ruthless attainment of it.

Aggression is conceived of in terms of the infant's attempts at the sexual mastery of the object with hate and aggression arising where there is frustration in relation to the object that provides pleasure; the aggression has a force broadly consistent with the level or duration of the frustration.

> *As part of an infant observation project, the observer notices that a 10-month-old infant has a pattern of crying to get his mother's attention but that when she comes to pick him up, he pulls away. The mother then has to engage with the infant to get his attention, which is usually successful. When the mother is unable to respond to the infant's cry for attention fairly quickly, the infant's rejection of mother, when she finally comes, seems longer.*
>
> *An analyst observes of a patient that the longer the break he takes for holidays or when sick, the greater the apparent indifference of the patient, to the analyst and the absence, when he returns.*

For a long time, Freud vigorously rejected any attempts to broaden the instinctual basis of psyche and this led to a number of controversies and fallings out within the early psychoanalytic movement, for example, with Adler in 1911 and Jung in 1912 (Freud 1914), both of whom proposed additional instinctual origins; Adler the 'will to power', Jung in a broadened (and Freud contended diluted) concept of libido.

Nonetheless, Freud's clinical findings increasingly drew his attention to the origins of hate and implicitly the part played by aggression, which demanded attention and explication. It was not until 1915 and the publication of *Instincts and their Vicissitudes* (Freud 1915), however, that Freud gave aggression an autonomous role alongside sexuality and a central place in his understanding of infant development.

In *Instincts and their Vicissitudes* Freud more fully developed his ideas about the origin of aggression in the infant's frustrated narcissism and the generation of hate in the ego's abhorrence of anything, which produces 'unpleasurable feelings'. In particular Freud explicated the role of phantasy, describing the frustrated infant's imagined destruction of the source of his or her hatred. This development of theory, envisioned something quite different to the mere eschewing of unpleasurable experience described before. In his elaboration, Freud assigned not only an autonomous role to aggression, but with his emphasis upon the role of phantasy, introduced a developed concept of mind and mentation. This may be contrasted with the *Three Essays*, for example, and the 'economic', mechanistic model implicit there.

Freud's changed formulation meant that the exclusivity previously afforded to sexuality could not be sustained; the origins of hate and aggression had become located in 'self-preservative instincts' with hate antedating love in psychological development.

With the publication of *Beyond the Pleasure Principle* (Freud 1920), the pressure upon Freud's existing model to contain his clinical experience necessitated modifying his ideas even further and to propose aggression as a further primary instinctual basis of psyche. This was in the form of an oppositional 'Death' instinct (Thanatos) to the sexual 'Life' instinct (Eros). In Freud's original formulation, aggression had became evident as a consequence of impingements, assaults or threats to the psychic or physical sense of well-being of the infant, for example, frustration, privation or deprivation of one sort or another. In this subsequent formulation, innate aggression, independent of any external precipitant, was identified. This set the scene for one of the great and continuing analytic debates. Are aggressive phenomena innate or reactive?

Perhaps in anticipation of the controversy that the assertion of innate aggression was likely to cause, not least as a challenge to the monopoly extended to the concept of Eros, Freud's introduction of the concept of the death instinct was low key, almost coy. There were, however, two psychological phenomena that he had struggled to explain. The first was sadism, the other unconscious and excessive levels of guilt, which latterly, he came to understand as a masochistic attack on the self. To account for the apparent contradiction of an instinct that hurried the organism to its own demise he proposed therefore, an 'ego instinct', whose aim is to get to the outcome of the process of life, namely death and the return to an inorganic state. In this account, rather than the conflict being between the desire for pleasure and the need to negotiate reality especially the demands of society (the pleasure principle and the reality principle), there is a conflict between the life and death instincts. The death instinct, Freud proposed, hastens personal extinction by promoting it directly rather than via the laborious process of building and development and loving promoted by the life instinct, Eros and the libidinal drives.

It would appear that Freud was not entirely happy with this revision and downplayed its introduction in *Beyond the Pleasure Principle* (1920), as an absurd hypothesis that would be easily be refuted with reference to other areas of disciplinary study; a refutation, however, that Freud contended was unfortunately incomplete so leaving the hypothesis partially standing. The new class of instincts was seen as particularly evanescent, 'silent' and difficult to see. It was to be detected only by inference and implication in phenomena such as sadism, where fused with a more clearly libidinal sexual instinct and via the convoluted processes that lead to the unconscious sense of guilt. An analogy would be with 'black holes' which cannot be directly observed but whose existence is inferred by reference to their effect on adjacent bodies.

One consequence of this theoretical development, which Freud had to apparently reluctantly accede to, was that the genie of a dualism of the instincts was out of the bottle. On the one hand, there are the erotic instincts focussed towards life, creation, building up and bringing together; to some degree concretized in the sexual drives, and whose developmental progress was charted in the *Three Essays on Sexuality*, through oral, anal and genital phases (Freud 1905). On the other, a much more silent thanatotic drive was envisioned, pushing towards a break down, destruction and reduced development moving back into an inorganic and lifeless state. Alongside the more readily observable drive towards life and preservation Freud contended there is an inescapable, ineffable and essential destructive element in the human makeup. This element came to feature more and more heavily in Freud's thinking right up to the time of his death so that his later writings are suffused with fatalistic pessimism regarding the human condition.

Freud's introduction of the death instinct has been attributed to a number of factors including his own pessimism, ill health and disillusionment in the face of the political and military upheavals of the first third of the twentieth century. Whatever the truth of this, clinically, Freud sought to understand the phenomenon of those patients who inexplicably rejected the progress obtained through analytical work, apparently preferring to cling to self-destructive and self-defeating patterns of psychological relating. In such circumstances initial progress appears to falter and may be reversed in what later came to be known as the 'negative therapeutic reaction' (Freud 1923). The help of the analyst is rejected and even treated as though it is a threat.

One version of this is the fable of a frog asked by a scorpion to carry it across a stream to the opposite bank. The frog refuses on the ground that from what he knows of scorpions this will lead to him being fatally stung. The scorpion dismisses this saying that it would be absurd for him to sting the frog, as the consequent death of the frog would result in the scorpion's destruction also. Convinced by the logic of this, the generous frog carries the scorpion into the river. Half way across, the scorpion stings the frog. As the venom works, and in its death throes the frog asks incredulously 'Why did you do that? Now we both will die.' The scorpion replies, 'I can't help it. I am a scorpion'.

> *A 43-year-old unemployed man has a long history of contact with psychiatric services. His psychiatric diagnosis is unclear, although he is not psychotic. A major difficulty is his serial, vexatious litigation concerning the 'inadequate' services that he is offered, perceived slights from staff and anger regarding inadvertent mistakes. He is a source of considerable anxiety to the hospital staff, who are reluctant to deal with him for fear of attracting complaints. He is referred to the psychotherapy department for a psychodynamic formulation, and hopefully, treatment. In several difficult assessment sessions and subsequently in treatment, a psychotherapist is able to make considerable progress in understanding his sense of resentment. His complaints are contained within the consulting room and their sense is understood within the transference relationship. A history emerges of early years in a children's home and of physical and sexual abuse about which he tried to complain only to be ignored or disbelieved. For the first time, the patient appears to feel genuinely understood, neither patronized nor treated with suspicion.*
>
> *In due course the patient learns, however, that the therapist had sent a brief letter to the referring psychiatrist months earlier, without the patient's knowledge or consent and this leads to a complaint to the therapist's professional organization about breach of confidentiality. The patient defaults from treatment,*

and refuses further offers of session, alleging no confidence because of 'breach of trust'. Although it is generally conceded that it might have been better for the therapist's letter to the psychiatrist to have been open and explicit, the patient's rage and sense of betrayal is felt to be entirely disproportionate and even in some sense affected. It is as though the patient is relieved at having the burden of the treatment removed from him and the complaint and accusations of bad faith, a rationalization.

For Freud, this 'biting the hand that feeds' emanates from a tragic, inevitable element which inevitably mars the human condition and from which humans are only partially able to escape the consequences. The painfulness of this perceived tragedy may be one reason why it was only reluctantly given a space in his ideas as a developed and worked out concept. Despite the profound pessimism implicit in Freud's latter work, for example, *Civilisation and its Discontents* (1930), Freud seemed to find it difficult to accept the shifting of sexuality from its exclusive position in the centre stage and give equal billing to aggression or accept a dualistic or even multiple, instinctual basis for mental life.

Klein

It was left to Melanie Klein, to develop the concept of the death instinct and explore the idea of an essentially innate origin for aggression. Taking up Freud's concept of the death instinct, she rejected his proposition that it is 'clinically silent' contending instead that it is both 'noisy and raucous' (Hinshelwood 1989, p. 54).

In her *The Psycho-Analysis of Children* (1932) Klein interpreted the play of children in terms of both aggressive and erotic drives and in particular the conflicts that arise between them. Drawing on material derived from adult analysis, but more importantly analytic work with children, Klein's account featured erotic attachment combined with faecal bombs and cutting teeth, the latter expressions attributed to innate aggression. Klein was clear that the force of this was not to be underestimated. In phantasy at least, all human beings are considered to have deep wells of destructiveness, murderousness, cruelty and sadism to draw upon, with the psychopath, murderer, torturer and robber to be found in every human soul. The difference is in their expression either directly, in fantasy, by sublimation, displacement or in realization of defence as opposed to enactment. At the base, in terms of primary process, there is nothing to be chosen between an infant's phantasy of scooping out mother's insides, Jack the Ripper's murderous evisceration or a scientist attempting to possess the secrets of the universe. The difference is in the acts and the gap between primary processes, adult realization, psychotic enactment or successful sublimation.

In addition, Klein viewed these matters as derived from essentially intrapsychic sources, rather than reactions to the external world; the mental world of children, she proposed, is only partially to be understood as a consequence of environmental factors but rather as dynamically derived from the interplay of innate elements. To put it simply, rather than there being an interplay between a single, erotic drive and the environment there is a vastly complicated mental life derived from internally derived instinctual forces, independent of external factors. This is consistent with later developments in the concept of instinct, for example, Tinbergen's definition of instinct as 'a hierarchically organized nervous mechanism which is susceptible to certain priming, releasing and directing impulses of internal as well as external origin ...' as quoted by the Kleinian Money-Kyrle (1978).

To Freud's attribution of sexuality to the innocence of youth, Klein added violence and aggression. In this the psychoanalytic discourse to some extent returned to the point at which Freud had parted company with both Adler and Jung.

A 29-year-old London City banker specializes in identifying medium-size companies on the stock exchange, which are in trouble, and pulls together capital for a takeover bid with the aim of gaining control and selling off the different assets. With his small and specialized team, the company is known as the 'target', and the takeover is referred to as 'fucking' the company. At any one time, the 'fuck list' is the roster of companies in his sight, and the 'corpse list' is those over whom control has been gained, and are being sold off. Recreationally, he has a predilection for violent thriller films, enjoying identifying in the plot those who are going to get 'fucked' (here meaning killed). He is extremely successful at his work, lives with his girlfriend of five years standing and complains of no psychiatric, psychological or other difficulties.

The co-centrality of aggressive phantasy in mental life was underlined in the Kleinian and later post-Kleinian accounts by reference to clinical material produced by children, which emphasized the central, affective part played by infantile phantasies and their later versions and surrogates, for example, the effects of attacks made by devouring teeth, the phantasy of hollowing out mother's body and the making of biting attacks upon mother's breast. An essential aspect of this is the crude, uncontained and extreme (often referred to in the literature by the perhaps sanitizing and misleading sobriquet 'primitive') quality of base, affective states and their phantasy mental representations.

The background to these attacks was conceptualized by Klein in her 1946 paper 'Notes on some schizoid mechanisms' (1946) which described the operations of what she called the 'paranoid schizoid' position. In this she drew upon the work of Fairbairn (1952) to talk about the intra-psychic consequences of the internal, dynamic erotic and thanatotic instinctual factors in relation to external objects and to their internal counterparts, the internal objects. In Klein's account, on encountering frustration, the infant's experience of the object, say mother, is bifurcated. In phantasy, both self and object are split into good and bad parts, the bad part of the self subjected to projection, the bad part of the object destroyed or rejected. The object is split into two parts, a sustaining nurturing part and a withholding hostile part. The infant experiences anxiety and terror of death brought about by frustration, hunger or whatever, and this is projected onto mother as if she (mother) is murderous and actively frustrating the infant. This intensifies the splitting both of the object and the ego so that the hatred of the bad part (the 'bad breast') is attributed to the 'bad' part of the ego and split off from while the relationship of the 'good' part of the ego (with the 'good' breast') is preserved. In Klein's account, the concatenation is the attack on the bad breast by biting it. Parents will know that the point at which an infant bites in frustration is salutary and that one will be a bit more careful in future. Later it is the concretization of the infant's rage that collapses the illusion of the split mother because the whole mother is hurt by the actualized attack; bad and frustrating aspects of the whole mother are a bit more careful or withdrawn in future.

In this account, the notion of a destructive part of the personality that leads to a violent polarization of the object into good and bad parts, and which then conducts an attack on the 'bad' object is a central developmental driving force. The developmental step that it moves towards is the second of Klein's psychic constellations, the 'depressive' position. The model proposes that the infant that has attacked the 'bad breast' as described, recognizes the whole mother's response of withdrawal or change and importantly recognizes that the 'good breast' or good mother also has been damaged. In the infant's mind, there is a realization that the polarity of mother into good and bad parts is an illusion, and that the attack has damaged the whole imperfect mother rather than simply the illusory bad part of her.

> *One of the companies that the 29-year-old banker 'fucks' turns out to be a start-up business that has been reasonably successful and run by an old primary school best friend with whom he has lost touch and forgotten. The banker regards as a perk of the job the meeting with the target companies' board of directors when the realization dawns that they have lost control. The meeting with his ex-friend's company is unusual in that there is the recognition of the acquaintance at the beginning. For the first time, the grim faces and tears of the vanquished have some meaning. The banker apparently inexplicably becomes depressed.*

The depressive position, intended by Klein as an account of healthy functioning, describes the state of mind that develops when there is a recognition of the damage that one's own aggression and destructiveness can do, sometimes leading to efforts at repair, 'reparation', in respond to the damage that has been done either in reality or in phantasy. True, as opposed to 'manic', reparation is not an attempt to undo or deny the damage, but an acceptance of the damage and work to repair or patch up. The acceptance and recognition of one's own destructiveness and aggression is seen as a very difficult but fundamental, developmental psychic task.

In reality, a mixed picture of depressive and paranoid schizoid elements is more likely to be found and some theorists such as Bion (1984a) have described a model that involves repeated and lifelong oscillations between the paranoid schizoid and depressive positions rather than a single successful or unsuccessful transition during infancy.

> *A man studying for his professional examinations, in a moment of jealousy and envy, secretly destroyed the revision notes of his best friend, whom he believed would easily surpass him in the examination results. In their university this led to a scandal, the authorities denouncing and threatening the unknown perpetrator, agonizing the man, who had regretted the act almost as soon as he had impulsively destroyed the notes. Partly out of fear (paranoid) partly out of guilt (depressive) he dedicated himself to reconstructing the notes, his guilt only deepening at the praise he received from lecturers and students for the 'selfless' way that he was helping his friend. In consequence the friend achieved a high result, the man doing poorly partly as a consequence of the time he had dedicated to his friend's revision.*
>
> *The man's actions remained a secret, until in later life he became convinced that this same friend was having an affair with his wife. This was patently untrue and had a delusional quality to it (although he himself had had extra-marital affairs). Over time, in analysis, the paranoid schizoid elements within an Oedipal transference to the friend became clearer so that he could tell the friend both about his convictions in relation to his wife and about the destruction of the notes. In this case, to his surprise and rather movingly, the friend said that he had been aware from the outset that his friend was the destroyer of the notes, intuitively aware of his struggle with the pain of his paranoid schizoid anxieties and appreciative of his attempts at reparation.*

Later Kleinians such as Bion came to conceptualize this movement not so much in developmental terms but rather as a pattern of apprehension and the way in which the self relates to the object with fluctuating movements between the positions. Bion annotated this as Ps↔d. Meltzer further revised this schema (1986) to propose a depressive phase preceding the paranoid schizoid position.

As noted, a further response is a manic illusion that somehow the damage caused by the aggression can be reversed or eradicated, and this needs to be distinguished from a reparative acknowledgement and effort to mitigate the damage. An ordinary example here might be the way in which in cases of domestic violence, an incidence of violence by a partner may often be followed by promises and undertakings that it will not reoccur, this accompanied by acts of 'thoughtfulness' and 'consideration'. Despite this, further incidents of violence take place after an interval. In this instance, the promises may not necessarily be false in the sense of not being meant when made. More likely the person is normally split off from the state of mind that exists when he or she is actively, physically violent and this is only tenuously available to ordinary consciousness. Again we will return to this later when we consider matters related to prognosis and the extent to which expressions of 'remorse' can be taken as an expression of real psychological change, even if remorse is traditionally given great weight, (regardless of whether it is cynically or manipulatively given), for example, when considering prisoners for release or privileges.

The centrality of the problem of destructiveness and violence in the Kleinian account can be compared with the more classical Freudian account of erotic development. Freud, over time, sketched out a line of development through which erotic or libidinal energy was invested in the world about it. In the first instance via orality, the infant learns the process of taking in of air and nutrition later modulating all processes of ingestion, and secondly, via anality, as the infant becomes fascinated by the process of expulsion and letting things out, as a prototype for all issues of power and control. The third, phallic phase introduces the idea of genitality, with the Oedipal recognition of the third person in the parent–infant triad, and an emerging idea of sexual difference, again generalized into experiences of separation and difference. This whole theoretical edifice is a developmental account of the erotic, libidinal or 'life forces'; an account of how the infant channels his or her drive to build relatedness with the world. In this account destructiveness is secondary; there is no word of that which is centrally problematic in the Kleinian model, as to how the thanatotic, destructive or 'death force' manifests itself, and how the infant explores and develops their propensity to destroy and withdraw. The Freudian developmental stages describe only how the infant is engaged in an exploration of their surroundings, in a task of building up knowledge and skills of how to survive in the world that they have been born into; how this process unfolds and the avenues and major concepts along the way; taking in (oral), putting out (anal) and engagement with others (phallic).

In the Kleinian account the erotic libidinal drives are considered in tandem with the thanatotic, destructive drives and the conflicts that arise between them. The difference is in the focus on developmental drivers. Usually this has come to be characterized as libidinal in the Freudian account, and as destructive/thanatotic in the Kleinian, although as we have seen this may be an unfair characterization of both Freud and Klein. As we noted in the last chapter, this characterized difference in emphasis probably underlies the fact that the issue of the existence or otherwise of the death instinct has become totemic.

In the classical Freudian tradition, the extreme position would be that aggression, destructiveness and violence are always a response to frustration or trauma in some way. That every instance of aggression, destructiveness or violence can be traced back to a frustration, to a repetition compulsion related to a trauma or as a reaction to some form of threat to either body or psyche. For example, the frustration of a child at being unable to ride a bicycle like his or her peers might lead to an aggressive attempt to acquire the skill. Here the aggression is being harnessed in the task of beneficial development. Or the self-defeating object choice of a young woman, who has had a sequence of alcoholic and abusive partners, might be seen as a repetition compulsion of an overwhelming and unassimilated reaction to abuse at the hands of an alcoholic and violent father, with the repetition compulsion being an attempt to gain mastery over the situation *this time round*. The young woman does not have a self-destructive wish or impulse to choose a man who will be violent to her; rather she chooses on the basis of a phantasy that with this man she will be able to make the trauma turn out differently. In phantasy, she will be taming her father, and overcoming the trauma. In reality, tragically, the repetitive cycle goes on round. This is not an example of masochism, with an innate destructiveness turned inward, rather a misguided effort at a libidinal drive towards creativity and development.

By contrast from a polarized Kleinian position the same material might be understood more in terms of the woman's destructive attacks upon the internal parents and her object choice would be seen in an overdetermined way as an identification with a denigrated internal couple, allowing no productive parental intercourse at the same time as she punishes herself for her destructive attacks in an attempt to avoid depressive guilt.

Narcissism

A further central contribution from the Kleinian literature has been the development of the concept of 'destructive' narcissism. Originating from the myth of Narcissus who in Greek mythology fell in love with his own reflection, in Freud's metapsychology, narcissism was conceptualized as the situation occurring where cathexes (instinctual attachments) were to the ego rather than to objects (people) in the outside world. In Freud's view it is this state that pertains at birth, with the infant existing in an illusory world of omnipotence in which there is no gap between wishes and their fulfilment. In this way, where all goes well, the baby is protected from the reality that he or she is absolutely vulnerable and dependant; the alternative is for the infant to be overwhelmed by unbearable anxiety. The primary caregiver's task is to initially support the defensive omnipotent illusion, for example, by ensuring that there is only the briefest of gaps between the infant becoming hungry, and he or she being fed; failure to do this prematurely exposes the infant to the precariousness of his or her situation. This illusion is gradually relinquished as the infant becomes less dependent and acquires increasing ego strength.

The focus for development is usually outwards; the baby tries to reach out; to stand and walk to one of its parents; to learn to ride a bike to be able to extend the region of exploration, then to be able to travel to a first girlfriend's house. All of this effort is in the outside world, with a striving towards relationships and creativity in the external world, and aggression is a component part of the feelings which underpin this; anger, frustration, determination, self-possession and so on. By contrast, a narcissistic focus is inward, with an eschewing of external connections and attachments and here the aggression is employed destructively.

This may be thought about in terms of different film endings; if a couple live 'happily ever after', this is an object-related ending, involving a capacity and commitment to sustained engagement with the 'other'. If the lonely gunslinger rides off into the sunset, this is narcissistic; the gunslinger needs no one and nothing but himself, he is strong and tough and needs no ties to weaken him.

Clinically, however, these patterns do not pertain in pure form in individual people. Inward-looking narcissism may be self-reflective rather than object denying and oscillations between inward and outward occur, albeit in a variety of ways, and in varying degrees that are entirely consistent with patterns of separation and attachment, aggression and affection, along with concomitant psychological integration. Inward reflection and imagination may be drawn upon as the basis for mental development as affective experience is married to thinking and affective elements are digested and integrated.

Problems arise where inward movements predominate and the capacity for imagination and inward reflection is enlisted not for the purposes of self-awareness, differentiation and individuation but in the service of defensive, omnipotent phantasy/fantasy. In such circumstances, aggression is brought to bear upon perception and the apprehension of psychological reality (or realities) or alternatively upon the organs of perception. This is the movement towards destructive as opposed to 'healthy' narcissism.

There are circumstances in which this destructive narcissism may lead to violent enactment and we will talk about this in due course. For the most part, however, instead of killing people off in the real world, the 'civilized' person kills people off in his or her internal world. The 'lone gunslinger' violently destroys his dependency on his 'gal' in his mind; he kills off the relationship and the attachment, and his 'gal' will be psychologically damaged as if physical violence had taken place. The 'lone gunslinger' also destroys his recognition of vulnerability and the recognition of the ways in which he is dependent; in short the things that make him human and fallible. Instead, he puffs up an illusory belief in his own self-sufficiency and omnipotence. The person enthralled to destructive narcissism and its illusions destroys or damages his recognition of reality, as well as his relationships. It is important to recognize, however, the difference between situations in which a murderous fantasy ('I felt like killing him', 'I wished him to Kingdom Come') is available for reflection upon so that the aggression may become available for integration and those situations in which the murderous fantasy becomes itself a source of satisfaction. As we will see such fantasies may also be a component part of violent action, where some part of the affective component, is felt to be intolerable.

This concept of 'narcissism' creates a theoretical model which includes the concept of a mental realm, a mind in which aggression can be discharged and given mental representation rather than being enacted concretely. It also provides a bridge between the psychoanalytic understanding of 'civilized people' outside the prison wall, whose murderousness is contained within their mind and is symbolic, and those within, for whom it is concrete and have failed to contain it. The difference between the murderer serving a life sentence or in some jurisdictions, facing execution, and the judge who sentences him or the jury who finds him guilty, is not in the degree of darkness of their souls. Both have the shadow of thanatotic aggression and violence over them. It is just that one group manage to engage with this psychologically, or in a manner that is imaginative rather than the concrete expression that constitutes enacted violence. We will consider this matter in detail in due course.

> *A 34-year-old successful lawyer is involved in an important case for her firm that is preoccupying her. She recognizes that she is beginning to find it difficult to switch off from it, and after discussing the problem with her husband, decides to take a couple of days off work to 'pamper herself'. She spends a day in a health spa, receiving massages, mud bath, hydrotherapy and various other treatments, and a second day having her hair cut and blown dried, her nails done and spends time at the beautician in preparation for being taken out to dinner by her husband. Over this time, her faith in herself is restored, and she returns to work refreshed and invigorated to take up again the challenges of the case.*

> *A 39-year-old psychiatrist with a history of depression is in analysis. Approaching his 40th birthday, he reflects on the two years he has been in treatment himself and wonders if he should continue or finish. In the discussion about these issues, he reflects that he is not really convinced that the treatment is doing him any good. When he is depressed, he does need something. He reflects that he feels he needs a friend principally. The analyst is familiar with this pattern. In an unassuming way, the psychiatrist repeatedly dismisses her contribution, and avoids engaging in a discussion about what this might mean. She feels that he is getting closer to recognizing this dismissal and*

squashing of the insights that she offers. She hypothesizes that this pattern is an articulation of his narcissism, and that the reason for his considering to terminate the treatment is because it is coming into focus in the analysis. He wants to destroy the treatment and his chances of making progress.

'Independent Accounts'

A Freudian criticism of Klein's concept of narcissism is that it 'pathologizes' a normal state. D.W. Winnicott's account of very early development and the role of aggression attempts to combine both the Freudian and Kleinian accounts. For Winnicott, from the beginning, the infant is a dyad with its mother; from the infant's perspective, it is not clear where he or she ends and mother begins, a situation which Balint describes as a 'harmonious mix up' (1968). There are, however, 'nuclei' of volition and agency that may have the capacity for object relations, although these are not yet formed into a recognizable ego structure. For Winnicott, the role of aggression is in the formation of the ego (the notion 'violence' being used by him, as with a number of other writers, as a measure of the degree of aggression used; therefore it is the employment of a large amount of aggression that constitutes violence). Winnicott seems to allow that the infant has an autonomous aggressive drive that leads to expressions, including violence, which serves to delineate the boundaries of the self and of the ego. He describes, for example, how spontaneous, aggressive kicks against mother's body allow the baby to identify its own will, and its affect upon the 'world out there'. Mother's response to the infant's activity is crucial for the infant in arriving at the meaning of its actions along with the affects which are linked to them. In this account, aggression is clearly being utilized to forward a more erotic drive, pushing forward development.

Winnicott's other contribution to the debate about aggression, destructiveness and violence is in his paper 'Hate in the countertransference', (Winnicott 1949). Here, the argument goes, at a concrete level although the thief steals from the victim out of a nefarious motive, at another level, the thief is stealing back maternal love, affection or whatever, of which they feel that they have been deprived, *feeling it to have been stolen from them.* An important distinction is to be made between privation, which generates only hopelessness and apathy and deprivation, which implies the loss of a quality, which has been experienced, at least a little. What is felt as having been stolen is in fact the due maternal attention that has been lost. At another level, therefore, the aggressive component in thieving (and indeed other anti-social behaviours) can be seen as an expression of hope that in some way, the debt he or she is owed will or can be repaid, and that this is more optimistic than a hopeless withdrawal. Thus for Winnicott, violence contains within it the hopeful (and constructive) sense that what has been damaged can be repaired and that the aggressive element can be regained. This would be consistent, for example, with the example of the young woman given above, in her cycle of abusive relationships, up to the point at which the aggression is used in the destruction of the woman's ability to differentiate between the current and the original situation.

In both these examples, the action (aggressive kicking of mother's body or thieving) which might variously be construed as aggressive, destructive or violent is being cast as something that is erotic in the sense of driving towards development, and therefore as secondary to an underlying developmental erotic instinct. The notion of an early developmental 'mix-up' as midway between a Freudian primary narcissistic state and a Kleinian terrifying infantile object relation at a time of life when one is totally dependent allows for the consideration of narcissism as a destructive and pathological withdrawal, at the same time as allowing for some very early object relations, or rather proto-object relations between the ego-nuclei of the infant and the mother, with a potential for problems identified by Klein.

However, in this understanding of aggression, violence and destructiveness, the Winnicottian model fails to dismantle the basic totemic polarity between the two views that man has a basic destructive drive on the one hand, and that aggression, violence and destructiveness can be understood in terms of a self-preservative reaction to trauma on the other. Rather it opts for the more Freudian perspective of the aggression being secondary, albeit via an even more optimistic motivation of destroying, as it were, in order to build, so that the Winnicottian position can with perhaps only a little justice be caricatured as being 'Pollyanna-ish' in the sense of believing that everything is for the best in the best of all possible worlds. As a result, while valuing aggression there may be a tendency to ignore or underplay intractable or irredeemable violence, the clinical manifestations of which, led first Freud and then Klein to develop the concept of the 'death instinct' in the first place.

Another theoretical position that has been proposed is that of Fairbairn (1952) who emphasized the role of the super-ego and especially of the development of a punitive super-ego in the production of aggression. In this account, part of the critical super-ego becomes an 'internal saboteur', which comes to dominate the personality, an idea later developed by Rosenfeld (1971), to create an illusory sense of safety, by foregoing ego development which would involve the apprehension of painful reality, in favour of omnipotent phantasy. This position can be seen as a development of the position that aggression and violence are a response to an initial trauma or deprivation.

In the philosophical debate about the epistemological basis of psychoanalysis, Popper was clear that neither psychoanalysis nor Marxism could be considered as sciences (Popper 1972) because science proceeds via a process of hypothesis and refutation. A hypothesis is proposed, and experiments or series of observations are carried out to test it in an attempt to refute it. The refutation of the hypothesis leads on to its review and reformulation, and the progress of the scientific discipline. In psychoanalysis, the hypothesis of (for example) infantile sexuality can be attacked, but with the theoretical mechanism of repression, the psychoanalyst can reinterpret the refutation of the hypothesis as a denial or repression that further strengthens the original hypothesis. Marxism achieves this similar irrefutability by the mechanism of 'false consciousness', which explains why oppressed workers might support capitalist systems because of a 'false consciousness' belief that it serves their interests. The elaboration that the owners of the means of production explicitly foster this 'false consciousness' in order to keep the workers from challenging the status quo provides more support to the central thesis of their exploitative power over the workers.

In the same way, the broad interpretation that aggression, destructiveness and violence are always secondary to frustration, trauma or threat is irrefutable. Any clinical situation where aggression, destructiveness or violence has been exhibited can be framed in a context that makes it explicable in terms of it being a result of frustration, trauma or threat. Meloy's (1988, 1992) descriptions of the activities of psychopaths using extreme violence in a series of killings can be understood in terms of a catathymic reaction to a perceived threat to mental integrity. The violence and cruelty of some parents to their children in the same way can be seen as the parent/carer's reaction to the psychological threat that children can present as they stretch the carer's sanity to its limits as part of their normal exploration of boundaries and behaviour.

One of the cultural spin-offs from psychoanalysis has been the debate, in the 1970s and 1980s, about the reality of non-accidental harm to children, the recognition that violence by carers towards children was common; in the 1990s, a similar recognition of how widespread sexual abuse took place. The realization arose that many patients who have histories of using physical violence have a childhood history of abusive or violent experiences. As a result, almost all violence, as a clinical phenomenon, can be 'explained' in terms of being a reaction to abusive childhood experiences even if more careful consideration is likely to demonstrate an association rather than a causal relationship (which is not of course to deny the possibility of a causal relationship). The supposed sequelae of childhood violence has, however, entered popular culture as a 'truth' and especially as an analytic 'truth and the obvious shortcomings of this 'fact' has had the effect of somewhat undermining the authority of the arguments regarding causation and lent itself to a somewhat simplistic caricaturing of the relationship between childhood experiences of violence and a propensity towards violent behaviour, for example.

It has become nonetheless something of a truism that experiences of violence lead to violent behaviour in adult life. The biographies of both Hitler and Stalin, for example, both give ample testament to violent fathers physically assaulting their sons. Most analysts will be able to provide ample clinical material that makes links of this kind whether the violence is to a greater or a lesser extent. It is also true to say, however, that most analysts will be able to provide equal amounts of material where violence experiences in childhood have not led to violent adults and indeed that violence and destructiveness may occur in the absence of any obvious, actively violent, formative experiences.

In this discussion the two competing positions have not been resolved. On the one hand, there is a thanatotic destructive instinct, and on the other, aggression and violence are a reaction to something which is perceived as traumatic or a threat. These two relatively common sense understandings have been considerably elaborated by psychoanalytic theory, but they remain essentially an irreducible dualism. Having established them, however, they can be used as triangulation points to explore and illuminate some of the more specific theories of violence that have emerged in the literature and in the next chapter we will go on to consider this in some of the literature which addresses aggression and violence as its focus rather than as subsidiary matters.

3 Mechanisms: Psychopathy, Attachment and Self-Defence

In the last chapter, we considered the ways in which competing analytic ideas about aggression and violence evolved during the development of the main psychoanalytic metapsychological frameworks. Part of the task that we have given ourselves in this book is to try to distinguish between metapsychological theories on the origins of aggression and violence on the one hand, and ideas about how the mechanisms work, on the other. The distinction we want to make is between where aggression and violence come from and how these propensities or impulses become manifest. Again, because the literature is vast we will be focussing upon two main accounts in order to illuminate these issues.

There are of course other versions, for example, Hyatt-Williams' idea of a 'Blueprint for Murder', (1998) or Fromm's 'Necropilic Personality' (1997), and we want to stress that their omission here does not mean that we consider them unimportant.

The first account that we will turn to concerns the notion of psychopathy and the psychopathic personality; the second resides in the work of Glasser and the Portman Clinic group who have made a distinction between 'self-preservative' violence on the one hand and 'cruelty' on the other. This we will couple with Fonagy's explication of the violent act as a response to psychologically threatening stimuli.

Psychopathy

In that part of the psychiatric field that specializes in managing and treating violent patients, a dominant, perhaps the most dominant, influence is that which relates to the Hare Psychopathy

Checklist or PCLR (Hare 1991). Some may contend that this has turned into something of a 'psychopathy industry' concerned with the application of the instrument, the development of the conceptual framework and the training of those who would use it. The psychopathy checklist itself is an operationalization of Cleckley's original clinical description of a 'psychopath'; this consists of a summary of disapproving and one might even say pejorative adjectives, such as violent, duplicitous, deceitful, feckless, emotionally shallow, etcetera, which may be used to describe an individual (Cleckley 1941). The individual's demonstration of such characteristics is arrived at by means of a 20-item questionnaire. Each answer is scored between zero and two, into a total score of up to 40. Scores above 25, and especially above 30 are empirically associated with a considerable increase in the likelihood of violent recidivism (Hare 1991).

> *A 22-year-old man on the way home from the pub, who has spent all his money, forces the door of a house with no lights on to burgle it. Finding nothing valuable downstairs, he goes upstairs to try the bedrooms, but wakes up the frail old occupant, a woman in her 80s. Using her dressing gown cord, he ties her wrists and continues to search the bedrooms. Angry at finding nothing of value, and irritated by her protestation, on his way out he kicks her in the head where she is lying on the floor. Satisfied that she is silenced, he leaves. She is found several days later by relatives, having died from the head injury.*

Hare's psychopathy concept relies on an empirical validation rather than a powerful and rhetorical presentation, but he describes the psychopathic as that small group in every society that cause mayhem with their violent behaviour. This is a group consisting of people whose psychological profile, in time of war, constitute the cruellest element of the Nazi SS or commit atrocities such as those carried out during the civil war in Yugoslavia. These are the people who provided the driving force in the groups that visited the villages to be ethnically cleansed, killing leading civilians and their families so that there was no resistance to the regular army that followed. The psychopath is conceived of as somebody drawn to the extremes of cruelty and violence as a lifestyle choice, in times of peace at odds with and disruptive of society; only in times of war finding a societal role that is temporarily in accord with the society's aims as a whole.

At other times or in other societies, psychopaths are deemed to be those who find themselves on death row, serving long prison sentences or wanted by the police for transgressing the law or at best societal norms of civilized behaviour. This is an elastic concept and Hare subsequently extended his concept and also its profitable application to industrial and business management identifying similar personality traits in managers in organizations.

A former soldier with a plentiful history of convictions for violent crimes is serving a life sentence for the murder of his spouse during a domestic argument. He is being challenged about his violence in a prison rehabilitation programme and it is being claimed that he gets violent when he is unsatisfied with things or when he is bored. He is then challenged about whether there is a time that he can remember when he has actually been satisfied with things. He thinks for a moment, and then talks about how 'fantastic' it had been in the Falklands; the weeks of combat had been exhilarating, exciting and adventurous. 'I was being paid to kill people' he said with an obvious glee.

The psychological concept of psychopathy has at its centre a lack of trustworthiness and evidence of callous and manipulative use of people for financial gain or sexual gratification; robbery, theft, deception and extortion are resorted to, to achieve these ends, purportedly without compunction. Life for the psychopath, it is contended, is a personal hedonistic journey, unfettered by deference to civilized norms of behaviour. This is a pattern, portrayed in books and the cinema, with endless permutations.

When a youth, a man seeing and coveting a Rolex watch belonging to a fellow bus passenger, follows and robs him. When the watch's owner resists the robbery, the man savagely beats him. In later life having acquired a taste for an easy and extravagant lifestyle he gets together with like-minded men who go to the places where money is to be found, such as banks, robbing them and violently assaulting anyone who gets in their way.

A variation on this might be the seeking to gratify sexual impulses outside of the constraints and difficulties of maintaining an egalitarian relationship disregarding the consent of the object or the consequences.

Whether the gratifications being sought are financial or sexual, the philosophical preoccupations of the psychopath are similar to those of anyone else, money, sex and death. These are not lived out, however, in the way caricatured and satirized by Woody Allen as a morbid preoccupation about sex and death, but rather in a concrete wish to kill someone, apparently just in order to see what it is like; perhaps as a variation on exploring the boundary between 'le petit mort' of sexual orgasm and 'le grand mort' of death. Alternatively there may be a fusion of the preoccupation with sex and death expressed as the formulation of a plan to kill a sexual partner or commit sexualized assaults or murder.

Empathy and Empathic Failure

An aspect of psychopathy that has come to be emphasized is the issue of empathy. While the preoccupations, desires, jealousies and envies of the psychopath may be no different than any other person, it is contended, the non-psychopath is inhibited from violent or exploitative enactment by an empathetic connection with other people. In distinguishing the psychopath it is argued that for the most part, people are prevented from simply enacting robbery, rape or murder by an empathetic identification with others and at least some sense of relating on the basis of 'do as you would be done by'. An ordinary individual will have some sense of what it might feel like to be assaulted, of being robbed of a valued possession, of death in terms of a personal value of life or the effect of bereavement on relatives. Without this empathy-producing taboo against violence, it is argued, the psychopath can pursue self-interest and hedonism irrespective of the wishes and rights of others. If there is something they want, they will do whatever they have to gain it. If they need money, they will say whatever they have to, to get it, by borrowing with promises to pay back, by extortion or theft. Whatever it takes will be done irrespective of the consequences to the other.

Meloy (1988) has proposed a psychodynamic hypothesis to understand this apparent empathetic failure. He suggests that the psychopathic individual's lack of empathy is a function of disordered developmental attachment relations. The psychopath as a child has had attachment figures; parents, carers, who consistently failed to establish an empathetic bond during childhood development, so that this is an aspect of human relations that is simply not learned or developed. For example, a psychopath may have had a mother who did not want her child or felt him to be an inconvenience, or who saw her child as representing a hated father who is in consequence resented and left to others to look after, or to bring themselves up; or the infant whose father establishes a jealous hateful relation which fails to identify anything in his child's existence other than as a potential rival.

A man in his 50s is a decade into serving several life sentences for murder. He had worked as a security guard, and as a hired hand of the local drug barons to beat up debtors, killing on a number of occasions. During therapy he is exploring why it is that he did not feel remorse about those who he maimed and killed and he notes that in all his adult life he has never cried nor ever felt any sadness. The therapist asks about childhood experiences, whether he ever felt sad as a child. The man thinks not, reporting the harrowing story of how when at age five, his mother had committed suicide. With further questioning, it emerged that he had found her with her head in the oven, unarousable. The therapist suggests that his mother's death must have hurt him very deeply, and that perhaps he decided to bury his feelings, so as not to be hurt again. The prisoner has a puzzled sense that he might be missing something, but is apparently otherwise unmoved.

Such individuals were identified and characterized by Bowlby as 'affectionless psychopaths', observing,

... this indifference was absolutely characteristic of everyone of these children ... we might imagine them saying 'do not let us care too much for anyone ... let us avoid the risk of out hearts being broken again'   (Bowlby 1971).

Bowlby's conception introduces a different perspective, however, when he talks in terms of the child's heart, being broken 'again'. This implies something more than the failure to develop an internal model for empathic relations with other people.

It implies rather the turning away from experiences of relations with another, in anticipation of them being painful. This of course links to Winnicott's distinction between, privation on the one hand and 'de-privation' on the other. The former generates only hopelessness, the latter angry and resentful 'anti-social tendencies' (Winnicott 1956b, 1986), for example, the violent act.

Part of the unbearable tragedy of working with such patients in prisons or other secure institutions, is to become aware of the depth of deprivation and abuse which often they have suffered. The violence and criminality of which they are convicted is the tip of an iceberg concealing the greater part of a life which is characteristically one in which they were themselves the recipients of violence, neglect and abuse. As we will see, this violence cannot be understood only in terms of bodily action or physical experience. This developmental victimhood teaches a strategy of self-sufficiency, of learning to survive and of no one caring, by shutting down the idea of care. A child unable to understand why a mother consistently sends him to a sexually abusive and violent carer and who is impervious to his complaints, cannot bear the idea that she might do this knowing the trauma of the child. So he sets aside his sense of the empathy of a mother to her child or the notion of empathy as a whole. At the same time, to survive the trauma of the sexual, physical or psychological abuse, as far as possible he shuts down his own feelings in the situation.

Through years of abuse and violence, and years of practice, an unfeeling survival strategy becomes the norm. The idea that others may have feelings, and that there is a resonance between people's feelings in relationships is simply not an issue. Fonagy and Target (Fonagy & Target 1999; Fonagy, Moran & Target 1993) for example, have extended this notion to the concept of mentation; that some individuals lack not only a concept of empathy with the suffering of another, but that they lack the concept of the other, or indeed themselves, having a mind at all.

Eric, a slightly dull witted 30-year-old is being challenged in a cognitive programme run by the probation service, about why he hits people when he is angry. The session is focussing on a specific example of an occasion upon which he hit his brother who had called him stupid when he had dropped a pint of beer. 'It was an insult, so I clobbered him', says Eric, 'what else is there to it?'. The facilitator suggests that in-between the insult and the punch, there must have been a thought, and that the thought was a decision whether or not to hit out. She points out that the decision could have gone differently. Eric might have decided not to hit him. Eric does not understand this.

There is also a corollary to this idea; rather than being absent, the emotion and feeling of the psychopath are simply dulled or psychologically cut off from, in order to escape from the pain. In consequence, to achieve a satisfying level of emotional arousal, things have to be much more extreme. Such situations are commonly to be found among self-mutilating women, whose cutting or burning becomes increasingly severe in their attempts to cause themselves pain; although the self-infliction of painful self-mutilation may be incomprehensible to the observer, to the perpetrator such pain is the only thing that they feel that they have, with which to reassure themselves that they are still alive or that they have not damaged their capacity for feeling or sensation irrevocably. Pain is gladly accepted (although this is a complicated matter and is often sexualized in a secondary manner) as an antidote to their terror that they have irreparably damaged or killed off some part of themselves.

Thus the non-psychopath may be frightened to a satisfying degree by reading about a shooting in the newspapers. The psychopath would be impervious to this, and would actually need to be in the hail of bullets to experience the same level of fear. In a relationship, a married couple might find a direct outlet for aggression, arguing over the washing up; a psychopath may require the fantasy or reality of a sexual murder to achieve the same level of emotional arousal. The psychopath is drawn to extreme things and experiences, hence their 'usefulness' in war, as well as their criminality in peace time.

A 50-year-old man serving a life sentence, created mayhem while in the community, and in a more limited way has done so in prison, by inciting riots, rooftop protests and being involved in numerous scams and violent altercations. Following another incident, he is being asked about this long history, and whether, in his sixth decade he is going to settle down. Having a good relationship with the prison governor who is asking him, he responds as honestly as he can that he just gets bored, and has to fill the boredom with something.

The persuasiveness and authority that the psychopathy concept has found, derives from the empirical evidence that links a score on a list of 'psychopathic' characteristics to violent recidivism. People who have these characteristics are more violent, and are at a higher risk of reoffending. Because of the predictive value of the psychopathy checklist, it has been adopted across the world. Perhaps regrettably this authority has, within criminal justice psychology (criminology and forensic psychology) led to it to become more than merely an indicator or a tool, but has lent itself to the establishing a system in which a particular score diagnoses a personality type, with certain immovable characteristics and implications. A psychopath (scoring above 25 or 30) is a 'them' not an 'us', becoming a different sort of species. The risk is that being at a statistical extreme divests the individual of their human rights or even of their humanity. The splitting off, of psychopaths from the rest of us, conceptually and emotionally, has a large defensive component to it which is intended to achieve a comfortable distance between those who are 'good' and those who are 'bad'. This is amplified in the criminal justice setting by three factors. Firstly, the accounts of the crimes committed are hateful and difficult to bear, leading to a wish by the staff to hate and exclude a particular sub-group. Secondly, there is an awareness of the relative ineffectiveness of all psychological and custodial interventions in actually reducing the risk of reoffending, so that there is a wish to clarify the groups that are less likely to change, in order to preserve some hope about the rest. High PCLR scoring psychopaths are a group easy to separate out and exclude because of the reality of their higher risk and the likelihood to their manipulative and pretend engagement with treatment programmes.

The third reason for the exclusion of this group is more fundamental. From the perspective of research methodology the psychopathy checklist lacks 'face validity'. Everybody who reads it can apply it to people in their work or social sphere, people who do not have a criminal record, but almost always, people who the reader dislikes. The lack of face validity derives from the idea that the PCLR is simply a list of the horrible things one can say about people, that they are cunning and manipulative, that they are lying and deceitful, that they are exploitative and ruthless and that they are remorseless and show a lack of concern. Specifically, people see PCLR characteristics in their managers or politicians, and there is an argument that being effective in society does require some of these characteristics. People successful in business and ruthless people might come into this latter category and as we have noted Hare has extended his concept of psychopathy to include the world of business and non-criminal organizations.

More specifically, the PCLR describes us all, but particularly describes the parts of us that we would prefer to ignore in ourselves. The violence and callousness that human nature is difficult to bear, and particularly difficult to bear when taken to its logical extreme in the commission of violent or sexual crime. Working with criminal groups, there is a need to disavow personal similarities of attitude and values with clients, and to project them firmly into a sub-group, the high PCLR scorers.

Alongside the criticism of the concept of psychopathy that it scapegoats a minority group, while enabling the rest of us to deny our own psychopathic traits, further criticisms can be made. It may be that the apparent lack of feeling and lack of empathic capacity ascribed to the psychopath is in fact just that apparent. From this perspective rather than lacking feeling or a capacity for identification, the psychopath is in a constant state of threat of being overwhelmed by unmanageable affective elements and in constant states of over-identification. The problem may be that rather than their having not learned the capacity for feeling, what they lack is the capacity to manage their affective states and in consequence are doomed to constantly attempt to distance themselves from these. Such evacuations may be in the hope that the other will process the affects and return them in a state that they can understand. Or it may be that the evacuation is intended to permanently rid the individual of an affective state that they consider that it is impossible to bear. This would echo Bion's concept of the maternal provision of what he called alpha function processing infantile beta elements (Bion 1984b), which may be unavailable to the individual or which the individual may be unable to use, for example, because of envy. Recently some evidence in support of this has arisen in relation to research into affective neurological processes. It has become clear that the part of the brain responsible for processing and managing affective states, the right orbitofrontal cortex, does not develop in human beings until around the age of about one (Schore 1994; Carvalho 2002). Until it is sufficiently developed, infants are dependent upon their carers to identify with and manage their affective states, for example, by protecting them from and helping them to make sense of and thereby contain, crude affective experiences. Neurological development of this area is dependent upon this taking place in a satisfactory manner. In its absence the infant is forced to adopt strategies which effect disassociation from some sorts of experience. Of course this situation in infancy is one that will continue to pertain in adulthood, with all the increasing opportunity that this provided for complex experience, without the concomitant complex mental function that is required to successfully negotiate it. It may be reassuring to note that unlike some sorts of neurological failures of development leading to brain deficits, this particular capacity seems to be one that can be developed at any time in life and not like some others dependent upon particular developmental stages to take place (Schore 1994).

In spite of what is perhaps the overuse or misguided use of the concept, the psychopathy construct provides a potent understanding of the mechanism of violence. Force, in the form of violence is useful to persuade people to do things that they may not wish to. Without an empathetic resonance with the object, the psychopath has nothing to rule out violence in the pursuit of these personal aims.

> *A man has strangled and raped a woman in a sadistic and cruel manner which included the alternation in his victim's mind between hope and despair by first tightening, then releasing a ligature until finally he killed her. Slowly, however, he comes to conceptualize the feelings, which underlay his murderous act. This is complicated but contains the desire to have the power over life and death, as an antidote to his more usual state of constant terror of being completely powerless and at risk of annihilation, which is especially evoked in situations in which he is sexually aroused.*

Self-Defence and Cruelty

The second theory we wish to consider relates to the work of Glasser of the Portman Clinic to which we have already referred in Chapter 1. We have already considered some of the problems with the definition of violence proposed by Glasser, especially his reliance upon action rather than psychological states as central to his definition of violence. However, in a series of papers (Glasser 1979, 1994, 1996, 1998), he draws a distinction between two different types of violence. On the one hand, he describes a primitive and archaic form that is a response to a perceived threat. This is a simple fight/flight mechanism seen in animals, and would be consistent with what we described in Chapter 1 as 'self-defence'. The objective of this form of violence is purely and simply to remove the threat. To take out, to obliterate, whatever that is threatening the subject. This violence is murderous in its intent, but murderous in a pure form, where the objective is the obliteration of the object that is perceived as a threat to the self. This form of violence is the 'fight' option in a 'fight/flight' situation.

> *A 25-year-old man, committing an armed robbery at a post office, is unexpectedly confronted by an armed policeman. He is cornered. Rather than surrendering, in panic, he shoots the policeman and tries to make his escape.*

The contribution made by this model is in proposing an archaic, animalistic self-preservative form of violence, which is distinct from what Glasser names 'cruelty'. Cruelty might be seen as the violence carried out when the subject is not being threatened, such as in situations of torture, sadistic torment and so on. A crucial distinction to be drawn is that for cruelty, the aim is not the death of the victim. If the victim of cruelty dies, then the cruelty stops. The aim of cruelty is the suffering of the victim, not their death. In this respect, the two types of violence are very different.

> *A 34-year-old man abducts a young woman whom he sexually tortures and rapes. Before eventually killing her, he alternates between making it clear that he intends to kill her and implying that she can save her life by adopting a compliant attitude to the man. Her survival will, it is implied, depend upon her capacity to identify the attitudes and wishes of the man with which she must comply. Part of the man's pleasure is in seeing the waxing and waning of the woman's hope that he will not kill her and her inevitably futile attempts at*

complying with his implied demand that the pain that he causes her is pleasurable to her.

Popular accounts of such extreme sadistic crimes involve the victim being subjected to cruelty, such as sexual sadism, for a period and then killed at the end of this. Often there is a purportedly rational reason for the killing at the end of the cruelty that has been rehearsed in the perpetrator's mind many times prior to the event; that 'dead men (or women) don't talk'. In the perpetrators' accounts of these instances, however, there is often another element that comes into play. Within the extreme cruelty that the kidnap and torture of a victim entails, the psychopathic splitting off of the empathetic reaction threatens to break down; the perpetrator gets 'spooked' in some way. Suddenly, the reality of the plight of the victim becomes a threat somehow, and a fight/flight self-preservative violent dynamic comes into play, such that the reality of the victim or the pleadings of the victim, pierce the defensive armour of the perpetrator and it is this that has to be silenced, destroyed or killed.

We have already touched on a model of violence proposed by Fonagy, which centres round the notion of a threat to the mind of the perpetrator (Fonagy 1991; Fonagy & Target 1996), a concept also alluded to in a different sense by Symington (1996). This may be contrasted with Glasser's self-preservative model which sees the violence as a reaction to a real physical threat and the violent act as an attempt to remove this 'real' physical threat. Fonagy's model emphasizes the threat as being one, which is experienced as a threat to the very existence of the individual because it involves a conflation of physical and psychological realities. Fonagy proposes that as a consequence of this a physically non-violent psychological stimulus can have the effect of collapsing or destroying an individual's identity. This is experienced as if it were life threatening or annihilating.

The significance of this extension is that an argument, taking place in the psychological realm, between bickering spouses, for example, gains the potential to become physically violent. If one spouse manages to get hold of some aspect of the identity of their partner that is crucial and fundamental to their partner's sense of self and challenge it effectively, this may have the effect of destabilizing the identity of the partner (Bateman & Fonagy 2003).

This differs from the simple argument about a fight/flight situation described by Glasser, where self-preservative violence (psychological or physical) may be brought into play to ablate the threat.

The majority of those serving a life sentence for murder have killed one person, usually a close friend, family member or spouse. Frequently, the account of what happened follows this pattern of a psychologically intimate relationship where victim and perpetrator know each other well enough to have a sense of the identity foundations of the other. An argument ensues, which becomes psychologically threatening, leading to physical violence and sometimes death.

> *A 40-year-old childless man, who has made his work his life, is told that he is to be made redundant. That night his wife finds him morose and uncommunicative; not knowing about the redundancy she verbally attacks him. Later the confrontation continues in the kitchen where she senses that it is to do with his work and taunts him about how useless he is in this sphere also. In a moment, the man seizes the knife he is using to cut himself a sandwich, and stabs her in the stomach.*

The extension of Glasser's model of self-preservative violence to include psychological threats raises a number of interesting questions. Firstly, it would imply that the robustness of the sense of identity or self becomes a variable. Those with a more precarious sense of self will be more likely to be significantly threatened by psychological challenges. There is some support for this model in clinical work with psychopathic people. The non-caring and aggressive exterior can indeed be frightening and dangerous, but in a psychodynamic engagement, this can be re-framed as being more like a frightened primary school child who fights aggressively to preserve a soft, fragile and vulnerable internal self. Rosenfeld (Rosenfeld 1987), for example, has considered this in relation to what he calls 'Thick and Thin Skinned Narcissism' which may have important implications clinically (Bateman 1999).

Clinically, it can seem that there is a relation between the severity and toughness of the external psychopathic exoskeleton and the degree of vulnerability within. The success of this defensive constellation can be seen firstly in the effectiveness of this group in projecting their fear into others who come to fear them, for good reason in view of their propensity to violence. Secondly, an analyst pointing out a similarity between the activities of a dangerous imprisoned murderer and schoolboy is ridiculed. The notion that the violence and aggression might be defensive against psychological vulnerability seems absurd, and yet in a psychodynamic setting, this driving dimension can be discerned, even grasped by the patient and understood.

The second question that is raised concerns the nature of the psychological challenge that threatens the self. In Glasser's terms, a violent event or a crime scene will have a perpetrator, a victim and weapons, one of which will have been used to threaten, and another which will have been used in the self-preservative violence. The task of the investigator will be to figure out what happened to lead up to the violence that took place, and the task of the courts will be to deliberate on this and other accounts that emerge. In Fonagy's understanding of the violent event, there will again be a victim and a perpetrator, but there will only be one physical weapon; the psychological challenge that threatened the psychological identity of the perpetrator of the physical violence will of course have no physical presence, but may emerge in the investigation of the events leading up.

Both of these investigations of violent incidents focus, understandably, on the actual, concrete crime scene. Within the actual concrete crime scene, evidence will be searched for to provide clues to what actually went on. Obviously this is easier where the threat is concrete in Glasser's sense. Where the threat has been psychological, the identification of the weapon and the perpetrator may not be difficult, but the whole story will be more difficult to establish, as the threat leading to the violence has been psychological rather than physical. However, the nature of the psychological challenge involved in a crime scene is more complicated than the threat posed at the time of the incident. The psychological challenge, experienced as threatening to the identity of the perpetrator may have its origins in earlier experiences and patterns. As well as a relevant external crime scene, there is an equally relevant internal crime scene. The threatening object, be they a person with a knife or a nagging taunting wife also has a transference dimension in that it echoes an overwhelmingly painful infantile situation.

The notion of the 'internal crime scene' captures the idea that the 'here and now' of the violent incident is only one aspect.

The constellation of the violent incident often has parallels with other significant events in the perpetrator's past. In fact, an exploration of parallels between the external crime scene and previous traumatic developmental experiences often reveals that the primary cause of the incident as a repetition compulsion of previous patterns. The nature of the previous patterns, their relevance and meaning together comprise the 'internal crime scene'.

> *A 32-year-old man is serving a seven-year sentence for rape. He is being assessed for parole, and the context of his crime is being explored. The concern in the assessor is that the reason for the incident (a violent date rape) is difficult to establish. What the man does not say is that between age 10 and 13 he was engaged in a sexual contact with his biological mother; he was in care at the time, but used to visit her. Feeling strange about it, at times he would be impotent. The mother was usually drunk when she would seduce him, and would laugh at him when he was impotent. On the evening of the offence, the victim had laughed at him in the same sort of way.*

One might draw parallels in this case with the man we have already described who had both raped and killed. The clinical importance of clarifying the nature of the 'internal crime scene' and exploring its antecedents are clear. The nature of repetitive-compulsive cycles is that they are repetitive. Although the persons and concrete situations may change, the internal crime scene will need to be repeated someway, until it can be explored, and the unresolved trauma that drives it can to some extent be put to rest. In clinical practice, the importance of the details of the actual crime and links with internal traumatic patterns is taken a stage further. The classic psychoanalytic account of a symptom is that it is a crystallization in symbol form of a neurotic conflict, and that the key to the conflict may be found in the symptom itself. For the violent person, the incident is the symptom. An exploration of the details and issues related to it will reveal the characteristic pathways of the perpetrator's personality, like a homunculus. The violent event itself often contains within it a summary of the issues, difficulties and developmental traumata of the individual.

In this chapter, we have looked at two theoretical strands to the analytic understanding of violence. The first, the concept of psychopathy, includes the idea that the perpetration of violence, for example, by the so-called psychopath occurs because he or she does not have the empathetic resonance with the victim that prevents non-psychopathic people doing the same things. There are various theories about the aetiology of this apparent lack of empathy, related to developmental difficulties with attachment. Such difficulties, it is suggested, may lead to a failure to develop a mental model of empathy or even the capacity for mentalization in a more global sense. Alternatively it is suggested that there is a blunting of the capacity for affective experience or finally that there is a failure in the development of the capacity for managing affective states, which leads to the evolution of psychological defences both against identification with the other and the experience of affective states which are feared to be overwhelming.

The second strand makes a distinction between self-preservative violence that protects the individual from a physical or mental threat by the attempted obliteration of that threat and cruelty, where the victim's suffering is the aim, not their destruction. Confusion between physical and mental phenomena is seen as playing an important part in differentiating normal self-preservative or self-defensive actions, by ordinary people and acts of violence, which on the face of have no self-preservative aspect.

4 Towards a Theory of Aggression and Violence

The Concept of Aggression

In the previous chapters we have considered some of the main developments in analytic concepts of aggression and violence. In addition to these developments, with their roots in differing analytic schools and traditions, we have noted that confusion arises because of the ways that they have been conflated with each other and with related concepts. Partly this is a consequence of the enormous complexity of the subject matter but there has also been a tendency to try to false fit earlier metapsychological concepts with later ideas to preserve the 'integrity' of particular theories. This has often flown in the face of new developments in alternative analytic and other non-analytic but relevant disciplines and one result of this has been the politicized polarization of the debate along the lines of particular theories or theorists. As we have seen, this has been particularly the case in relation to the genesis of aggression where it has been allocated a totemic role in relation to the location of the origins of aggression.

To try to strip away at least a little of the confusion without adding too much of our own, we would like to reconsider the concepts of aggression and violence separately in an attempt to distinguish them one from the other and also to establish the relation between them. As we will come to see in subsequent chapters, this has important implications for clinical practice.

The word and concept 'aggression' makes most sense when it is used in a way that implies a broad-based phenomenon, the set, as it were, of which 'violence' along with other phenomena such as 'brutality', 'destructiveness' and 'sadism' are sub-sets even where these terms are used interchangeably.

As we have noted different words are often used to mean the same thing; in both Freud and Klein, for example, the words 'aggression', 'destructiveness' and 'sadism' are frequently used interchangeably. Over time there have also been shifts in the meaning given to words. Freud's early use of the word 'sadism' to denote the fusion of the sexual and aggression, had for example, by the time of Klein's later writings, come to mean something closer to a concept of normal, innate aggression.

The need for a more adequate theoretical framework is an urgent one because violence and aggression are by their nature difficult things to think about. If affects, including aggression, are essentially visceral and 'non-mind' in the first instance then violence is by its very nature 'anti-mind' and diabolic, rather than symbolic. The tendency is towards discharge, action and somatization rather than mentalization and this produces considerable problems both for thinking in the clinical situation and for the development of psychological theories of violence.

Freud of course attempted to develop a framework that encompassed both mind and body at the beginning of his career with the, in his lifetime unpublished, *Project for a Scientific Psychology* (Freud 1895a). This was intended to tie psychological phenomena to underlying biological substrata. In its own terms the Project failed, lacking both adequate concepts or the experimental or research tools to test and develop his hypotheses. It is only recently that Freud's ideas have been empirically explored and reconsidered, for example, by the psychoanalytically orientated neuropsychologists, Kaplan-Solms and Solms (2000). They, among others, have tied recent developments in neuroscience to his ideas about psychological structures and mechanisms.

In the same vein, Freud's reliance on theories of infant and child development lacked empirical and research evidence to back up his hypotheses and conjectures. In this field too it has only been recently that the research and conceptual tools have been available to test out his hypotheses, in part confirming his observations and remarkable intuitions, elsewhere refuting them. Important in these modern developments and for our consideration of aggression has been advances in understanding of the nature and role of affects.

Animal ethologists were the first people to systematically explore the idea of an instinctual basis for aggression in particular allied to survival, territoriality and both interspecie and intraspecie dominance. Although their ideas came to be influential for a number of analytic thinkers until recently, while analytic writers tended to talk in terms of the operation of single, discrete psychosomatic structures or a relatively limited number of instincts, drives or archetypes, such notions had long been abandoned by ethologists. Lorenz's 1963 book *On Aggression*, for example, made clear that the explanatory value of discrete instincts as directly causative of discrete behavioural or mental phenomena was limited. Lorenz suggested a model, which supposed the interaction, combination and conflict of a range of instincts, in what he called a 'great parliament of the instincts'. In his view it is the interplay between the constituent parts, which lead to the various manifestations of behaviour and the somatic basis of mental life. So while these ideas were clearly capable of integration with analytic ideas, these links were only partially or patchily capitalized upon. Some analytic writers, particularly Jungian, drew on animal ethologists such as Lorenz, Tinbergen and Goodal for evidence of the origins of aggression (Fordham 1957; Storr 1982; Stevens 1996) in particular, linking this to the existence of innate psychic structures, for example, instincts and archetypes; elsewhere these were also linked to psychoanalytic concepts such as 'unconscious phantasy' (Isaacs 1952) and 'deep psychic structures' (Ogden 1986).

Questions remain about the validity or status of these concepts of innate psychic structures and we will turn to this shortly but the question of making links between neurological systems and processes, states of mind, consciousness and their dynamic interaction has recently raised fresh interest with the advent of more adequate means of researching neurological processes such as PET scanning. Important in this is the growing understanding that affective states, including different varieties of aggression, are important in organizing mental experience and have complex relations with other sorts of mental functioning. Siegel, in a recent review of the literature concerning affects generally, cites emerging evidence that,

> ... emotion is *not* limited to some specifically designed circuits of the brain that were once thought to be the centre [sic] of emotion. Instead these same "limbic" regions appear to have wide ranging effects on most aspects of brain functioning and mental processes ... emotion is found throughout the entire brain (Siegal 1999, p. 122).

Kaplan-Solms and Solms (2000) have developed a line of theorizing, which has explicitly linked neurological processes to psychoanalytic concepts of structures such as the ego and mechanisms such as denial and splitting. Aggressive affects are located in the 'primitive areas' of the brain but not in a simple manner; rather aggression appears to be only one component (although as we will seem itself sub-divided into different forms and origins), capable of combination with other affective and cognitive elements. This suggests an even greater degree of diversity and combination between discrete neurological structures than envisaged by the ethologists and certainly by analysts. In the light of this, it may be possible to reach some tentative conclusions about the nature and origins of aggression as a starting point from which both to have a theoretical framework for considering all aggressive phenomena and from which to consider the various ways in which aggression is encountered clinically.

In reality it may be less helpful to think about aggression as an instinct or as a drive but rather to think about it as *instinctual*. From this perspective, aggression can be conceived of as an affective component or potential with a particular function. In the case of aggression the function appears to be one of mediating distance and difference in relation to the object. Jung, for example, early on proposed a definition of 'affect', which involves both psychic and somatic elements, in effect, bridging the two (Jung 1921). Bion's concept of the grid, proposed much the same (Bion 1989). The combination of both psychic (subjective experience) and somatic (bodily processes) elements is important to the understanding of aggression; as we have seen there has been a tendency to emphasize either one or the other, but an understanding of the links between the two has remained elusive. The debate about this continues with Panksepp and Watt (2003) criticizing Damasio (2003) for proposing a concept of affect, which does not include an element, which involves an impulse to action, even if this may be overridden.

To oversimplify, a function of aggression would be to establish and mediate difference and separation; one could contrast this, for example, with 'erotic' affects, where the issue is of alikeness/complementarities, togetherness and so on. Affects and their more psychologically differentiated development, 'feelings' can be understood as serving the function of orientating the subject to the object and mediating the relationship with them. Of course this is not a simple matter, as exemplified by the situation where violence (or perhaps more usually violent projective identification) is brought to bear in order to deny the reality of separation, say by a baby in relation to its mother or the schizoid individual in relation to his or her abandoning love object. However, as we will show, these would be instances of the failure to integrate aggression and examples of the development of specific pathological forms of aggression, to which we wish to confine the use of the word 'violence'.

Recent developments in neuropsychology have suggested a number of new models for affective functioning. Panksepp, for example, conceives of affective states as

> ... the psychoneural processes that are especially influential in controlling the vigour and patterning of actions in the dynamic flow of intense behavioural interchanges between animals, as well as with certain objects during certain circumstances that are especially important for survival. Each emotion has a characteristic "feeling-tone" that is especially important in encoding the intrinsic values of these interactions ... (Panksepp 1998, p. 48).

In infant development the interplay of affective elements including aggression, can be seen interpersonally, as important in the establishment and valuation of object relations. An example of this might be intrapsychically in defining internal objects and the differentiation of 'I' and 'not-I' objects.

Whether in an infant or an adult, this is not, however, a simple matter, involving as it does the interplay of a hierarchy of affective elements itself interplaying with other neurological systems. The exact nature of these affective systems is poorly understood and the categorization tentative, but Panksepp, for example, (1998) proposes four basic affective systems, at a neurological level; the so-called Seeking system, the Fear system, the Panic system and the Rage system. The Rage system, most relevant for our discussion here, itself consists of five sub-systems providing a sort of 'paint box' for the production of affectively coloured states of mind, from which a multiplicity of mental states may be produced.

This is more complicated still by the extent to which basic affective potentials ('primes') may be modified by experience (including perhaps at the level of neurological structure). So although some researchers assume that all affects are a kind of basic, 'given' others suggest there may be complex interactions with, for example, cognition that produces modified forms of affect. Primary affects may become the basis for derived affects, as they are subjected to alteration by cognitive processes. So guilt may have as a substrate a primary affect of 'separation distress' (Panksepp & Watt 2003), altered by the extent to which it has been 'cognized' (p. 206) during the development of relationships with others. Shame too, may be seen as having a similar evolution, although this may be an evolutionarily earlier development, with its group, as opposed to individual, psychological character; the relation between say sadness and depression, clearly sharing similar origins, might be considered in this light also (Panksepp & Watt 2003).

Un-Integration, Aggression, Integration, Disintegration, Splitting and Projection

Central to our consideration of aggression is the idea that there exists innate psychosomatic potentials which are important for the way that the world is apprehended and experience processed. As noted, this idea has a long history, notably with Plato's concept of the archetypes: Freud attempted such a development in the *Project*. Subsequently it has been hypothesized about in various ways (and rejected in others; see, for example, Stern 1985). Examples are Jung's rather different concept of archetypes (although based on Plato's), Klein and Issacs' developed concept of 'Innate Unconscious Structures' (1952), Fordham's concept of 'Primary Integrates' (1976) and Ogden's concept of 'deep psychic structures' (1986).

A detailed consideration of the existence or non-existence of such innate psychic structures is beyond the scope of this book but all of these structures imply a relatively complex degree of innate capacity to apprehend the world in particular sorts of ways. In our view it may be that these concepts all imply a level of complexity and a tendency towards 'ready made' and person-ified or part-personified concepts, which are not borne out by the evidence; instead complex psychological constructs of the kind envisaged by the above writers, may in reality be the consequence of multiple developments at much simpler levels of innate func-tioning, which then develop in characteristic ways, but shaped by individual experience. Stern's concept of 'Representations of Interactions that have been Generalized' (RIGS) (stern 1985) may be an example of the sorts of processes that are involved. Viewed from this perspective, babies' apparent attraction to breasts or human faces arise not from an innate capacity to relate to a breast or human face but rather a consequence of a much more simple, innate attraction to concentric circles. Contact with an actual breast or a face, would lead to the realization, in psychological terms, of the innate attraction to concentric circles.

The various ways in which innate potentials are realized, will of course be highly dependent upon the specificities of any indi-vidual's personal, familial, societal, cultural, economic and other material circumstances. It should be noted that these are likely to work in more or less complex ways. The concept of the instinct, for example, allows for the possibility of '... certain priming, releasing and directing impulses of internal as well as external origin ...' (Money-Kyrle 1978) which must with further com-plexity, react with one another, in 'feedback loops' in allowing for the production of, to all practical purposes, infinite potential patterns of mental experience. The innate structures may give rise to characteristic patterns of imagery and behaviour, although these are themselves not innate, even if their characteristic forms regularly lead people to the conclusions that they are.

Clearly innate structures exist because there are innate phys-ical brain structures. However, new understanding has empha-sized the role of primary caregivers in giving meaning to the infant's experience of his or her perceptions including affective states. Some of the psychic structures proposed by analysts as basic must now be understood as too complex to be primary but instead belonging to more sophisticated and advanced stages of infant development. Stern, for example, points out that concepts such as 'good' and 'bad' are complex compared to concepts such as 'pleasurable' and 'unpleasurable' and imply a fairly high degree of development of the concepts of intentionality and agency by the subject, and by extension, on the part of the objects to which these qualities are attributed (Stern 1985).

The concept of innate psychic structures may be better stated, at least in its undeveloped or original form, as innate psychic potentials, which require interaction with the environment in order to be realized. The way that the potential is realized will be subject to the exact environmental influences to which it is exposed. Certain affective states may perhaps be linked to certain situations or substances in an undifferentiated way. A small child will, for example, find bitter tastes unpleasurable and at least at first be averse to them. The origins of this could be understood in evolutionary terms as a protection against eating poisonous plants or substances many of which have acquired a bitter taste to ward off predation. Later, with the acquisition of experience, knowledge and a capacity for discrimination, such a broad prejudice may unnecessarily exclude important foodstuffs; bitter tastes may no longer be so off-putting and the 'taste' for them may be acquired by an elder child or an adult.

If innate potential coupled with experience mediated by care givers can be seen as providing the basic building blocks of mental life, this has implications for our understanding of the early processes of psychic development and in particular the nature of infant experience. From this perspective, it makes more sense to place centre stage the concept of un-integration in the development of mentation and mental development. This suggests a developmental model, with a different emphasis from the traditional analytic one stressing states of 'unintegration/integration' in normal development as opposed to disintegration/integration.

Such a model places emphasis on the combination of cognitive and emotional development. Fordham (Fordham 1987), for example, has pointed out that in such a model there is no need for a defensive bifurcation in normal development. Initially an infant's immediate affective experience of an object is central to its conception of the object. An 'unpleasurable' (more usually in analytic conceptual terms talked about as a 'bad', in our view a too sophisticated concept: see above) feed will be experienced as a quality of an 'unpleasure' giving ('bad') breast and a 'pleasurable' feed a quality of a 'pleasure' giving ('good') breast; the infant will have no *perceptual* grounds upon which to link the experiences of pleasure (good) and unpleasure (bad) as qualities of the same object (Fordham 1987). Only over time will the pleasurable and unpleasurable come to be perceived as qualities of the same object.

The concept of splitting is then best reserved for those circumstances in which the mental pain created by linking pleasurable and unpleasurable (good and the bad) experiences to the same object, is felt to be overwhelming. In this circumstance the illusions created during the early processes of concept building (the separate existence of entirely 'good' or 'bad' objects') is exploited for defensive purposes, by means of a retreat to the illusion (or delusion) of pure 'good' or 'bad' and a refusal of the too painful reality.

Meltzer (1986) talks about this in similar terms proposing, for example, that birth can best be thought about as an 'emotional experience', that is, one dominated by massive affective experience of an undifferentiated kind. This has within it the potential for the infant to respond in numerous different ways within a structure of innate potentials. This may be thought about, for example, from the perspective of Fordham's model as a 'massive deintegration', suggesting the possibility of an infinite number of responses to the experience depending upon the particular conjunction of internal and external factors active at a given time. This will be a matter of reintegration and mediation of the experience is dependent upon the mother (or mother functionary) providing what Bion has described as 'alpha function', which enables the infant to digest the raw elements of experience in order to effect a reintegration and establish related and organized individual mental contents. Repetition of experience over time, gives increasing sophistication and complexity to mentation.

Elsewhere the role of the right orbitofrontal cortex has been identified, as responsible for mediating and regulating the raw experience of affective states (Schore 2001; Cavalho 2002) and as this brain structure is not developed until an infant reaches the age of about one year, infants are wholly dependent upon their mother or other carers during this period to mediate affective experience. Faults in identification or failures of attunement, may lead to subsequent faults and failures in the development of the infant's, and later the adult's, capacity to manage their own affective states including their capacity to manage aggression.

For our purposes the important mechanism is the one which gives meaning to unintegrated affects contingent upon experience, noting the extent to which experience is a complicated matter, which includes internally generated experience, and experience as a result of complex interactions between external and internal stimuli. These are also the basis of increasingly complex psychosomatic and mental structures developing probably *in-utero* (Piontelli 1992) and increasingly quickly after birth. Important in this for our purposes are aggressive affects, which are capable of integration and providing motive power to development, in the face of psychic conflict subject to ego defences or where not integrated, subject to psychological defences such as splitting and projective identification. Integration is dependent upon the availability of a caregiver being available to process both the perception and the affective response in a way that gives it meaning (it is good, it is bad, it is dangerous, it is interesting and so on) setting it in context and giving it a name and the capacity to be thought about (symbolization); failures in relation to this means that the affect is not available for thought or for containment within a mental world, but becomes instead somatic and concrete.

The Concept of Violence

Taking into account what we have said so far, we think that it may be possible to begin to say something about the nature of violence and its relation to aggression.

If aggression is an affective state which, with other affective states, serves the purpose of orientating the subject to the object then the infant is dependent upon its mother or other caretakers to help it to make sense and give meaning to its experience; initially at least to provide for the absence of the function of the right orbitofrontal cortex functioning which has yet to develop (Carvalho 2002). This involves the kinds of processes that Bion and Winnicott, among others have described, even if they seem to have thought about this in terms of modulating extremes of emotional arousal rather than emotional experience across the range. Failures of attunement or identification with the infant may mean that the experience is not integrated but become intrusive. Stern, for example, has demonstrated the ways in which unpleasurable experiences such as occlusion of the nose during feeding, can have a longer lasting effect upon the infant's expectations relative to the pleasurable feeding experiences that have gone before (Stern 1985). In such circumstances the unpleasurable and particularly overwhelming, unpleasurable experiences need to be cut off from. The affect has to be got rid of relative to the experience of the non-symbolic unthought realm. Violence may be thought of then as the resort to aggression in order to distance the subject from its own experience of its own affects, including aggression, which is felt to be overwhelming or threatening.

In this context the word violence perhaps makes best sense, when used in more than a colloquial way, to denote aggression that at least in a clinical context, belongs to the somatic realm and is essentially 'action', serving a particular function. This concept of 'action' is consistent with Bion's usage. Bion (1989) describes action in this sense as,

> ... Something which ... is thought, even though it is thought apparently instantaneously transformed into action, or to reverse Keats's formulation of negative capability 'action which is used as a substitute for thought and not thought which is a prelude to action' (Bion 1989, p. 7).

Violence can be understood therefore, as a type of action, fulfilling a psychological function; the ridding of unwanted mental contents. We will turn in due course to the nature of the contents being got rid of. There are subtle distinctions to be made here; this definition of violence might include speech, and some other sorts of mental activity, for example, obsessional rumination, as having the essential quality of 'action'. These phenomena may be clearly seen in patients in the grip of psychotic functioning, for example. This sort of action, which is essentially mindless in its intentions, is carefully to be distinguished from 'behaviour' and is characterized by the operation of splitting and projective mechanisms with the aim of getting rid of unwanted parts of the mind in fantasy and in subjective experience.

Violent fantasy and actual acts of violence are linked but represent essentially different phenomena, so that fantasy about violence needs to be distinguished from violent phantasy, which may or may not involve violent fantasy. Fantasies of violence may be relatively sophisticated psychically speaking and concerned with psychic development rather than the obliteration of mentation. Childhood games of soldier or cowboys and Indians come to mind here as primarily concerned with finding of ways of thinking about and emotionally processing aggression, including forceful action and of being able to distinguish it (or more perversely or defensively learn how to confuse it with) from the destructive uses of aggression. Dreams of violence or death, for example, disturbing to the dreamer, may in fact be a correlate of psychological development. By contrast violent individuals, for the most part do not entertain violent fantasies (although dominated by violent phantasy). They may consciously plan or imagine violence and especially their own violent behaviour, but this is not to be confused with fantasy violence, in the same way that some children's obsessional manipulation of toys is not to be confused with play.

If the function of violence is to 'empty' the mind of unwanted contents, by means of splitting and projection, it may also be possible to consider the part of the mind that is being got rid of. Meltzer's concept of 'violation' (1986) seems relevant here including as it does the implication of intrusion either emotional or physical without distinction or rather emotional and physical intrusions experienced as though they are concrete intrusions by alien (that is non-ego, non-body) elements. The experience of violation is not, however, a direct quality of the emotion evoked *per se*, but of the force with which it is felt. We would contend here that the sense of violation is produced not by the quality of the emotion evoked, but by the overwhelmingly uncontained/uncontainable quantity of it (Mizen 2002). The sense of violation may be created as much by a surfeit of 'pleasurable' affect, for example, sexual excitation as by painful feelings such as shame or guilt, which may more obviously be seen to play a part in violence (Symington 1996).

It may be argued that to this point our proposed differentiation is only an exercise in semantics or hair splitting and that we are proposing a merely idiosyncratic concept of violence. Our view, however, is that such distinctions are very important because they can be critical clinically. Confusions and conflations not only in the common, but also the technical languages available to us are a reflection of internal conflations and confusions which are very likely to become important matters in therapeutic and especially the transference/countertransference relationship. These confusions are for the most part defensive and intended to keep out of consideration painful, frightening, even terrifying matters and analysis of the clinical material and especially the therapist's own countertransference is of great importance in order to understand the missing affective elements. The identification of their actual qualities, aggressive or violent are likely to be crucial to the success or failure of any particular therapy or analysis.

We have already noted that gross enactments of violence are rare in analysis and psychotherapy even if by no means unknown. Obviously, potentially violent patients tend to be rejected for treatment, as 'unsuitable'. Bion, following Freud commented that good manners are likely to be a 'minimum necessary condition' for analysis and violent behaviour is usually not least, a breach of courtesy, even if acts, such as the breaking of the furniture are, on occasion, temporarily tolerated (Bion 1980, pp. 11–12). This does not, however, mean that violence is absent from analysis, even if it is, by its very nature, 'anti-analysis'.

In what ways then does violence manifest itself in the analytic relationship if violent behaviour is absent and when generally the prejudice is in favour of its absence? In its absence, is violence unavailable for analysis in an analytic or psychotherapeutic relationship and especially the transference relationship? More generally can violence be considered to be absent from violent individuals when they are not behaving violently? In order to consider these questions and because clinical examples of a more dramatic and sensational kind tend to, and indeed are intended to, obscure the essential psychological components of violence we will attempt to give an example of how violence may occur in analysis. It concerns a patient whose material has aggressive aspects to it, but who is not manifestly violent in her behaviour. With this example we may run the risk of being accused of using material, which is not 'real' violence at all but drawing upon our definition we hope to demonstrate that there are invariant elements which are essentially violent and which need to be distinguished from those aggressive elements, which are in the service of psychological development.

A patient informs her analyst that she will be missing the last session of the week before a break. There follows a long statement which is apparently an attempt to show that this is a matter of great regret to her, a reluctant absence in order to spend time with her mother who is frail and whom she knows will soon die. The analyst feels that this may be an important expression of her wish for self-determination and ability to separate from the analyst/original mother, and a little guilty at the implicit criticism in her talk to the effect that she is persecuted by incorrect, critical, interpretations about resistance to the analysis and so on. In consequence, the analyst refrains from commenting on the patient's explanation.

The patient then misses the session. On her return after the break, the analyst felt profoundly shocked by the extent to which the patient felt emotionally absent. This was underlined a few sessions later by her commenting, not all together unexpectedly, that she intended to end the analysis as she cannot for the life of her think what point there is in going on with it. In the same session, a little later, the patient recounts how, over the break, she disagreed with her mother over whether or not she should miss one of her daily telephone calls to her mother. When the patient had said that she might not telephone because she had another commitment, her mother had replied 'that is not my daughter talking'. The analyst then put it to the patient that before the missed session, she had both wished to distance herself from her murderousness towards her frail and dying mother (and whether her murderousness was responsible) and had simultaneously felt that a child part of her had been murdered by both her ruthless, self-absorbed mother and by the part of her that defensively identified with this mother. She needed the analyst to help her to be clear that she herself needed the analysis not least to differentiate between her aggression which was necessary to both separate from her mother and establish her own identity, and her murderousness which both sought to deny the reality of the separation and her own murderousness towards her mother. Thus she felt that murder had taken place prior to the break and that the analyst was complicit in it. This led to the reestablishment of the emotional link that had been broken and the analysis could then continue.

With most patients there is considerable potential for confusing aggression in the service of development with violence; deprivation with destruction and progression with regression. In the example given, the analyst confuses his own aggression with the patient's protectively identified aggression. Patients may seek to exploit this confusion for defensive purposes, in order to keep at bay depressive feelings contingent upon guilt about destructive aggression, for example. In such circumstances, patients wishing to avoid painful psychic realities may play upon the analysts' own anxieties about his or her potential for uncertainty and confusion around aggression. Clinically this can be very tricky because it is important to apprehend the nature of the aggression in order to avoid perpetuating confusions and this is coupled with the analyst often being limited in the time that they have available to make the necessary distinctions and to understand them. Because the whole matter is suffused with anxiety and often with anxieties of a catastrophic kind, the analyst's potential for containment may be limited. While interpreting an example of a patient's striving for autonomy as a violent attack upon the analysis may be commonly recognized as having the potential to damage and even ruin an analysis, the potential for interpreting a patient's violent attack as an attempt at self-determination is less commonly recognized as damaging. Not least this is because such situations are most likely to lead to unconscious collusions of a sadomasochistic kind and remain masked.

This has important implications because the analyst may need quite quickly to form an idea about how much room for manoeuvre they have in the clinical situation because the question of the nature of the aggression will be more important for some patients than for others. So the importance of being clear will vary from patient to patient as will the latitude that is therefore available in the clinical situation. Some patient's will have more capacity for tolerating the confusions than others, for the most part depending upon the extent to which the patient experiences the aggression as potentially catastrophic. Thus for some patients the emergence of aggression within the transference will be feared as a disaster, although there may be a considerable range of consequences envisaged from breakdown of a valued relationship to annihilation of either the patient, the analyst or both. The confusion, which has been conveyed to the analyst, will need to be carefully considered.

On the one hand, there is the possibility that the conveying of the confusion may be an attempt by the patient to communicate his or her pain in the hope of having it contained and mediated; on the other it may be an attack upon the analyst's ability to make any links which lead to painful realizations and this may have as its intention not containment but ablation.

In contradiction of Walker's definition of violence, as adopted by Glasser, the essential ambiguity of the behavioural and verbal aspects of this example illustrate the extent to which it is the psychological rather than the behavioural, which is essentially 'violent'. It is the unconscious meaning of any given act or interchange that is important even if this is obscure and indeed may remain so for long periods including during a therapy.

Is it possible to say something more about the quality of the psychological experience, which is characteristic of violence? We have considered already the important part played by the sense of violation to which violence is a response but it may be important to qualify this, in particular what is meant by the word 'response'. In using this word we do not mean to suggest that violence has its origin in the environment, in any simple sense; that it is simply reactive. This idea has considerable currency, however, with many writers explicitly or implicitly contending that violence is a reaction to something that has, as it were, been done to patients (see de Zulueta 1993). As we have seen, this question has been extensively played out in the 'innate/environment' debate. Nonetheless the strength with which the 'reaction' idea is adhered to may have its roots in the fact that a subjective recourse to violence is likely to be experienced subjectively as reactive. This may not just be a matter of rationalization, justification (or hollow self-justification, depending upon your point of view) but be a consequence of the fact that subjectively, aspects of the self are likely to be experienced as alien, at least initially, and as it were 'coming at one'. Problems of integration, which may or may not be accompanied by active splitting, may lend themselves to subjective experiences of violation or insult felt to have an origin in the environment.

In consequence, it is common for people to describe their violence and their experience of using violence as a *reaction* even in circumstances in which to an outside observer such a contention is absurd. Intellectually the person may (although often they will not) be able to see that such a position is absurd, but this will be in contradiction to their feeling and to their experience, which precipitated the violence. Often the violence is conceived of as an action which is directed, *as though* it were against an object in the environment. In this context, it may be seen too that violence *per se* is neutral. It has no content. It is merely a mechanism whereby content – whatever the content might be – is moved around.

The central quality of violence, however, is its evacuatory function having as a particular quality the reversal of a sense of violation by means of creating a sense of violation in the other. I want also to draw attention to the extent that the violence seems related to situations in which there is *nearly* a conscious *experience* of an affective state which is feared to be unbearable.

The 'Mindlessness' of Violence

In formulating our concept of violence we wish finally to turn to a quality which it is commonly supposed to possess, namely 'mindlessness'. It will be seen in our consideration of the analytic definitions of violence, as well as in everyday life that it is common to stress the extent to which violence is conceived of as occupying the somatic realm. So we talk of 'mindless violence' and something about this expression is felt intuitively to be true. And yet it is not quite right. In reality although there is a mind, by means of violence, the violent individual appears to be trying to get rid of it at least in its all consuming hurt, pained and angry condition, by getting it into another object. A perpetrator does not want to mind; he or she wants somebody else to mind. And so it transpires that violence is not mindless, but that the expression conveys that its user is somebody who knows something about having a mind but wants to get rid of it into somebody else. They do not 'mind' the other person 'minds'. It is the violating operation of these mechanisms of splitting and projection, which in aggregate constitutes 'violence'. This also accounts for the apparent absence or unreality of pain or death in cases of completed suicide, para-suicide, deliberate self-harm or self-mutilation.

This area of mental experience has been thought about by a number of theorists considering the somatic substrata of mental life, perhaps most notably Bion. Jung, early on proposed a concept of the somatic substrate of psychic phenomena, which he called 'psychoid', and the ways in which 'mind' develops out of 'body'. Jung conceived of the psychoid in 'energetic' terms and as bridging psyche and soma (Jung 1948, paras 368–370; Jung 1968); implicitly there is the potential for two-way traffic between them. This he linked to his definition of 'affect' or emotion, as a precursor or earlier version of 'feeling', crossing the bridge.

Bion's grid describes a similar conception schematically, mapping movements across a spectrum that at one end is, or is indistinguishable from, physiological activity moving through proto-mental activity on to dreams, unconscious phantasy, fantasy, cultural expressions, thinking and so on. Bion's formulation also makes explicit, what is implicit in Jung's energetic model; that these movements are available for defensive reversal from psyche back to soma, which Bion called 'reverse alpha function', the workings of which can be mapped through the operations of a 'negative grid' (Bion 1989).

From this perspective, violence can be seen as the means by which the psyche attempts to reverse the progression that moves from the physical to the mental with increasing complexity and sophistication, when such a development would lead to a perception which for whatever reason, would be felt to be intolerable. In this way, mental elements are transformed into physical activity (this may be gross or it may be subtle). In the case of violence a special quality of the experience that is refused is that of violation. It may be too optimistic to say in the hope of finding a container as suggested by Winnicott (1949) but this may be so.

A variety of circumstances may lead to this situation. A mother (or the internal mother) may fail to provide a container for a violating experience. Alternatively, rather than providing a container for the infant's experience by means of alpha function or maternal reverie, the internal mother may be experienced as evacuating or may through projective identification indeed evacuate her own unbearable internal contents into the infant. These processes may be global in nature or they may be discrete. Gianna Williams (1997) has described the latter instance as *omega* function to distinguish it from the former, which would be consistent with Bion's notion of minus alpha function and the operations of the negative grid.

There may be a variety of reasons why the experience of violation cannot be borne. Fatigue, toxic states, threats to the ego from dystonic, psychotic or neurotic elements or overwhelming anxiety may all evoke a threat of being overwhelmed. Such circumstances also promote confusion between internal and external reality, about what is fantastic and what is external reality. Violence is intended to discharge or undo the threatening experience of violation. Paradoxically the phantasy may be the part of the experience that is felt to be dangerous and an enactment is likely to be an attempt to discharge or get rid of what is experienced as a dangerous affect. The man who punches another man on the nose is likely to be the man who is afraid of *feeling* like punching the other man on the nose. Violent acts are attempts not to have violent feelings (or be subject to violent affects).

It may be argued that experience does not accord with this description and that for example, violence and say criminal violence does not operate in this way but is in support of exploitation as in the case of theft or related to questions of status or control. But as we have already considered in Chapter 3, this objection is likely to be negated if one takes into account the motive behind the offence and the actions of splitting, projection and particularly the operation of narcissistic defences such as adhesive and projective identification. If according to this definition, theft is inherently violent, it is intended to elicit a sense of violation in the victim and violence can be seen not as in the service of the theft, but as its very *raison d'etre*. As Freud noted, thieves do not feel guilt because they steal; they steal, because they feel guilty. As we have already suggested, in this way violence may be manifest or it may be obscure in terms of behaviour.

In this chapter, we have considered some of what we believe to be the essential elements of violence. Violence can be distinguished from aggression, but is related to it, aggression being a substrate of violence. Aggression is capable of integration during psychological development being an instinctual, affective aspect of the psychosomatic processes that occur as innate potentials meet with experience. The emergence of aggressive feelings and affects (along with other feelings and affects) has the function of orientating the self to objects, including self-objects.

Violence cannot be integrated. Failures of integration are likely to lead to aggression becoming split off and violence may be one consequence of this. Violence has the particular characteristic of 'undoing' a mental experience along the lines that Bion seems to have been describing with his concept of reverse alpha function. Unbearable mental experiences are in phantasy and subjective reality evacuated and got rid of. This involves the somatization of mental elements and so may often present clinically in a form distorted by the defensive operations of splitting and projection and in particular projective identification. Considering the qualities of the experience being evacuated and their affective corollaries, we have referred to Meltzer's idea of 'violation' as an essential component of that which is being evacuated (Meltzer 1986). Violation is not, however synonymous with violence and violence does not beget violence in any simple sense. Rather, it is the experience of violation, uncontained, that begets violence, which has the evacuation of the experience of 'violation' as its aim. The purpose of the evacuation is the transformation of what is anticipated as being an unbearable mental experience into action (action used in Bion's sense), which in this context is an expression of a phantasy of omnipotence. Somewhat misleadingly this giving rise to the idea of 'mindless violence'. The apparent mindless attributes of violence are in fact a consequence of the purpose of violence, which involves the emptying of a sense of violation out of the subject into the object.

5 Types of Aggression and Violence

In earlier chapters we considered the ways that descriptions of aggressive or violent behaviour are misleading because behaviourally identical acts can have quite different psychological meanings; the naïve correlation of behaviour with motivation has made considerably more difficult both the theoretical and clinical understanding of aggression and aggressive phenomena.

The Neurological Basis of Aggression

There have been numerous attempts to develop criteria with which to distinguish different types of aggression. Moyer (1976), for example, has created a taxonomy of aggression related to behavioural manifestations. His categories are *fear-induced aggression*, say were an animal is trapped or cannot escape from a threat, *maternal aggression*, in the service of defending an immature offspring, *irritable aggression*, caused by frustrating experiences, *sex-related aggression*, in the presence of sexual stimuli, *territorial aggression*, in relation to rivalry for living space, *intermale aggression*, between males in relation to rivalry for females and *predatory aggression*, in relation to food seeking.

What we have criticized, on the basis of a false homogenization of heterogeneous psychological states of mind, the neuroscientist Panksepp has criticized on the basis that diverse behavioural manifestation may share the same underlying brain circuitry so that, for example, aggressive rivalry between males, the so-called intermale aggression and maternal aggression seem to share 'the same brain circuit, even though the two can be distinguished taxonomically by the different psychosocial/cognitive precipitating conditions' (Panksepp 1998, p. 193).

Research has so far provided an incomplete description and understanding of the neurological processes underlying aggression. The nature of the interactions between differing neurological affective systems and their categorization and delineation becomes the less certain the finer the distinctions that need to be made. Nonetheless, as we described in the last chapter, there is general agreement that there are four basic neurological, affective systems, 'Seeking', 'Rage', 'Fear' and 'Panic', which in turn are sub-divided into sub-systems (Panksepp 1998; Solms & Turnbull 2002). These affective systems and sub-systems do not necessarily operate in 'pure' form, but interact and combine with each other. We have used the analogy of a paint box of affective states, in which primary colours can be combined to give different colours, different shades of colour and varying intensities of colour. Damasio has proposed a hierarchy of neurological systems each level built upon the other. Using the analogy of a tree, Damasio locates at the base, physiological self-regulatory systems, immune responses, basic reflexes and metabolic regulation. Built upon these are pain and pleasure behaviours and upon these drives and motivations. Above these, branches on Damasio's tree are emotions proper with 'feelings' representing the most developed level of neurological functioning, the twigs. Each 'higher' layer incorporates the 'lower' level neurological systems. It is also to be noted that this represents a development from entirely unconscious functioning, through behaviours towards the development of mind (Damasio 2003).

Neurologically, what is commonly considered to be 'aggression' will be a consequence of one of at least three different affective systems, in interaction either with each other or with other affective systems. The three main systems are the so-called 'Rage' system, a system for 'cold' predatory aggression, and a final system called intermale aggression, which, as we have noted, includes, for example, female aggression in relation to the protection of offspring.

Thus it is probably misleading to think of aggression as a homogenous entity, but rather a collection, or even a diversity of affective systems and states. Similar behavioural patterns, for example, may be underpinned by quite different neurological systems. This underlines our contention that behaviour is a poor basis for understanding aggression.

Only one affective system, the 'Rage' system underlies the type of 'hot', angry states of mind, sometimes referred to as 'affective attack', often treated as synonymous with aggression (Panksepp 1998). Observation of the animal world quickly makes clear, however, that much aggression does not necessarily include a 'rage' type emotion; hunting, territorial or mating displays are obvious examples. Rage may be involved in a secondary way, for example, if an animal is hurt or frustrated in the course of hunting its prey, likewise bulls or stags locking horns over territory or access to females may become enraged; but this form of aggression does not have as its primary source affective attack. The kind of aggression involved in hunting may closely involve affects derived from the 'quiet biting attack' aspect of the 'Seeking' system, and defensive aggression from the 'Fear' system. Conversely predatory aggression may be involved in the 'Lust', 'Seeking' sub-system. The combinations of affects in a relatively simple way may often be observed in the non-human animal world and of course affective combinations are also to be found in the human world, albeit in ways that may not be immediately obvious. This is because of the much more complex forms in which they exist, disconnected from simple patterns of behaviour which link appetitive impulses to the objects of their gratification. In addition, the capacity for self-conscious reflection is either absent or very limited in the rest of the animal kingdom as is the capacity for the symbolic use of language, except in very specific special circumstances in the primates. Finally, there is the extent to which internal mental processes (for example, the not necessarily visio-spatial images which form aspects of an internal world), which are not necessarily expressed as behaviour, become themselves objects to which the self relates (Damasio 1999).

Traditionally, analytic concepts of aggression have not made these kinds of distinctions and at its worst there has been a tendency to attribute all kinds of aggression to the affective attack type of emotional experience. Lack of a conscious experience of rage emotion is then attributed, without differentiation, to repression or other defensive relegation of the emotion to unconsciousness. As we have seen, such may indeed be the case. Situations eliciting overwhelming affective experiences may be avoided or defensively cut off from, but this precludes those aspects of aggression, which are primarily free of rage type emotional experience. This may mean that clinically there is an emphasis upon the rage aspect of the experience to the exclusion of other aspects of aggression. Clearly, issues of aggression associated with dominance or the acquisition of food, territory or defence of the self, both physically and mentally, play an important part in orientating all higher living organisms to their environment, objects in their environment and others of their kind and this may be quite separate from rage type affective experiences.

If, according to our proposal, in the normal course of development, aggressive affects of diverse kinds are available for integration and are instrumental or functional, then it must also be true that there will be failures of integration, which will give rise to varieties of aggression, other than of the rage type, in ways that can be considered violent. On this basis it may be possible to propose a model of development which includes a diversity of potential affective states which fall under the rubric of 'aggression', in unintegrated, integrated and disintegrated (i.e., violent) forms. Aggressive or violent behaviours may be underlain by a variety of 'aggressive' affective states quite separate from the affective attack variety.

At this point, there is the temptation to speculate about the extent to which different sorts of aggression may be responsible for different sorts of violence. It may be, for example, that the violence associated with what has come to be called 'stalking' (although the mere choice of this term may perhaps say something about a dimly perceived intuition about the instinctual elements in the activity) might have its roots in predatory aggression, disintegrated by means of the mechanism's projection, splitting and projective identification. Likewise the range of disorders often referred to as psychopathic would seem to lend itself to the idea that non-affective attack, aggressive elements play a component part. It seems to be reasonable to suppose that these affective states are as capable as an other of being submitted to projection and splitting and of elaboration in phantasy, for example, of eating and of being eaten, of being dominant or subjected to domination by the other. Indeed it is just these kinds of processes that both Freud and Klein understood to be important in psychological development both in normal development and in pathological development and including complex patterns of introjection, incorporation, identification and so on. The question arises, however, as to whether these states necessarily include the 'affective attack', emotional experiences, either in consciousness or unconsciously, that is normally assumed to be the case. Certainly the absence of evidence for rage type experiences as a driver for development in infants, during normal development (Stern 1985) is at odds with what Klein envisaged, but would not seem to preclude the importance of non-rage aggressive affects, mediated and embedded within the developing structures of the self.

As tempting as such speculations are, however, they remain, for the time being at least, just that and not enough evidence currently exists to support such hypotheses. Possession of a better understanding of the natural history of affective development clearly has important implications for both theory and especially clinical work with patients who have difficulties in managing or understanding their affective experiences.

Oedipal and Pre-Oedipal Elements in Aggression and Violence

If aggression of one sort or another is a constant in the affective repertoire, then the ways in which it manifests will be dependent upon the processes of both physical and mental development. One of the most powerful contributions that a psychoanalytic perspective has brought to understanding human nature is the casting of different mental phenomena as developmental sequences. Freud's account of libidinal development through oral, anal and phallic stages in his *Three Essays on Sexuality* (1905) has been the most influential analytic account although there have been others including Klein's notion of paranoid/schizoid and depressive positions, notions of pre- and post-Oedipal two and three person relationships and so on. Later writers have questioned this phased schemes, notably Bion suggesting the lifelong oscillation between paranoid/schizoid and depressive positions (Bion 1984a) more akin to 'fields' than stages and Meltzer proposing a pre-paranoid/schizoid, depressive position (Meltzer 1986). Bowlby considered the development of the capacity from attachment and more recently Stern has described the development of the sense of self (Stern 1985). These different accounts together constitute a rich and often complementary (although of course elsewhere conflicting) developmental perspective with which to understand mental experience.

Curiously, neither Freud nor his successors extended his developmental approach into the realm of aggression. It seems as if the moral abhorrence of the idea that aggression might be as natural and integrated in the personality as a libidinal wish to explore, to love and to build has prevented a more objective and rational debate about its nature. If one takes a position of assuming that aggression is one of a number of instinctually derived affective systems balanced and acting in tandem with others to orientate the subject to the object (sometimes precariously or sometimes to disorientate the subject to the object) then it would seem reasonable to suppose that the development of these will follow a developmental line.

If this is true then firstly, aggression and the capacity for destructiveness are manifested differently at the different developmental stages, secondly that problems of integration at different stages of development line will lead to problems at the points that the developmental task cannot be resolved and thirdly, that in the adult patient, violence will be phenomenologically distinct depending on the developmental stage at which the problems occurred.

The concreteness of Freud's original conception of developmental phases has been found to be unsubstantiated by more recent researchers both in terms of his discrete chronological succession and the media through which he imagined infants experiencing the world. His contention that the mouth is the primary medium of early infant experience, for example, has proved to be wrong; gaze is much more important (Stern 1985). Nonetheless the 'taking-in' quality of an early infant's experience holds true and this has important implications for the immediate experience of infants and in the development of mental structures; the concept of developmental faults being expressed as pathology during later development remains valid.

Early Development, Aggression, Violence

The dilemmas arising at the earliest stages of development would seem to be around the issues of basic survival. Erickson has put this in terms of 'trust vs mistrust', orality and dependence (Erickson 1951). Aggression during this phase arises in relation to feeding, warmth and the rudiments of survival; the carer's task is that of protecting the infant from exposure to overwhelming emotional states, which are likely to be experienced as unbearable if unmediated. Unmediated aggression gives rise to the development of defences against anxieties, which have the quality of being total and annihilatory. This quality has its roots in the perceptual and cognitive limitations of the infant as well as in the lack of brain function with which to manage affective experience. In addition, explicit memory has yet to develop and implicit memory lacks definition or narrative structure (Kaplan-Solms & Solms 2000). This means, for example, that a child, who has experienced violence after the age of about two, has the capacity to remember it as an event (if the memory has not been subjected to denial or splitting). A child younger than two years will have acquired not an explicit memory but rather the expectation of the world as a place in which one is subject to violence. A result of this will be that in later life, the child older than two years when subject to violence might have an expectation that there are terrors in the world; the younger children whose anxieties emanate from a period prior to the development of explicit memory might later feel themselves to live in a terrifying world or even a world of terror.

These recent advances in understanding of child and neurological development mean that the exact details of Klein's theory of infant development are also to be doubted. Her contention that ordinary development arises out of enraged states in the infant, which ordinarily arise during the interactions between carer and baby, seems to be untrue. Although these states do arise they are perhaps more to be thought of as the beginnings of failures in the mediation of the infant's experience; as warning signals to the carer that, left unattended, problems will arise; and as a temporary means by which the infants can manage their overwhelming experiences. Sufficiently attended to, the potential for psychological damage can be obviated. Only if the 'bad' experience persists for too long or reaches an overwhelming intensity does the infant have to resort to the systematic patterns of forceful, splitting and projection which we have described as being the essence of violence. Ordinary development seems to take place in the quiet moments between mother and infant, in which the infant's experiences are given meaning and context within the mother's interactions with the infant. The enraged, angry, terrified, undifferentiated scream of the hungry or uncomfortable infant, who seems to feel that the world is going to end because their feed is not instantaneous, needs a response which will mitigate the painful intensity of their experience. Pathological states arise where this fails to materialize and it is in these circumstances that the infant's fear of annihilation becomes relevant. In this case, the rage, as well as representing a fear, involves a projection by the child of an overwhelming experience of aggression outwards, and this is then perceived as a threat. As we have noted, an important quality of these earliest experiences is that they are total and undifferentiated.

In adult life, problems with aggression arising during this early period may be manifest as violence in the form described by Glasser, for example, as self-preservative. These are where the anxiety is about being annihilated and therefore the threatening object simply has to be annihilated. Accounts of catathymic violent events, where (to quote from a gangster film script) 'you've just gotta kill every mother in the room' are often precipitated by a perceived or real threat to the psychological or physical self. This form of violence is also underpinned by the more primitive mental states described by Klein, where the aggression is totally split off and projected into the object that is perceived as attacking. The world is perceived as a violent and dangerous place, where you are either good or bad, 'with us or against us' and if against, to be destroyed.

Subsequent development does of course have an affect upon the consequences of earlier development. For example, satisfactory subsequent development may either mitigate or circumvent problems that were experienced earlier. If development has been 'good enough' then the vestiges of earlier bad experiences, which unmediated, would have had the potential for becoming pathological in a structured sense, may be retained in psychological form as opposed to a compulsion to action. Or if untouched by satisfactory subsequent development then the problematic area may exist in a way that is split off from, so called vertical splitting, which cystic aspect of the personality may come to the fore at times of stress and particularly in circumstances that repeat in some way the circumstance of the original, unbearable situation.

So a threat that leads to undifferentiated catathymic violence can be physical or psychological and the violence perpetrated can also be physical or psychological. Both an annihilatory remark or psychological attack intended to stop the threatening object in his or her tracks has the same function, and derives from the same developmental stage as the annihilatory physical attack. Clearly there is a distinction in that the physical attack is concrete, whereas the verbal or psychological one is more symbolized, and draws upon a capacity for mentation absent or unavailable to the person who resorts to physical violence. At the very least the physically violent man in a fight/flight situation will retain his physical developmental achievements such as agility and physical fighting skill at the same time as loosing all or part of the capacity for mediating his emotional experience.

Aggression, Violence and Power

The developmental dilemmas that need to be negotiated in the phase described by Freud as the anal stage of development are those that concern power, control and expulsion. In Freud's account, typically the toddler becomes aware of his or her bodily functions and bit by bit the control that he or she has over them. Defecation is generally regarded as the paradigm case, although this might now be regarded as exemplary rather than causal. The child's awareness of his or her capacity for control exists alongside the awareness that he or she is likely to be the subject of the other object's controlling wishes. So the mother may want the child to defecate in a particular place, a potty, for example, and in this way the issue of control enters into the relationship with the mother. The toddler becomes aware of matters that the mother is sensitive to (such as faecal mess or emptying the contents of cupboards), and he or she may begin to use these to express and articulate hostility to the mother in a much more targeted and controlled way. The balance will be between the aggression in the service of the growing sense of autonomy, individuation and identity which will be linked to bodily and then to emotional needs and in the face of emotional pain, the wish to subvert this and transform ways of relating away from the realization of these realities and turn it into a matter of power and control (Meltzer 1966). Power and control then ceases to be in the service of preserving and servicing the bodily reality of the child or later on the adult, but instead makes power and control an end in itself. This targeted and controlled aggression or violence is very different to the simple undifferentiated scream of the enraged and terrified infant.

In Glasser's account of 'cruelty', which he distinguishes from 'self-preservative' aggression, the cardinal characteristic is that the victim is under the control of the perpetrator. Torture is not a hot, immediate form of violence where the victim is a threat to the physical or psychological life of the perpetrator. Torture is cold, calculating, controlled, infliction of violence where the degree of control that the perpetrator has over the victim is of central importance. Aggression is not expressed in an incontinent rush of annihilatory violence, but instead is continently and in a controlled manner meted out, like small pellets of faeces. Elsewhere Meltzer has explored the psychological correlates of anal evacuation in the service of projective identification, linking the underlying phantasy to the bodily experience (Meltzer 1992).

There has been a recent cultural awareness of 'bullying' and intimidation as a psychological expression of violence. Bullying and intimidation are principally about cruelty and control, and aggression from this period of development is an important component part of this. The purpose of the bully is to divest him or herself of the sense of being powerless, by evoking this same feeling, overwhelmingly in another person. I do not feel powerless; I feel powerful because he is powerless within my power. There may be a symmetrical unconscious intent on the part of the person being bullied; that they fear their own aggression and so this is a quality that is invested into the bully. The consequent absence of a sense of aggression in the person being bullied, reinforces his or her sense of helplessness and powerlessness in the face of the aggression invested in the other. The resulting intrusive and persecuting sense of guilt and anxiety about aggression gathering apace, in the bully being experienced as driving their wish to attack. Feelings of powerlessness may be exacerbated where there is room for confusion regarding the legitimate and illegitimate expressions of power and control; a confusion between authority and authoritarianism, for example. So relationships may exploit this confusion if the relationship is part of a legitimate hierarchical authority, which exists in order to facilitate the performance of a set task, but this is used instead, to exercise power and control as an end in itself.

At this level of aggressive development, there may be considerable ambiguity; the faecal is felt to be both 'shitty' and at the same time overvalued and precious, expressed for example, in the notion of the purifying effect of suffering; the dwelling on techniques of torture by both its practitioners and by some human rights pressure groups illustrate this perverse idealization. These elements are particularly important in the development of perversions, the form of sexualized violence that in Chapter 9 we will be considering as one of the more common pathological manifestations of aggression.

Aggression and Violence, Jealousy and Rivalry

Freud's third phase of development was the phallic, which he considered as coinciding with the onset of the Oedipus complex. Children become more aware of the significance of the parent of the opposite sex, and aware that mother has other interests and attachments with which they compete. The child struggling to negotiate the phallic phase of development will fantasize about power and sexual potency in a way that is inflated and unrealistic. Identification with idealized masculine or feminine stereotype images such as Action Man or Barbie Girl illustrate their involvement in a wish to be the idealized form of their own sex in order to trounce the same sex parent and take the opposite sex parent for themselves.

Problems arising in the phallic phase exemplify the extent to which defensive psychological arrangements are essentially backward looking. So the preoccupation with the phallic qualities of objects is not to be understood as essentially masculine even if it contains within it the possibility of an increased developmental maturity. Preoccupation with the phallus is based upon an earlier preoccupation with the breast and especially the nipple. Penises are considered to be a sort of super-nipple and the preoccupation with phallic objects is an identification with an idealized mother. The essence of masculinity is the testes; it is these that carry the fertilizing genetic contents and the penis is merely the delivery system, but the testes are hidden and as such the antithesis of phallic display. In the similarities between bodily orifices and bodily effusions lay considerable potential for increased differentiation in the relationships that evolve out of the conjunctions between holes, protuberances and body fluids; by the same token under the sway of unintegrated aggression is the same capacity for confusion and conflation, in the service of defence against feelings of loss, as the reality of the loss is disavowed, buoyed up by specious substitution (Chasseguet-Smirgel 1984).

In this partial account of development as it touches upon aggression we have emphasized the ways in which the traditional psychoanalytic account highlights the ways in which psychological structures arise out of body experience. As Freud emphasized, the ego is a body ego. We might, however, have emphasized the development of the sense of self and the ways in which aggression bears upon this but we hope that we will deal with this in greater detail when we move on to discuss transference and countertransference. The developmental line as a way of describing the vicissitudes of aggression demonstrates a clear move from primitive ablative forms of violence towards more organized, and arguably less harmful manifestations even where aggression has failed to be integrated; in the exploration, toleration and elaboration of separation, individuation and differentiation, for example. Some have argued that the arms race and preparations for war prevented a resurgence of international hostilities since 1945. The energy and ingenuity that go into the research and development of new ways of killing people is an important sink for mankind's unintegrated or disintegrated aggression. During the Cold War, not many Russian soldiers were actually killed by American soldiers, but millions were killed in fantasy during military training. The problem is that investing all of this time and energy into these 'phallic' form of aggression has made the methods of killing people very effective indeed, should there be another collective regression into a more primitive, ablative form.

Aggression, Integrated and Disintegrated

In children's psychological development, following the phallic phase there is a period of latency, Freud contended, where libidinal strivings become less obvious for several years. As children become more physically and intellectually able, erotic drives become sublimated into creative, artistic, sporting and intellectual channels. Children become little painters, musicians, footballers and so on. In following the path of the aggressive elements, these too, in increasingly sophisticated combination may be seen to feature in the energy and enthusiasm with which these new sporting and artistic activities are engaged. Klein has described the ways in which the combination of erotic and aggressive elements combine, first in masturbation in which, if all goes well, there is a turning away from both the parents and the incestuous focus of attachment and identification with them (Winnicott 1958), and later on the development of an interest in playing sports and so on (Klein 1923).

Freud considered that children emerge out of the latency period with the onset of puberty, and begin the task of establishing fuller, intimate relationships with other people; subtly dependent upon the patterns of the preceding relationships with the parents, but only in neurosis or psychosis, compulsively repeating this. Other theorists have considered the matter differently. Jung, for example, saw the 'latency' period as the beginning of sexuality proper, considering the foregoing phases driven by 'nutritive' drives and the like. As we have seen, modern neuroscience sees these matters as being much more complicated so that sexuality is in practice inextricably linked to other affective elements, for example, the Seeking system to produce the lust sub-system or to intermale aggression or predatory aggression.

In Freudian development the (fluctuating) movement is towards a position that extends beyond solo, autoerotic, phallic posturing towards related genitality which, at least in its ideal form, encompasses difference, dependence and equality. In the complementary Kleinian developmental account, aggression is given greater prominence in the notion of the depressive position, which acknowledges the aggressive elements that exist side by side with the erotic ones. This involves recognition of the power to do harm and the reality of loss and death that is the corollary of acquiring the fundamental necessities of life.

One of the riddles about aggression and violence, which underpins this book is how to distinguish between a surgeon who cuts open the stomach of a patient, and a knife-carrying robber who does the same. While the contexts and motivations for these two acts are entirely different, the physical act is the same. The difference is in the motivation of the two people cutting open the stomach. With the surgeon it is to be hoped that the motivation is constructive. The cut is administered in a situation where precautions are taken to minimize the possibility of the suffering of the subject, anaesthesia and a sterile environment, and the cut is administered with the aim of reducing the suffering of the individual by treating the disease. Nonetheless the surgeon has to draw upon his capacity for aggression either consciously or unconsciously and his motivation cannot be naively considered as simply benign. In the same way, for the robber, the aim of cutting the victim is more confused than simple evil intent, containing as it does desperate acquisitiveness followed then by delusory self-preservative attack. The perpetrator may be blind to the potential suffering of the victim at the outset of the robbery, Nietzsche's 'rosy criminal' (Nietzsche 1961); alternatively it may be its very *raison d'etre*, the actions of the 'pale criminal' (Freud 1916).

While the motivational context of the two instances of cutting can make a moral distinction between the two acts, for our purposes, more important is the developmental perspective, which highlights psychological differences in the two situations. The violence of the robber may initially involve a fantasy of the power over the victim, say the ability to obtain compliance using the threat of the knife; but because this may stir paranoid anxieties, further regression to more anal-sadistic cruel taunting may result, in turn further breaking down into phallic, fight/flight quasi-self preservative forms of violence and in a scuffle or a struggle, a stabbing takes place. The aggression of the surgeon, on the other hand is integrated, genital and genuinely creative in the sense that it includes taking responsibility for the aggression and a sense of there being at least a degree of mutual dependency between patient and practitioner; it involves the use of skill and professionalism in the administration of a procedure that includes the potential for violence in the course of the work. Destruction and destructiveness is accepted as necessary corollaries and costs for the therapeutic advantage conferred by the surgery. In this circumstance the aggression is explicit and the aggressive act is carried out in the knowledge of its possible adverse consequences and appropriate preparations to mitigate them are made.

Neurotic Violence, Psychotic Violence and Violence in Between

We have made a distinction between forceful aggression, which is related to real threats, and aggression that concerns illusory or delusional threats, which nonetheless are felt to have the quality of violation. In the former case, the reciprocal use of force does not in our view have the essentially psychological quality of violence. It may be self-preservative (although we use this in a more limited sense than Glasser) or it may be in the service of protecting others, including others from the violence that they might do to their own self or to their own self-interests. Equally, force may be used against objects in ways that are destructive; a builder pulls down a building or digs up a field. A woodman cuts down a tree and a slaughterman kills a cow. But in these cases the quality of violence is likely to be felt to be absent because there is the expectation that this destruction is in the service of subsequent construction; a house, a wooden table, a meal. These examples, may illustrate the degree of ambiguity that is often felt to reside in such actions because there may be also disputes about the legitimacy or otherwise of these activities either in specific cases or as a general principle. Often the reparative benefit will be an important factor when considering whether the act is felt to be legitimate or illegitimate. So in addition to the sphere in which aggression is entirely psychological and lacks the quality of violence there are forceful actions which in our terms lack violence also.

Where the anxiety about hurt is illusory or delusory the aggression drawn upon by way of reciprocation may be violent, but is likely to be limited to action intended to drive away the source of the hurt that is felt, or at least modify the source in a way that means it is no longer felt to be threatening. Implicit or explicit threats towards the analyst or what the patient perceives the analyst to have an emotional investment in, fall into this category. Probably most violence, pub brawls, domestic violence and public order offences are a consequence of this.

More difficult are those patients whose sense of self may be fragile and lacking in ego structures alternating between integrated, neurotic and psychotic modes of functioning. Patients who fall into the 'borderline personality disorder' group present particular difficulties as a consequence of the fluidity with which they move between modes of functioning. These patients are likely to have particular difficulties in managing their affective states and in consequence resort to projective and splitting mechanisms of defence in order to maintain some sense of psychic and emotional equilibrium. Important in this, especially as it comes to be portrayed in the transference relationship, will be the extent to which the borderline patient invests the unwanted parts of themselves in other people, with whom, nonetheless, they have to retain a close relationship in order to maintain the pattern of splitting and projection. Threats to dissolve such relationships are likely to be experienced as an overwhelming threat, as the split-off parts threaten to return and destroy the fragile equilibrium that has been built; in such circumstances violence against either the self, the other or both may be likely.

Finally there is violence, which is related to the fear of annihilation. Both the sense of hurt and the fear of annihilation involve a sense of violation, but the former implies the survival of an enduring sense of self while the latter only a fragile or flawed sense of self, liable to disintegration in situations which evoke affects felt to be overwhelming or incapable of being processed.

Winnicott described four kinds of 'unthinkable anxiety, each being a clue to one aspect of natural development'. He listed these as:

(1) Going to pieces.
(2) Falling forever.
(3) Having no relation to the body.
(4) Having no orientation.

These are the ... stuff of the psychotic anxieties, and these being, clinically to schizophrenia, or to the emergence of schizoid elements hidden in an otherwise non-psychotic personality (Winnicott 1958, p. 58).

In both psychotic patients and patients with hidden psychotic elements, the psychotic aspects may not be apparent. In the former case, a patient may be in the prodromal phase of a psychotic mental illness but defended against the emergence of the psychotic anxieties, for example, by recourse to omnipotent fantasy or patterns of idealization or denigration. Alternatively with borderline or narcissistic patients, the area of psychotic functioning may be circumscribed having a cystic or split-off quality; perversions, addictions or anti-social behaviour may perform this function so that the anxiety is both expressed while at the same time being triumphed over by recourse to an auto-erotic or sadomasochistic manipulation in phantasy.

> *A man had a psychotic, 'depressive' breakdown when his wife left him. During the demise of the relationship he had comforted himself by stealing toilet rolls from lavatories. He had then masturbated while imagining the discomfort of people who having defecated found themselves unable to wipe their bottoms. Their imagined shame and sense of being trapped was a central feature of his fantasy, however, he had increasingly come to feel that terrible retribution would be a consequence of his actions, in particular that he would be publicly exposed and shamed.*

Important for this man was the sense of powerlessness imagined to exist in the people he had placed in the position of either having to hold on, in a painful way to their internal shit stuff, or otherwise having evacuated the shitty-ness, were unable to clean themselves up feeling instead merely smeared with it. Initially, by evoking this situation in others he was able to keep the anxiety in projection. Over time the paranoid nature of the anxieties resulted in an accumulation of fear of exposure, and the return of that which had been projected, in a catastrophic way.

Alternatively patients may resort to obsessional rituals or manic activity in order to keep at bay anxieties of a fundamentally depressive kind. Ideas of being important or special, shored up by external world 'success', may collapse in the face of what appears to be relatively minor reverses in the world of work. Paranoid anxieties may be hidden by the extent to which a person unconsciously encourages 'real' persecutions of one sort or another or idiosyncratically interprets the 'slings and arrows' of everyday life as personal insults.

Analysts hearing accounts of persecutions, of unfortunate and painful reverses, the exercise of compulsive ritualized regimes or of relationships carefully delineated in black and white, good and bad terms, may want to think carefully about the erotic and aggressive, hating impulses that they might disguise and in particular the anxieties that might be contingent upon these. This is not to say, however, that all such phenomena are a defence against psychosis and even less that violence is the automatic corollary of psychotic anxiety.

Psychotic patients who do become violent are likely to become violent in the context of their delusions. Analysts or other mental health professionals may be included in patient's delusions especially within a delusional transference. We will consider this further in Chapter 8, but the analytic frame is intended to encourage the constellation of the patient's transference within the analytic relationship and this will include psychotic elements. Considerable care and thought needs to be given to how far the delusional aspects of the transference can be held by the analytic relationship and the analytic frame and in particular, omnipotent countertransference responses especially of the omnipotent, messianic kind, need to be considered and guarded against.

Internal Relations, Aggression and Violence

We have considered above, some of the ways in which aggression manifests during development, in particular the extent to which bodily experiences have an important role in structuring, organizing and giving form to mentation and mental experience. Another aspect of this is the ways in which this is realized in the context of relationships and this is important for analytic work, in the extent to which it is the transference/countertransference relationship which gives access to the individual qualities of the patient's mind. While it may be possible to make broad generalizations about patterns of human relation and behaviour it is only in the intimacy of the transference/countertransference relationship that the individual can come to be truly known. It is in the qualities of the patient's internal relations that the meaning of their material becomes apparent and the kinds of ambiguities that we have been considering can be resolved.

Too frequently the concept of internal objects is equated with whole objects, a tendency reinforced by the need to personify them in terms of 'mother' or 'father'. We will consider this in more detail in due course, but the later concept of 'part objects' has done better justice to the idea that internal objects consist of aspects of objects linked to complementary aspects of the self. More recently still, particularly in the clinical situation it is the affective qualities of the link (although in more primitive or defensive states of mind these might be felt to be concrete qualities of the object) that have come to be emphasized, as well as the links that are felt to exist *between* objects. As we have noted, aggression presents particular problems because of the extent to which it may be that aggression is the affect that is defended against while at the same time being the affect that is brought to bear in order to affect the defence. Paranoia is the obvious case in point, with its characteristic escalatory tendency.

The relation between earlier more primitive modes of relating and later more complex modes has been the subject of much debate, summed up by Bion in his statement, 'Winnicott says that the patient *needs* to regress: Melanie Klein says that they *must not* regress: I say they *are* regressed' (Bion 1992). In our view, subsequent development does not supersede earlier ways of relating, but rather supplements them and it is in this way that modifications take place; earlier ways of relating remain where matters proceed satisfactorily, linked to later modes of relating. These then take the form of internalizations, which operates in much the same way that mothers mediate their infant's experience. Matte Blanco has talked about this in terms of the psyche operating in dissonant ways simultaneously (Matte Blanco 1975) at different levels of experience.

In this way, later modes of operating may either manage or alternatively disguise problem affective states and flaws in the integrity of the ego. The conflict may then be between object relating and narcissistic relations with potentially destructive aspects of the personality disguised. The examples that we have already given are of the outwardly successful businessman who is later found to be corrupt, or the person who exploits a position of trust for sexually perverse ends. Such patterns of internal relating, expressed in external world relations with objects may have a compulsive pattern involving the fixed projection of aspects of the self which are felt to be unbearable. Hyatt-Williams (1998) discussed this related to murder, calling it a 'blue print for murder'. Although for long periods of time the destructive aspect remains obscured, it will from time to time emerge, perhaps in explosive violence, the 'catathymic crisis', described by Wertham (1949).

Violence with the objective of expelling the unbearable object may be either unstable or stable. Where unstable the violence has a reactive character in which its projective quality may be explosive. The violence is intended to actively void mental elements, which are experienced as violating or potentially violating of the existing psychic system; the force of the violence will be commensurate with the force of the threat to the psyche. In the stable set-up the arrangement is also essentially projective but the evacuatory function is arranged in a way, which fixedly projects the unwanted aspects. This latter set-up may take the form of a psychic structure, which is a defence against psychotic anxieties. As we have seen, the 'stable' set-up is inherently weak in reality and likely to lead to the kinds of unstable, explosive situations, outlined by Hyatt-Williams, Cartwright (2002) and Meloy (1992) among others.

It will be seen that it is in the pattern of pre-Oedipal relating that the anxieties generated are more likely to be to do with annihilation rather than with being hurt, and associated aggression and violence more problematical in consequence. The specificities of the anxieties as they arise may be expressed in the external relation to their world. Menninger, for example, has considered the ways in which people's choice of suicide method symbolically expresses their internal phantasy (Menninger 1938).

The component parts of the phantasy will be dependent both upon the level of development and how this level of development is realized in the relationship between internal objects. The actual qualities of this may be deceptive, however. Oedipal elements, for example, may be to the fore, but these are predicated on the earlier patterns of development so that problems mediating aggression in the pre-Oedipal arena may mean that the anxiety which is generated by the Oedipal situation and its successors will not be about being hurt (castration anxiety) but may be to do with annihilation (of being killed say); of course the psychic reality of death itself has different connotations for different people; a sad loss, an unbearable abandonment, a terrifying disintegration, castration, annihilation and so on.

The pattern of primary object relations will be important in establishing a sense of safety and freedom from overwhelming anxiety and for the gradual development of a core and then an enduring sense of self. In the absence of this, paranoid anxieties in particular may give rise to violence. Violence may also arise where defensive, excessive projective identificatory processes create delusional phantasies of fusion with maternal objects, which in turn generate subsequent anxieties about passivity, feelings of being trapped and annihilatory loss of self, in the way described by Glasser (1979) in his concept of the 'Core Complex' or Meltzer (1992) in *The Claustrum*. Elsewhere de Zulueta (1993) has emphasized, actual experiences of deprivation or 'trauma' in the genesis of violence or alternatively brutalization, as have Gilligan (1992) and most famously Bowlby (Bowlby 1944; Holmes 1993). Violence in these circumstances has the qualities attributed by Glasser to 'self preservative violence' (Glasser 1994, 1998) which he contrasts with sadistic violence, which is more predicated upon the wish to locate unbearable aspects of the self into the other, often with secondary sexualization. Joseph (1997) has described the way in which sexuality may be an essential quality in a relationship, which links the subject and the object and compares this with sexualization as a means of defensively denying painful feelings which link subject and object. The obvious example here is the way in which sexualization may be used in a manic, antidepressant way. As we will consider further, in the chapter 9 on sex and aggression and violence, sexuality associated with violence is defensive and intended either to deny its essentially violent quality or in a perverse way, turn shit into sugar, the turning of a medium for relating and mutuality, into a denial of humanity and the exercise of power and control.

Some writers have also emphasized the role of fathers in the genesis of violence including Stoller (1985), Perelberg (1999), Fonagy and Target (1999) and Campbell (1999). Violence has been variously conceived of as arising simply as a consequence of an identification with a father who was violent in reality, in terms of the wish to displace the father in the Oedipal situation by violent means, as an identification with a degraded and perverse distortion of the penetrative aspects of sexual intercourse, out of the wish to attack the parental couple in the primal scene or in the absence of a reliable father figure, failure to make a transition from the incestuous attachment to mother. This latter situation can be seen as complementary to the phantasy of fusion with the mother.

The capacity for symbolization and for distinguishing between fantasy/phantasy and reality are also important and noted by Hyatt-Williams (1998), Fonagy and Target (1999) and Segal (1997), among others.

All of these factors have a bearing upon the form that the violence takes and on the meaning that is to be found in it as an expression of the relationship that exists between an individual's internal objects. There is, however, an important exception, which concerns violence that takes place in groups or violence legitimized within an authoritarian institution. It is outside of the remit of this book to consider this at length although we will give further consideration in the penultimate chapter when we consider violence and aggression in institutions. As was noted by Freud (1921) and by Bion (1968) groups have the tendency to act in ways which are stereotyped and at the level of the lowest common denominator of psychological development. In this way psychotic elements may predominate and individuals can be carried along by the dynamics of the group to perpetrate acts, which in any other circumstances they would not countenance.

6 Aggression, Normal Development and Transference

Central to our discussion has been the drawing of empirically and clinically derived distinctions between mind and body, mentation and action, which link these without resorting to Cartesian dualism or 'ghost in the machine' type explanations. The task has been to find a model for human manifestations of aggression and indeed for other affective states, that allow them to be explored as psychological phenomena, separate from but related to patterns of aggressive behaviour or aggression that is merely autonomic. Such a model is necessary to link violence with the possession of a mind; the alternative is to propose that violence is indeed mindless and automatic. In support of our contention we have already given the example of the way in which humans may be described as 'violent' but not animals. Ascribing violence to animals would generally be considered insupportably anthropomorphic and imply the possession of a capacity for a degree of self-consciousness, autonomy and elements of a mental world that we do not believe animals possess. Thus it is intuitively understood that violence is contingent upon possession of a mind however much we may also see it as involving the ablation of mind and hence the idea of 'mindless' violence. Our contention that violence, as a particular form of aggression, is a fundamentally psychological phenomenon rather than just an exaggerated example of aggressive behaviour, with the psyche as epiphenomenal corollary, is predicated upon this.

Unfortunately, adequate theoretical models have been lacking. The advent of neuro-imaging techniques with which to explore neurological processes and structures *in vivo* has, however, made it possible to begin to evolve them. Such models need to account for a truly psychological, imaginal realm, alongside autonomic patterns of action in a way that causally links psychological phenomena to physiological processes at the same time answering objections to the direct correlation of affects with bodily states, as proposed by James and Lange.

A number of theories have been proposed. Damasio, for example, has posited a model of mental functioning, which provides an account of the way that the core sense of self is created and maintained at the level of brain functioning (Damasio 1999). He proposes that maps of internal states are created within the brain. These maps take the form of an image containing the interoceptively derived information about the internal state of the organism that is required to monitor and maintain internal body homeostasis within defined narrow limits; oxygen, temperature, blood sugar levels and so on. It also includes information about the state of the viscera, vestibular and the musculoskeletal positioning of the organism. This together, Damasio refers to as an unconscious 'proto-self',

> ... a coherent collection of neural patterns which map, moment by moment, the state of the physical structure of the organism in its many dimensions   (Damasio 1999, p. 154).

The organism then comes into contact with an object 'a face, a melody, a toothache, the memory of an event ...' (*ibid*., p. 170) which is represented neurally as an image along with the ways that the organism is affected by the object. The sense of self arises as,

> another level of brain structure creates a swift nonverbal account of the events that are taking place in the varied brain regions activated as a consequence of the object-organism interaction ... one might say that the swift second-order nonverbal account narrates a story: *that of the organism caught in the act of representing its own changing state as it goes about representing something else* ... the knowable entity of the catcher has been created in the narrative of the catching process   (author's italics, *Ibid*., p. 170).

In this way, affects are not derived directly from bodily states, but from the neurological mapping of bodily states. Apprehension of the organism, the object and indeed of a constantly changing multiplicity of objects is continuously repeated. The image of the organism *in its relation to the object*, not to be thought of as confined to representations only in visio-spatial terms, are stored in various types of memory system (Siegal 1999); these in turn may become objects to which the organism relates if and when retrieved.

Damasio's model may be seen to offer a basis upon which truly psychological development can take place. It is the retrieval, elaboration and modification of images stored as information at varied brain sites that forms the basis for autobiographical memory and the capacity for an enduring but at the same time changing sense of self. Of itself this does not of course account for the development of an individual sense of self or identity; these neurological processes only provide one of the necessary prerequisites. The images created, in turn, need to be given context and meaning and this is achieved in the first place by the organism's affective response to the object. Again this is not of itself sufficient so that the organism, let us say a baby, is dependent upon the availability of adequate objects, which actively attune and identify with his or her affective states, in order to mediate, modulate and give meaning to the raw affective experience that the object evokes. As we described in Chapter 4, Panksepp and Watt (2003) suggest that the 'cognising' of primary affects, leads to the development of first social and then more differentiated affects so that, for example, basic separation anxiety in the social context leads to the development of guilt, shame or sadness and in pathology depression. The mechanisms of projective identification and introjective identification in relation to primary care givers are important in the processing of affective states, providing the potential for the capacity for more differentiated feeling and thinking and the development of mentation and a mental world. We will go on to consider this further shortly.

At its most basic level this means that the physiological systems, which constitute the human organism, are constantly redefining themselves relative to objects in the environment. The mechanism for so doing is, according to Damasio, the first and second order maps which are generated by the organism's contact with objects. If 'objects' are any stimulant to which the organism relates, including of course, the organism's experience of itself (the relationship between first and second order maps), then the organism is constantly redefining itself relative to these.

Crucially this model allows the individual to relate to him or her self or to aspects of him or herself, as though they are objects in the environment. The individual 'images' him or herself and it is to this image, or rather multiplicity of images that the self, a cumulative agglomeration of such images modified by the processes of first and second order mapping, relates. Affective responses to objects are central elements in these images and the self not only experiences affects, but also *is* affects. The self is always self-apprehended as the object affects it and the object includes aspects of the self as the object affects it. This provides ever greater complexity and individuality, within the limits imposed by innate capacity and experience, as the self is structured by its development of complex and sophisticated 'internal objects' and 'object relations'.

These matters have significance for the concept of transference and not least in the ways in which affective states manifest within the transference relationship. The original concept of transference was formulated in terms of whole objects and later part objects, this latter subsequently emphasizing the affective states attached to part object relations. Our understanding of the origins of self means that this now needs to be revised to include the ways in which the psychosomatic entirety of the individual is structured around relationships with objects including selfobjects. The individual does not just relate to objects; the individual's self is structured by its relations with objects and this needs to be included in what is usually thought about in terms of the transference relationship and the concept of transference.

If we propose a concept of the Self that includes the whole human being in his or her psychosomatic entirety, then the sense of self has, at its very core, the relationship between the subject and the object. Mental life does not originate or develop in isolation, but as manifestations of relationships. There are innate, inherited structures and potentials, but these only come to be realized in each individual's unique fashion, in the complex interaction between the individual and his or her environment. This is not of course a simple matter but one, which involves interaction, the interaction of interactions and in mind boggglingly complex feedback loops the potential for nearly infinite variation, within the defined parameters which neurological structure and the individual's environment provide. It takes place not just at the relatively superficial levels of social and interpersonal relations but at multiple levels, including basic physiological functioning.

Transference

Although the idea that the mind is a *tabular rasa* upon which experience produces character form, has gained intermittent popularity, at the core of most analytic theories of mental development is the idea that there is an interaction between innate elements on the one hand and experience upon the other. One of Freud's great achievements was to both realize and then to begin to systematically explore the centrality of relationships as the arena in which this takes place and to conceptualize this as 'transference', the unconscious patterns of expectation and assumption with which the patient imbues the analyst. Such expectations and assumptions may be straightforward or they may be complex in part subtly dependent upon the qualities of the objects that the patient has met in his or her past and in part upon the ways in which an individual has brought their experience to bear upon these objects.

The concept of transference like its corollary the counter-transference, which we will address in Chapter 8, has been expanded and elaborated upon in ways, which both illuminate and confuse. Freud's original notion represented the straightforward sense that objects in the present were obscured by the way in which objects from the past were transposed upon them, most particularly objects representing the parents in relation to the infantile subject (Freud 1920). Initially this phenomenon was conceived of as a barrier to treatment. Breuer fled in the face of the illusory and intense passion of a patient, presumably alarmed by the passion and failing to notice that it was illusion (Freud & Breuer 1895). Freud came to recognize the illusion and in this eventually saw a way of mining transference as a rich seam in the patient's mental life.

Damasio's model has been disputed particularly with regard to his concept of affects and the mechanism by which the self apprehends its self (Panksepp & Watt 2003); undisputed is the evidence that the relationship between self and object is central to the generation of mentation and that furthermore this relating takes place at multiple levels simultaneously including, as we have described, at the most basic levels of physiological functioning. As we have seen, historically, transference and countertransference have been progressively conceived of in ever greater degrees of complexity and this new understanding may perhaps suggest that the concept needs to be seen as operating at deeper levels still.

Freud, at least originally, conceived of the transference in relatively simple terms, as what came to be thought about as whole objects; for example, that the analyst represents the mother or the father or a sibling. This might be characterized along the lines of the analyst interpreting the patient's experience as something like, 'I represent your father whose aggression towards you was frightening'.

A 40-year-old woman in analysis wishes that she had met her (male) analyst ten years earlier, so that she could have married him instead of her husband, with whom she is chronically dissatisfied. In discussing these feelings in her analytic sessions, she is uninterested in the analyst's attempts to interpret this.

This idea continues to hold some sway (Blum 1994, 2003) but elsewhere the concept came to be viewed more in the light of defence mechanisms such as splitting and projection giving rise in infancy to part objects. These might be expressed by the analyst in the transference along the lines of 'I represent a frightening, aggressive, bad aspect of your father'. This is complicated where the analyst is conceived of in a way that is distorted by splitting, projections or the evacuation of unwanted parts of the self. 'I represent a frightening, aggressive aspect of your self, which you have projected into your father' (Klein 1952) or 'I represent the unwanted, aggressive parts of you' in the total situation (Meltzer 1968; Joseph 1985). Finally the transference may be conceived of as including, in addition, those aspects of the self that are unintegrated in the sense of never having been integrated (Fordham 1985a). This might be along the lines 'I represent potentials/experiences that you have yet to become/have'. This has been developed further to include the ways in which, the internal world of the patient has come to be conceived of as the relationship between internal objects, including the way in which internal objects may act as containers for each other (Bion 1984d) and where in unconscious phantasy, the analyst is a repository for aspects of the self, which are disowned, unwanted or yet to be integrated aspects of the self (Fordham 1985).

> *A 38-year-old man who has served two sentences for deception and theft struggles in his psychotherapy because he is constantly convinced that his therapist is lying to him to trick him.*

Objects may in part be understood here as the personification of maternal functions, which in phantasy the infant experiences as either the provider or the withholder of that which meets a need. Thus there is an object that meets the need and a different object that produces the pangs of hunger. This latter is felt to be a present, 'absent' object. In the Kleinian account it is the unwanted aspects of the self which by means of splitting, projection and particularly projective identification (conceived of as being inherently violent) are evacuated into the analyst (or mother), as a consequence of the ego being unable to tolerate those affective and affectively laden contents too painful for the individual (or infant) to bear. Although frequently denied (Hinshelwood 1989) the logical implication of this is that infantile states of mind are inherently pathological and adult pathology a consequence of the failure of the individual to develop beyond infantile states of mind.

> *A 46-year-old man is serving a life sentence for a murder committed in his 20s, one of a number of killings carried out while he worked for the local drug dealers as an 'enforcer', a hired hand beating people up and worse for failing to pay debts incurred. He is asking for release on licence, but has so far been refused because he is unable to get good reports from the responsible prison and probation staff. After a further failed attempt, in discussion with the prison chaplain, he realizes that the staff do not trust him because they do not know him, and they do not know him because he avoids them. It emerges that he assumes that they think he is filth and beneath contempt, and then with the chaplain's help, that in fact he believes that anyone who works in a prison is filth and beneath contempt.*

Bion implicitly rejected this (1987) by proposing a concept of 'normal' projective identification, by which means the infant (and the infantile aspects of the patient) communicate primitive, undifferentiated and *potentially* overwhelming affective states into the object, say mother or analyst, as part of the normal developmental process. It is the mother/analyst's role to mediate the experience and Winnicott talked about this in terms of both the analyst's and the mother's role as one of 'dosing' the infant/patient's exposure to the affect. Violent, that is, pathological, projective identification is resorted to when there is a failure by the mother or analyst to mediate the affective experience, in a way that makes it bearable for the infant or patient. In this situation the projection has the aim of evacuating rather than communicating the unbearable experience. The consequence of 'violent' or 'excessive' projective identification is not then the increasing capacity for symbolization (Segal 1997) and sophisticated, complex and realistic perception of the self and other, afforded by normal projective identification, but rather an ever increasing distortion and alienation from the self and objects.

Bion's work implicitly proposes a developmental model that differs from Freud and Klein (Bion 1989) in that he takes as his starting point not pathological, but normal development. Such models have been explicitly proposed elsewhere, for example, by Fordham (1976). These have as a base line, infant states of *unintegration* rather than *disintegration*, and distinctions between objects imposed by perception rather than active splitting. 'Normal' infantile states are not then characterized by disintegration; such states are seen as arising only as a consequence of defensive splitting and projection, which arise in relation to failures of containment and mediation of an infant's affective experience.

The operations of projective identification are crucial in this for the development of mental life in both normal and pathological forms; what Freud thought of as 'ego consciousness' (1895), and more recently Fonagy has conceptualized as 'mentalization' (Bateman & Fonagy 2003). If projective identification initially between self and object and later between internal objects, is the basic means by which experience is processed, especially the affective corollaries of perception and cognition, then as Damasio suggests, these allow for the development of images of the subject in his or her relation to the object, to be conceived of as objects, to which the subject relates. Normal projective identification allows for the (relatively) coherent assimilation of self/object-images as the basis for a flexibly coherent sense of self, drawing on various types of memory including autobiographical and procedural memory. By contrast, violent projective identification is likely to produce feedback loops of split off, disintegrated and rigid, self-dystonic images and flaws in self-structure and the capacity for 'mentalization'. The processes of projection and identification are the means by which we either find ourselves in our relations with objects or alternatively, lose ourselves.

Such physiological/mental processes account for the existence of an imaginary world (or world of conscious fantasy and unconscious phantasy) which may be related to on the same basis as objects in the external world. Such a model has important implications for our understanding of phenomena such as omnipotence as well as transference and countertransference.

'Normal' Developments in the Affective Experience of Infants and Patients

If this revision is accepted then the analyst's position in relation to the contents of the patient's mind and material can be considered to have two aspects to it. The first will concern those aspects of the patient's functioning which are non-pathological and relate to ordinary developmental patterns of projection, identification, attunement and empathy; these are the ordinary, nonverbal mechanisms of communication and capacity for relating to objects and these convey the range of aggressive category affects linked to a variety of vitality affects (Stern 1985). The second will be concerned with those aspects that touch upon pathology and the development of defensive organizations and defensive ways of relating with objects and the environment, relevant to our subject in the origins of violence.

The first consists of facilitating the 'unpacking' or unfolding of the patient's experience and exploring and particularly drawing links between proximate elements in the patient's material. This may be a complex rather than a simple matter with the analytic situation merely providing a condensed or concentrated version of the 'mental space', which is ordinarily available in the good enough environment. This is not passive but involves, for example, a baby's primary caregivers or a patient's analyst seeking to establish what might be thought of as the punctuation and organization of the grammatical structure of the baby or the patient's material in a way that allows the sense of it to become clear. This kind of relationship will vary in its qualities according to the protagonists, but constitutes the ordinary pattern of all human interactions of a non-'beta-screen' type.

In the relationship between analyst and patient, this does not address pathology of the patient as such. Pathology involves the inability of patients to structure their experience in a way that is integrative, usually because to make such links leads to painful realizations, which the patient feels cannot be borne; by the same token there is resistance to the analyst's attempts to make links. Astor (2001) has considered some of the ways in which analysts need to carefully consider the structure and grammar of their patient's communications in order to identify the severed links and understand the painful elements which have been cut off from. Elsewhere Carvalho (2003) has described this as 'parsing' the patient's material.

Such parsing, however, may also be considered as a more general phenomenon and the equivalent of the ways in which a mother attunes to and identifies with her infant in order to give his or her unintegrated experience, in its perceptual, affective and sensory experience aspects, context and meaning. It is out of this in both infant and patient that an evolving sense of self (Stern 1985), ego strength, complexity and identity grows. The ordinary parsing of affective experience by the infant's carers will include the mediation and placing in context of experiences of aggressive affects allowing for the development of a capacity for tolerating emotional, and then later differentiated feeling states, which the infant and in due course the adult can use to evaluate and orientate him or her self to his or her environment and to his or her own internal affective states. This process in infancy mediates the development of neurological structures, which provide the infant with the capacity to gradually assume from carers the function of mediating his or her own affective experience.

In an infant observation project, the observer is curious about the child (by now about a year old) saying 'taa' enthusiastically while playing. Mother repeats the 'taa' sound back, to the child's satisfaction, but acknowledges that she does not know what the child means. In a subsequent visit, mother explains that over the weekend, when an older brother got a new toy car, the infant had been very excited, saying 'taa, taa' – so they had surmised that he was trying to say 'car'. Several months later, the infant is making a noise like 'taa, mmm'. Mother responds, 'yes, daddy's car goes brumm; very good, car goes brummm'. When the child is about two, the 'taa mmm' discussion has evolved, such that it is linked to 'da da bye bye'. 'Yes, that's right', says mother in response, 'daddy has gone away in the car; brumm, bye bye daddy'.

As we noted in Chapter 4, failure to adequately encompass the infant's affective experience by his or her objects may lead to a failure to develop the neurological structures involved in the management of affects (Schore 2001; Carvalho 2002). 'Cruder' mechanisms of mediation equivalent to splitting are substituted for finer emotional differentiation and differentiations based on feelings.

A 29-year old man is known to the police, having been involved in incidents of domestic violence with several different women. The pattern seems to be that a new girlfriend is a 'good girl, not a slag like the others', but as time passes, the man becomes jealous, the girlfriend transgresses and so becomes a slag, leading to arguments that frequently become violent.

Fortunately it would appear that later provision of the circumstances in which the affective experience can be more finely differentiated leads to the development of those neurological functions, which had previously failed to develop (Schore 1994).

The processes that we have described above have as their starting point, ordinary developmental processes rather than pathological processes; we will go on to attempt to describe pathological processes from the standpoint of normal development in the next chapter. Historically, as we have noted, analytic theory has involved the modelling of normal states from pathological ones. Some analytic theorists have uneasily attempted to introduce notions of primary states of unintegration against the background of established analytic metapsychology. In particular the role of the carer in mediating the infant's affective experience through identifications and attunement has been explored by analysts drawing more closely upon research into the psychological development of children and especially of pre-verbal babies. This started with the work of Bowlby (1971) and has most recently been developed by writers such as Stern (1985) and Fonagy (Fonagy, Steele, Steele, Moran & Higgins 1991).

For these writers it is the emotional qualities of the transference that are important along the lines of 'I provide those functions that you do not have access to because your development has been distorted by privation/deprivation'. For Fonagy (Fonagy & Target 1999; Bateman & Fonagy 2003) this involves the provision of a model of mind in the other, by analysts with patients and mothers with their babies; pathology is to be understood in terms of the failure of the individual to have their experience mediated in a way that both establishes an internal sense of an increasingly complex and related subjectivity at the same time as there is a failure to develop a sense of an increasingly complex and related mind in the other. This has links to an earlier Freudian 'economic' model from which violence may be merely a matter of expediency as the object, which is not conceived of as possessing a mind, is exploited for impulse gratification. As we saw in Chapter 3, this model conceives of a lack of differentiated affect as a failure of mental modelling in the mentally disturbed individual, compared to say a Kleinian model, where the absence is considered to be primarily illusory in the sense that it is a consequence of splitting and projection and the evacuation in phantasy, of affects which are experienced as potentially overwhelming.

One of the most cogent criticisms of the 'normal developmental' thread of theorizing is the extent to which, for example, in infant development, the tendency is towards attributing passivity to the baby and 'simplistic' models of psychological functioning (Holmes 1993). Much of the subtlety and complexity of development and especially the growth of self-generated states is lost in what tend to be rather mechanistic accounts and the tendency has been to consider development primarily in terms of environmental adequacy or deficit when although the environment is crucial, it is not adequate of itself to account either for normal or pathological development. From this perspective, the baby's mind is in essential ways only a reflection of the parental mind and pathology a reflection of pathology in the parental mind also, again usually conceived of in terms of privation/deprivation. This may be contrasted with a 'Kleinian' position where objects in the baby's environment are experienced through the lens of distorting projection and splitting. This is caricatured as painting a picture of the baby's world, essentially of its own creation.

An alternative is a model for the development of mind, which depends upon objects for the realization of the infant's innate capacity to develop a mind. Mind arises in the relation between say infant and mother or analyst and patient, in which experience and especially the affective experience of the infant or patient is given context and meaning allowing for the development of an increasingly complex sense of self, derived from the multiplication of images of the self relative to objects. The ordinary parsing of the patient's experience underlines the extent to which it is not only unwanted aspects of the self that are projected into or onto external objects. Rather it is by this means that raw and unprocessed, particularly affective aspects of the self come to be first projected into the carer/analyst, mediated and then virtually simultaneously, subject to introjective identification (Galway 1996). Bion came to talk about the raw unprocessed elements of emotional experience as beta elements and the 'maternal' function, which processed and mediated these as alpha function. This idea has not, however, sat particularly comfortably with the Freudian/Kleinian position, which has taken as its starting point a primary *disintegrated* state for the infant, dominated by the 'death instinct'. Bion and Meltzer's ideas implicitly challenged this by implying the existence of primary *unintegrated* states, Bion deeming it necessary to introduce the concept of reverse alpha function to account for the existence of as it were 'de-mentalized' beta elements in pathology, particularly in psychotic states of mind.

This highlights the distinction between aggression, which is in the service of development and aggression, which is in the service of various forms of psychological defence. As we have seen aggression or more correctly, the aggressions have, along with other affects, the function of orientating the object to the subject. Thought about in slightly different terms the affects, of which aggression is one, forms a link between the subject and the object. In practice the affect will be unlikely to be experienced in pure form, decontextualized relative to other affects or modification by cognization. So we might say that the subject is linked to the object by hate, contempt, derision, revulsion, repulsion, dislike, irritation, disapproval, abhorrence, detestation and so on. All of these words describe states of feeling which have some form of aggression as a component part, albeit modified by the extent to which other affective components or cognitive elements are also present. Such states of feeling are links, which orientate the individual to the objects in his or her environment and by which means he or she in part evaluates them. Affects allow rapid evaluation, whereas cognitive processing takes longer. Affects and cognition may be dissonant or complementary in a 'second thoughts' manner. We will consider in the next chapter the ways in which aggression may be brought to bear in order to destroy the link or affective or perceptual qualities of the link between subject and object, where the making of the link results in what is feared to be unbearable psychic pain. Affective states, unmediated by other affective elements or cognitive processing are experienced as being unbearable, so that, for example, being dropped may be experienced as a fear of falling forever (Winnicott 1962).

Aggression in combination with other affective elements, such as those produced within the 'Seeking' affective system, are important for both physical and mental development and obtaining access to food, safety or warmth. Aggression is also related to effecting separation, a sense of separate self and of having individual and personal boundaries that contains individual and personal qualities. Where this goes well, this will include an increasing sense of continuity of self (Stern 1985) contained by a skin (Bick 1968) and an increasing capacity for managing affective states. One may think about this in terms of an infant's moves towards self-determination and autonomy or the adult's developed and expanding sense of self, individuation and of his or her own identity. These are all elements that come to be played out and may be explored in the transference relationship especially where they are in conflict with oppositional affective states. These matters may be affected by or be impinged upon by pathological elements, but are not to be confused with pathological processes.

A professional woman in her 30s with a history of depression and self-harm is in her third year of analysis. At difficult times over the three years she has, on several occasions, become incandescently angry and stormed out of the session in tears, slamming the door hard, leaving the analyst anxious about whether she might impulsively self-harm. However, these incidents have diminished, and from accounts of her life outside, things have stabilized. In one session, the analyst informs her of a disruption to the sessions, such that the patient has to miss several. The patient is angry and critical, which the analyst interprets as linked to her disappointment about her father leaving the family when she was young. She is again incandescent at this, but in a different quality, and she does not leave the room. She calmly recalls five or six occasions when similar disruptions have occurred, and points out that in their initial discussions about session times and breaks, such periodic disruption had not been mentioned. The analyst feels uncomfortable because her criticism is accurate, and reflects on a more integrated and healthy use of aggression in the patient.

Aggression then consists of affective psychic elements which contribute to the child and later the adult, locating themselves in their environment, social and psychological situation. It is necessary for the development of the capacity for self-care, location of danger and self-preservation. It is linked to the ever present and inevitable reality of death and for guarding against this. Such achievements depend upon the ability to integrate aggression; to both experience it as an affect, or rather spectrum of affects, linked with other affects and to objects, producing the capacity to think, take action or refrain from action, as necessary.

It is these developments in mentation, psychological functioning and mental life that come to be constellated in the transference/countertransference relation with the analyst.

Aggression in the Transference

In the light of these ideas, how can experiences of aggression and violence come to be represented and thought about in the analytic relationship and in particular as transference phenomena? As we suggested in Chapter 5, the prevailing tendency in analytic thinking to conceive of aggression as a single affect, albeit subject to qualitative and quantitative variation, has been largely undermined by advances in the neurosciences (Panksepp 1998); in reality there are a variety of affective states which may be subsumed under the heading of 'aggression' and the 'affective attack', rage aspect is only one component type. Furthermore these aggressions are rarely present in 'raw' form but are for the most part arrived at in combination with other affective systems (Panksepp 1998). It is the combination and embeddedness of these affective experiences along with the capacity for reflection, which renders the experience of affects, tolerable as opposed to overwhelming. Unmediated either by balancing affects or the capacity to reflect upon their value or context, it is the rawness of the affective states which is felt to be overwhelming and which, in excess lead to cruder forms of protection against mental pain, in the form of gross splitting and in phantasy the ridding of the painful content. It is as a consequence of the ways in which affective states combine as elements in internal relations that constitute the qualities of an individual's mental life. It is the ways in which the internal objects are constellated that creates the individual qualities of the patient's mind which is in turn reflected in the transference relationship. The analytic setting allows for the creation of a mental space in which to elucidate and explore these constellations as artefacts, in the total situation of the transference (Joseph 1985), in what Britton has described as 'the other room', (Britton 1998) facilitated by the relative anonymity and continence of the analyst.

Amplification of the transference dynamics, identifying the relations between internal objects allows patients to both entertain and reflect upon emotional and feeling states and the extent to which they are experienced as belonging to bounded entities of self and object or if there is confusion about the location, meaning and value of the affects. One example of this is the way in which 'Implicit Memory' operates as opposed to 'explicit' memory, in the generation of 'atmospheric', affective or mood states, which are not immediately available to explicit explication at the level of conscious reflection. Gross failures of integration, along the lines that we have described are manifested as defuse but pervasive anxieties of an overwhelming kind. Bion described some of these as feelings of 'nameless dread' (Bion 1987); Winnicott as 'psychotic anxiety'

(Winnicott 1962). Implicit memory as opposed to explicit or auto-biographical memory (Fonagy 1999, 2003) is experienced not in terms of images of events (although images and events may be appropriated in order to rationalize the experience) but rather in broad, overarching terms. One patient described this as a sense of living in a terrifying world as opposed to living in fear of a terrible event; of living in a 'concentration camp' world rather than in a world in which concentration camps exist.

In the transference, an adult exposed to violence before the age of two and the development of the neurological capacity for explicit memory lacks an overt memory of assault. They will, however, be likely to live with the conviction that the world is an assaultive place and the expectation that this will feature in their analyst's attitude towards them. This will be different from the patient who has an explicit, autobiographical memory of an assault even though, because it is painful, it may have been 'forgotten' or set aside (Fonagy 2003). This clearly has implications for the ways in which the patient communicates his or her experience within the transference/countertransference and how far the analyst needs to consider, both their explicit, focussed attention to images, ideas and cognitive processes and how far to the emotional atmospheres generated within the analytic relationship.

The processing of the unintegrated, implicitly retained affective states may be dependent upon the extent to which they can be modified and given explicit form within the present transference relationship. This includes the development of feelings out of emotional states (Jung 1921; Damasio 2003; Panksepp 1998) in the sense of finer distinctions, less tied in to global, somatically located experience.

A 23-year-old man is on remand for various offences, but his solicitor is suspicious of the police assault charges, understanding the incident as a rather chaotic brawl outside a pub, into which the police may have stuck a boot as well. The solicitor, therefore, is trying to get an accurate account of what her client remembers, but is hampered by his reticence. 'Look' she says, getting his attention and meeting his averted gaze, 'I'm on your side – I think that these charges are not the whole story. What really happened?'. The man is amazed. The notion of someone senior or in authority being 'on his side' has never occurred to him before.

Much analytic work, therefore, consists in the kind of affective, perceptual and cognitive sorting, which might be characterized as 'knowing ones own mind'. If it reprises the relationship between mother and baby then it is for the most part the ordinary interplay of reciprocal, affective influences. In this situation the transference aspects of the analytic relationship will involve the analyst's quiet reflection upon, and parsing of, the patient's experience that enables the development of mental space in which experience can be processed and integrated along with the development of narrative, autobiographical accounts.

> The idea each of us constructs of ourselves, the image that we gradually build of who we are physically and mentally, of where we fit socially, is based on autobiographical memory over years of experience and is constantly subject to remodelling [much of which] building occurs nonconsciously [as does] the remodelling   (Damasio 1999, p. 224).

In the transference the patient's phantasies may be explored through the evocation of their fantasies, their dreams, the elucidation of their perceptual experience and affective and sensual relation to the analyst. This will include the parts played by aggression in their fantasy life and the ways in which the unintegrated or disintegrated aspects of their aggression come to be located in the analyst.

By way of illustration we might consider the analogous case of children playing with guns. This is frequently a matter of some concern to both parents and children, to the extent that parents may try to inhibit their children's use of toy guns while on the other hand children might feel inhibited in playing with them.

Through the medium of play with guns a child might explore the limits of his or her aggression and its role in self-assertion and self-defence in contrast to exploitation and domination and to understand such distinctions. Such explorations are not violent in themselves. For the most part, children are sufficiently anxious about their play to make it clear to themselves and to each other that it is just play and the guns are only toys, while at the same time allowing themselves to suspend disbelief for long enough periods, to expose themselves to the affective states in an authentic, but bearable way. For this to happen the parsing function of the parent will have to have been internalized at least to the extent that the child has developed the capacity for playful elaboration and exploration of their imagination and affective experience. They will also have to feel free enough of parents' projections concerning aggression and violence, not to feel to be vulnerable to any confusion that they feel between fantasy aggression and violent reality.

Such play may be considered to be aggressive as opposed to violent; those parents who try to stop their children playing with guns are likely to be projecting their own aggression or anxieties about aggression into the children's play. This is likely to produce a situation in which the children, lacking the capacity to integrate their own aggression, are likely to become either the masochistic recipients of violence or alternatively violent, at least in the circumscribed sense, we have described. This paradigm may be repeated in other situations; sexual fantasy, for example.

Pathological Developments in the Affective Experience of Infants and Patients

We have considered at some length what we have described as the way in which more ordinary aspects of development are expressed in the transference relationship and the analyst's role in relation to the patient's experience. For the most part the analyst is able to take this part of the relationship for granted and allow it to 'take care of itself'; not to do so risks intruding, in a perverse way, into the patient's primal scene (Meltzer 1973). Some analysts have, therefore, taken to talking about this aspect of the analyst/patient relationship in non-transferential terms as 'the real relationship' or the 'rational transference' (Greenson 1965; Zetzel 1956). In our view this unnecessarily splits the analytic relationship and in particular risks overlooking the important relations that exist between pathological and non-pathological aspects of the patient. Perhaps more importantly this split is illusory and therefore unnecessarily defensive on the part of the analyst.

It is in the nature of analytic work, in any case, that for the most part analysts are concerned less with unintegrated affective states and more with disintegrated states because these are the matters that are troubling and lead patients to look for analytic or psychotherapeutic help. It is, however, very important clinically to be able to distinguish or at least to make clear that distinctions are sought between pathological and non-pathological elements especially bearing in mind the potential for confusing the two; from the perspective of our topic to distinguish aggression from violence. From the point of view of aggression and violence, one of the main tasks of the analytic work will be to distinguish aggression which is in the service of development from aggression which has come to be split off from and has taken the form of violence, either as behaviour or as a pattern of relationships between internal objects.

Anxiety is generated not only by the excessively painful or overwhelming affective states, or by the inherent instability of the defences erected against them but also by the potential to confuse normal and necessary aggression with violence; this confusion is an important component in depressive anxieties as well as the confusional states found in paranoid and schizoid states of mind.

An example here might be the inevitable aggressive component in genital masturbation. Winnicott has pointed out how masturbation requires both an identification with the parental couple within the primal scene and, in the resolution of the Oedipus complex, an aggressive rejection of them (Winnicott 1962). In this way there is a fine balance in relation to the aggression. There has to be sufficient love towards the parents to want to be like them, but sufficient hostility towards them to want to move away from them. In this way in the normal course of events, masturbation forms a transitional role, away from the primary engagement with the parents' sexuality towards the establishment of a separate sexual identity and private sexual experience. The extent to which aggression towards the parents is always present in masturbation means that it is always a source of guilt; if integrated depressive, where unintegrated persecutory and paranoid/schizoid. The ordinary and necessary aggression becomes essentially violent if the masturbation takes on a compulsive quality as a consequence of the anxiety about aggression which prevents a non-parental focus for erotic interest; in this way masturbation becomes not a way of imaginatively exploring sexual experience but moves towards withdrawal of sexual experience as a means of relating and becomes perverse.

This masturbation may then be considered violent in the extent to which it represents an attack upon those objects, which are experienced as outside of the individual's phantasied omnipotence, particularly the maternal object. At the same time the phantasy may include possession of, or an intrusive entry into a maternal object, within the individual's omnipotent control. This may give rise to the sense of being in a vicious circle, *claustrum* or trap (Meltzer 1992) and violent action then becomes likely as an attempt to break out of suffocating, incestuous situations (Cartwright 2002; Schachter 1999). The phantasy of the parents in bed is not then the template for relationships outside of the family but the compelling source of erotic interest, at the level of identification with part objects, within the family situation. The elaboration of the primal scene phantasy is not then in the service of an expanding capacity for relating to the other, but becomes an essentially addictive attachment, which 'goes nowhere'. We will consider this further in Chapter 9.

Such patterns of relating are constellated in the transference and in the face of failures of integration the 'ordinary' parsing functions of the analytic work become important in delineating the analyst's engagement with disturbed, pathological aspects of the patient. In these, past failures in the mediation of the patient's aggression are expressed in terms of the ways in which the patient invests split-off aspects of their internal world in the analyst, which as we saw earlier involves the destruction of awareness of aspects of affective links. As we saw in Chapter 5, the nature of the defences will be dependent upon the quality of the anxiety; if fear of hurt, for example, of the type characterized by Freud as 'castration' anxiety, neurotic defences will arise, specific to the type of damage anticipated. Where the anxiety is of annihilation, the defences will have the quality of omnipotent, delusional, withdrawal from reality.

Failures in the mediation of the infant's affective experiences of aggression are productive, for example, of adult paranoid states of mind where the aggression is experienced in projection or states of powerlessness, disorientation or compulsive compliance. Alternatively the aggression may be expressed in acts of sadism intended to evoke fear of aggression in the other or masochistic states in which the sadism is disguised in an attempt to escape the guilt or the fear of retaliation which the wish to attack evokes. All of these operations are to be found in the transference relationship with the analyst. Where in the transference, the aggression is located in the analyst the patient may be distrustful of the analyst.

In some cases there may be an intractable lack of a capacity to trust other people. The patient may be convinced that the analyst is motivated by a wish to control the patient in order to avoid aggression or that any aggression that is felt to reside in the analyst is an attack upon the patient. Thus the patient may experience the setting and the keeping of analytic boundaries only as an expression of, or a defence against, the analyst's own aggressive feelings in relation to the patient unmitigated by any sense that they exist in order to preserve the analysis and the analyst for the patient's use. The patient may be unable to distinguish between aggression that is in the service of preserving the object from violent assault upon the object.

A 35-year-old woman in analytic therapy, anxious about revealing too much is usually silent at the beginning of sessions, and in the last five or ten minutes begins to bring up more relevant issues in a way that can be taken up. She regularly felt disappointed that the session was ended just as she was beginning to engage, and silently resented the analyst for this. Following some other material that suggested that her mother had been a rather critical figure, the analyst linked this with the phenomenon of only bringing material at the end of the session and suggested that she was afraid of his criticism. The woman exploded in rage, asserting that the analyst hated her, and this was why he always stopped her just as she was getting going.

Aggression also makes for a more complicated picture because of the extent to which aggression may be both the affective state which is defended against *and* is also drawn upon in the production of the defence. So, for example, violent projective identification will add force to the phantasy of evacuating the unwanted affect, which may itself be an aggression in one form or another. It may be seen that there is within this, the potential for escalating recourse to aggressive projection, in an inevitably futile attempt to evacuate the aggression. This is a common characteristic of paranoid and delusional mental structures and the dynamic may be important in understanding a characteristic pattern of escalation in an individual's resort to violence, often culminating in an explosive violent climax or patterns of catathymic violence.

7 Aggression, Violence, Pathology and Transference

A young man has just become engaged following a nine-month relationship with his new girlfriend. Introducing her to his cousins at the engagement party, in the slightly inebriated banter, one of them teases him about how his fiancée has red hair and a shy demeanour just like his mother, unlike his previous girlfriends. The man is struck that he has never noticed this before, but immediately forgets the conversation in the bustle of the party.

A 22-year-old man is convicted for the murder of a close friend who he stabbed in a drunken brawl. His friend had laughed at him for being stupid in front of some other friends. Many years later, in therapy, he recalls being totally humiliated by his step-father repeatedly and regularly in front of the family and his friends while growing up. He concludes in therapy that while it was his friend who he killed, the person who he had really wanted to murder all his life was his step-father.

Unintegration and Disintegration in the Transference

If it is true that it is in the 'other' that human beings find themselves, it is also in the other that they seek to loose themselves. If the essence of 'normal' transference is integration, then the essence of pathological transference is disintegration.

Unintegration is the ordinary state of the invoked, psychosomatic potentials of the individual. These depend upon the environment and especially objects in the environment for their realization and upon relationships with objects for their integration. Within a spectrum, defined by the characteristics of the element to be integrated, a particular cognition or affect, for example, each individual achieves each aspect of integration in their own unique way. As we have seen, such relationships are stored as images including, but not necessarily, visio-spatial images in various types of memory and these contribute to and structure the internal world of the individual. As part of the person's 'landscape' internal and external, they too become objects in the environment to which the individual relates; from this the sense of self, consciousness, the mental world and mental life arises. The relations between objects, as embedded in images, means that we may come to understand patterns of object relations not as innate, although perhaps taking up characteristic forms, but rather the elaboration of what are in the first place the minutiae of the interactions between organism and objects, including internal physiological events.

In the last chapter we sought to make a distinction between those aspects of aggression that are unintegrated but seeking integration, and those which have been disintegrated and therefore resistant to integration. It is in the nature of the ordinary transference that it concerns movement towards integration. This assumes that transference is an everyday, indeed an every moment matter, not a phenomenon unique to analysis. It is only that analysis is uniquely structured to explore transference.

It can no longer be held that transference is only a reprise of past relationships (Fonagy 2003) and especially not of relationships in the whole object sense. The ordinary operations of the transference are consistent with Freud's descriptions of sexual development characterized by linking and change involving what Bion emphasized as the capacity for reflecting upon affective states as a prerequisite for emotional differentiation and development; the extent of the infant's ability to use the maternal object. With a somewhat different emphasis Winnicott highlighted the availability of a usable maternal object.

By contrast the pathological transference or rather the pathological aspects of the transference are characterized by malignant splitting, projection and especially violent evacuatory as opposed to communicative projective identification. If normal development depends upon the function, part-personified as the 'thinking breast', pathology is intrinsically connected to what has been part-personified as anality and anal expulsiveness. Within this, aggression plays a part not only as an affective element subject to communicative projective identification in a non-pathological way, but also as the force used to effect projective identification which is pathological. It is only the quality and quantity of the aggression employed in effecting the projective identification, which is pathological.

In the pathological aspects of the transference the disintegrative fragmentation of the self and object that goes with violent projective identification, is expressed in the ways in which the analyst is imagined by the patient to be orientated to his or her disavowed aspects. In the patient's unconscious phantasy the analyst either carries the fragments of the patient's self or is assiduously protected from them. This may leave the analyst either as a repository for the patient's unbearable thoughts and feelings (Carpy 1989) or aware (or even more problematically unaware) of lacunae in his or her affective, cognitive or even perceptual, relation to the patient (Symmington 1996).

Fragmentation can of course take place at a number of levels. Meltzer, for example, lists three, firstly in relation to 'raw sensory data', secondly the 'mythic constructions' that are stories about emotional experience and finally in relation to symbols (Meltzer 1986, p. 230). All of this will be recorded within the transference relations and the quality of the intercourse between analyst and patient. They may be described in the patient's material but it is the appearance of their affective components within the analyst's countertransference, which enables the meaning of the material to be discerned, hopefully in increasingly accurate ways as the analytic work progresses.

This is not to suggest, however, that a clear dichotomy exists between integration and disintegration. In contrast to unintegration, disintegration is always costly, psychologically speaking because it involves an act of not knowing; the disowning or denying of what in reality is known, equivalent to Jocasta turning a 'blind eye'. This is quite different from unintegration where something is truly not known, even if intimations exist. Thus where Meltzer describes the analyst's experience of fragmentation at the level of 'mythic construction', as the equivalent of discerning that the 'fallen columns of a temple contain architectural qualities' (Meltzer 1988, p. 230), our view is that this must be carefully distinguished from the architectural *potential* inherent in the raw materials available for new constructions which is present in an analysis in increasingly worked-upon forms.

The burden of the analytic work will be in ascertaining and making distinctions between the constructive and the violently destructive aspects of aggression. This is assisted by the reality that, as Bion notes, while truth 'just is', lies have to be manufactured and liars have to tread with care lest they inadvertently stray into the territory of truth (Bion 1970). Thus denied, an individual's reality is always seeking expression even while at another level it is disavowed and following Freud it has become something of an analytic truism that symptoms encapsulate what is denied even as they at the same time express it; so too do dreams. An individual must put considerable effort into 'not knowing' something that is unpalatable, anxiety provoking or painful; inevitably there is also a counterforce, which seeks to reintroduce the split-off element and this gives power, for example, to repetition compulsion and obsession. As a consequence, in the transference it becomes possible for the analyst to know about and even to feel the aggression that the patient feels that it is impossible to feel.

The Aggressive Contents of the Transference

Aggression is part of the content of, but is also involved in structuring, mental life and in the same way aggression provides both content and structure in the analytic relationship. Depending upon the capacities of the person for integrating aggressive affects, it either supports or undermines the capacity for separation and individuation. Aggression in relation to aspects of the self may be used by an individual in the service of effecting containment or may be brought to bear in order to, in phantasy, get rid of by projection, aggressive wishes and impulses. This may be reflected in an analytic relationship on the one hand by the establishment and acceptance of the need for the analytic boundaries or on the other by violent attempts to break or undermine them, for example, subtly by locating their authorship, not in the relationship between analyst and patient, but in some third party, for example, analytic professional organizations or an analytic theorist. Analysts too may seek refuge in such fictions under the compelling pressure of the phantasy that the emergence of aggression, with its connotations of separation, will be catastrophic.

In this way aggressive impulses in relation to the analyst or what are imagined to be the analyst's aggressive impulses towards the patient (which may or may not be accurate) may be aggressively denied. Paranoia is the classic manifestation of this, which at its most intractable gives rise to a 'nice' variety that is extremely resistant to psychotherapeutic intervention because of the implacable violence that is believed to be the dominant part of relationships.

An elderly woman was obsessed with proving that she was not responsible for the damage that she had caused to somebody else's car, which she had driven into when she was distracted. When the irate driver of the car pointed out the damage to her, she protested that it could not possibly have been her as she had just finished working a shift as a volunteer with an animal 'rescue' organization. The incident troubled her deeply and she spent considerable time and energy trying to prove that the, in reality, rather minor damage was pre-existing and somebody else's fault. It was intolerable to her that she might be a careless or thoughtless driver capable of damaging the object. In her mind it was critical for her to preserve the idea of herself as a helpful, caring person devoid of aggression in both intention and action. The thought that she might possess aggressive qualities was violently rejected to prevent the emergence of depressed feelings; she made a considerable nuisance of herself, tinged with threat, in her attempts to maintain her guiltlessness.

Such 'nice' paranoid people rarely allow themselves to enter analytic work, suspicious and anxious about the possibility of intolerable states of mind emerging, and attached to the gratifications contingent on their idealized sense of self. They may, however, enter therapy or even become therapists on the basis of a phantasy that analytic ideas afford them possession of, and omnipotent control over, internal and external objects. Such patients are particularly problematic as analytic trainees, placing considerable unconscious pressure upon their analyst to identify with their conscious wish to become the 'analyst' or 'therapist'; at the same time the fear and hatred of limitations and separation which analytic understanding provides is disavowed. The processes of adhesive identification upon which these patients rely, in part as a defence against their uncontained, unintegrated aggression, depend heavily upon the idea of sameness between analyst and patient. Relations with the analyst on the basis of realistic dependency are severely inhibited and only occasionally may it be possible to engage analytically with such patients if, for example, their ways of defending themselves temporarily breaks down.

Such patients assume a kind of 'those who are not with us are against us' attitude in relation to the analyst with a countertransferential corollary in the analyst, of being in the hands of a 'terrorist'. This is along the lines of Rosenfeld's 'internal gang' (Rosenfeld 1982). The patient may take up a position in relation to the analyst which limits the options to addictive dependency on the one hand or suicide or murder on the other. This presents the analyst with a situation in which the interpretation of the underlying phantasy is likely to lead either to the breaking off of treatment, self-harm or harm to a third party or entry into a protracted collusion which acts out the patient's central assertion that the only alternatives are addictive dependency or death. It may be possible for the analyst to be silent and to pick his or her moment to unravel the Gordian knot of this particular kind or transference, thread by thread; but it may also be the case that the narcissism of the patient is impenetrable and that the patient is unsuitable for analytic work. However, collusions between patients and analysts, in the face of these terroristic phantasies are common, the analyst getting caught up either in the anxieties generated within the countertransference or as a consequence of his or her own anxieties about unintegrated and uncontained aggression.

In less-defended patients or patients less in the thrall of fixed patterns of splitting and projection, the aggression is manifest in the aggressive location of unwanted aggressive affects outside of the analytic dyad. Here too unconscious assumptions about the similarity of the analyst and the patient prevail but differences are denied or located in other people or in force of circumstances.

A patient complained bitterly about the ways in which his friends were 'fair weather' and never available when the patient wanted them for support, despite the patient feeling that he endlessly put himself out to help them.

By contrast the patient noted the limitations in the availability of the analyst and that there were many times when the appointment times were a burden, but discounted these as a source of discontent on the basis that the analyst had to be endlessly available to 'more demanding' patients and in any case the analytic 'powers that be' dictated the analyst's arrangements.

These rationalizations are intended to deny the reality of the patient's hate towards a present object and the possibility of the analyst's (albeit contained) present hatred of the patient. Aggression, manifest as hate is not seen, for example, as having a place in the service of the analyst's preservation of him or her self and the analytic setting, not least for the patient's use.

If aggression has the function of modulating distance and difference, the issue of separation is the medium through which aggression is most often manifest within the transference. The meaning of separation will be highly dependent, however, on its significance for the patient. For the analyst considering the patient's material, perhaps with a view to deciding upon whether or not analytic treatment is indicated, the question will arise as to whether separation for the patient intimates varieties of mental pain associated with rejection and exclusion in the Oedipal situation. Or more seriously does it signify abandonment by the primary caregiver in a way that threatens the patient with overwhelming fears of annihilation? In the latter case, is then the significance of the Oedipal situation, that it is the prelude to annihilatory abandonment?

Neurotic Anxieties about Aggression

Where the prevailing anxiety is of loss, classically Freud's concept of 'castration', the defences erected are ego defences (Freud 1930), that is, mechanisms which are used by the patient to set aside those aspects of their mind which they think are incompatible with the retention of their object's loving feelings or approval or alternatively their love for the object. Unmodulated or unmediated aggression with its implication of uncontrolled distancing easily comes to be felt as a threat. Within the transference, in a symmetrical manner, the analyst is likely to be assumed by the patient to possess the same ideas. Disguising or cutting off from the aggression is intended to hide those qualities that it is feared will evoke the aggression of the analyst and prevent the emergence of those qualities of the object that the patient feels will destroy or damage his own good feelings for the object. The phantasy of possession and would-be-omnipotence dominates the mental life of neurotic patients as they contort, if not distort, themselves in order to try to control their objects and in particular their access to their idealized love of their object and their object's idealized love for them while at the same time denying their hate. Cutting off, para-suicidal and amputating states of mind involving dismemberment and the breaking of mental links prevail over holding in mind, the making of emotional links and re-membering.

> *A man begins psychotherapy, but abandons it when he finds that although the analyst's interpretations give him relief during the sessions, he is unable to retain enough of his understanding between sessions for him to feel that he is making any progress at all. This situation is exacerbated by him frequently missing sessions when he 'forgets' appointment times or sessions altogether.*

These people by one means or another, consciously or unconsciously, avoid those external or internal circumstances likely to evoke the kinds of affective states that they anticipate as being unbearable. These individuals may present with phobias or neurasthenia with the narrowing or impoverishment of their lives. Often they are set in their ways, adopting obsessional and ritualistic patterns of life, which support the illusion of omnipotent control over potentially threatening forces.

> *A woman campaigning against the depiction of sex in the media, complained to a television company about a play, which she said portrayed a man anally penetrating a woman. In fact the play made it quite clear that the intercourse was vaginal even if the pictorial representation lent itself to misperception. The woman's protest was not, therefore, about the televised depiction (which according to one's lights may or may not have been worthy of complaint) but about her own excited, but denied, sexual fantasy which had been transposed upon the images in the play.*

In the analytic situation these patients may unconsciously attempt to limit the scope of the intercourse between themselves and the analyst. Often they will say that they cannot think of anything to say or dismiss anything other than a limited number of well-rehearsed subjects as 'irrelevant' or unlikely to be of interest to the analyst. The analyst may indeed feel bored, not however, as a consequence of the patient's lack of potentially interesting material, but rather as a consequence of the patient systematically stripping their material of affective content beyond the anodyne.

Such people stand in contrast to those who tend to try to locate the split off and projected parts of their experience into external objects, for example, the analyst. For these people rather than avoiding the circumstances in which the painful affective states arise they seek to actively evoke them in objects. The various varieties of sadism, masochism and intrusive provocation would fit into this category.

> *A patient habitually paid his bill by throwing the cheque into the waste paper bin at the end of a session. When he left, he made it clear that he imagined the analyst as humiliated by having to dirty himself rummaging through the rubbish, to obtain the money. This excited fantasy, however, also hid and denied his pain at having to give up something that was very valuable to him; if the cheque was in the bin it must be rubbish and constitute no loss. In reality the cost was not least in the exacerbation of his envious feeling that he could contribute nothing of any value to the analysis.*

The distinctions that we have made do not, in reality, appear in pure form; they are characterized by the extent to which the threat, whether believed to be latent and passive or manifest and active, is felt to reside outside of the self. A breakdown occurs when the stability afforded by defences is lost, typically when events, internal or external, bring together the elements that have been split off from and projected, accompanied by the emergence of the feared and painful, affective experience. This will often be felt by the patient to be something that the analyst cannot bear and include the denied reality of separation between self and an external object, where the object carries an aspect of the self. The loss of the object is then experienced as a loss of a part of the self and therefore, effectively speaking, a painful amputation. This may be compounded where the object is imagined to be retained as part of a phantasy of possession and omnipotent control over the object. Once the defensive phantasy collapses, if the emergent affective states cannot be either worked through or alternatively reinstated in a manic fashion, the patient is likely to feel overwhelmed by states of vulnerable, powerlessness and helplessness. Violence may then take place as an attempt to reverse the feelings of vulnerability, powerlessness and helplessness by instilling them in the other, either in reality or in phantasy.

In the transference situation, the anxiety is likely to be about the patient's phantasy about the destructiveness of their aggression and its impact upon the analyst coupled with what the patient imagines is the analyst's anxiety about the patient's anxiety, complicated by the imagined overwhelming anxiety that the analyst feels about their own aggression along with their fear of the effect upon the patient. This phantasy may have been carefully avoided in one of the ways described above, but the reality of separation may be brought home, perhaps by a break, for example, so that the patient's aggression towards the analyst becomes manifest, along with the anxiety that the break is an expression of the analyst's murderous aggression towards the patient.

It may be the breakdown of defences or threat of breakdown that leads to a person seeking analytic help. Prior to breakdown, whether of neurotic, psychotic or borderline kinds, there may be no obvious signs of either pathology or distress except perhaps a sense that the individual functions in somewhat rigid or stereotyped psychological ways. An individual's sense of this and of there being something 'missing' or wrong in themselves or in their life, may lead them to seek help from analysts or therapists. Overwhelming or ruminative, preoccupying fear of other people's aggression or violence, or fear of political, environmental or military disaster, in contrast to the patient's sense of their own defencelessness, may be examples of the ways in which an individual's aggression goes 'missing'.

An analyst discerning the existence of such 'missing' elements may be a prelude to the development of a so-called 'negative therapeutic reaction'. If aggression is felt by a patient to be inimical to the existence of a 'good' relationship with the analyst this may be countered by the patient nurturing a defensive phantasy that any aggression is located outside of the analytic relationship. If in the light of the analyst's interpretations, the patient looses the capacity to sustain this phantasy, this may give way to the patient coming to feel that all of the aggression is located in the analyst. The analyst may then be experienced as unfeeling, unempathetic, a crook, a charlatan, incompetent, critical or attacking (Fordham 1974). The patient may imbue the analyst with aggressive wishes or violent impulses, the wish to control the patient or perhaps to humiliate or denigrate them. This can take on the character of a stuck, sadomasochistic transference relation in which the patient maintains a fixed, violent projection of their aggression into the analyst, which becomes resistant to interpretation or change. Rosenfeld has described this in terms of 'impasse' (Rosenfeld 1987) presenting as it does considerable problems of technique.

If, however, the analyst is able to tolerate such attributions and rely enough on his or her own experience of analysis to bear the uncertainty that goes with such assertions, it becomes possible to work out what is felt by the patient to be unbearable, and how this is being voided by means of the patient's projections or projective identifications. It may then be possible not to enter into defensive collusions or effective denial and explore the origins and meaning of the patient's painful or frightening affective states, based on direct rather than dubious, 'hearsay' evidence.

Borderline States

For some patients, anxiety about separateness will have the quality of annihilation consequent upon infantile abandonment rather than 'just' painful loss or hurt (Fordham 1985b). Such anxieties originating at the earliest phases of infantile development may be characterized as psychotic. Winnicott lists a number of what he calls psychotic anxieties including 'falling forever', falling to pieces and depersonalization to the extent of feeling that one ceases to exist. The nature of the psychological defences against such anxieties will depend upon the degree of capacity for relating to objects that has developed in the patient. Where the destructiveness of the aggression is relatively unmitigated by the establishment of organized internal relations, which can provide a degree of containment by virtue only of their existence, frank psychosis develops. We will return to this shortly.

If, however, some internal, organized, object relations exist, the psychotic anxieties may be contained, in a more or less unstable way, by resort to 'neurotic' defences, especially insofar as they allow for the development of the omnipotent phantasy which 'controls' the separateness of the external objects into whom the patient's internal objects are projected. It is the patient's sense of being in 'control' of their internal sense of the separateness of their objects that their equanimity depends. Such patients tend to breakdown or act out, becoming violent or self-harming when the realization of the reality of the separateness of objects upon whom they depend is rendered undeniable; a partner may leave them or they may loose a job or suffer some other reverse. In the absence of a capacity to draw upon aggression for the establishment of separateness in self or others, violence is brought to bear upon self and/or object in order to try to obliterate the capacity to discern the reality of separation.

Violence may be offered or threatened in order to coerce the object to conform to the phantasy of identity between self and object. Alternatively violence may be directed at the organs of apprehension or parts of the body associated with autonomous existence. Often these will be the patient's sexual organs or parts of the body felt by the patient to have a sexual significance. The patient's phantasies about the analyst are likely to be centred upon such part objects. The violence implicit or explicit is directed at the analyst, if the analyst is felt to embody aspects of the patient associated with separation. Typically, but not confined to borderline patients, this may include the analyst's capacity to think or have their own ideas, or smearing violence against the analyst's integrity, for example, by attempting to establish that the analyst is dirty, dishonest or mad, bad and dangerous to know.

In analysis it is to be hoped that a growing awareness of separateness along with the capacity to tolerate this, may be achieved as a kind of controlled 'breakdown'. But violence directed against the body of the analyst or objects belonging to the analyst, becomes a distinct danger where the patient feels that his or her existence is threatened by an assertion by the analyst of his or her autonomy which may be experienced by the patient as an annihilatory attack. The kind of impasse that we described above can then emerge and it can be a very difficult matter technically, because the situation is reached where the withdrawal of the analyst is felt to be a threat, but so too is the continuing presence of the analyst felt to be a manifestation of the patient's aggression, and as such a threatened and therefore threatening object. Very careful thought needs to be given therefore, to the setting in which such patients are treated, both from the point of view of being able to maintain a sufficient sense of containment within the patient, but also from the point of view of the safety of analyst, patient and third parties.

A distinction has been made between neurotic splitting, characterized as 'horizontal', with the unwanted mental contents subject to repression, and 'vertical' splitting, where complete aspects of the personality are cut off from. In the latter situation these cut off parts can have the qualities of being sub-personalities (Redfearn 1985), a 'cohabitee' (Sinason 1993) or even so called multiple personalities. Often the nature or even the existence such sub-personalities can be obscure or even completely hidden. Rosenfeld describes the case of an apparently respectable woman doctor, whom he has been treating for some time in an apparently satisfactory manner, whom he discovered through a newspaper had been operating as a drugs dealer (Rosenfeld 1987, p. 136).

The relationship between adaptive, superficially integrated and functioning states may alternate with much more, apparently disintegrated states. The latter may be precipitated by painful affects or realities, breaching the patient's defences. The 'more' disintegrated, frankly psychotic states may represent increasingly desperate attempts to re-establish would-be-omnipotence.

A patient was compulsorily detained on a psychiatric ward and a diagnosis of manic depression was made. A member of staff began regular meetings with the patient. The patient talked at length about his situation, initially seeming to find relief in having somebody in whom he could confide his worries. The member of staff made little comment, but felt increasingly surprised at the diagnosis as the patient spoke lucidly and with considerable feeling about his home and family life and with no sign of the dramatic and flamboyant talk and behaviour, which had previously been reported. After a few meetings and towards the end of an interview the staff member said to the patient, 'From your description, your relationship with your father seems to be a painful and difficult one'. The patient immediately stood up saying 'I am Jesus Christ and this is the kingdom of God and I cast you out'. The patient then struck the member of staff who had to beat a hasty retreat.

In all probability the member of staff's comment was both accurate and pertinent, if partial and lacking in understanding of the transference implications of what the patient had been describing in relation to his father. But his articulation of the patient's pain and his understanding of the reasons for it were more than the patient could bear. Among other things it was experienced as a humiliation and an assault. He responded 'in kind' with an assertion of omnipotent power, on behalf of the Father, with the rather heart-rending implication of his being both his father's much loved son and a son who felt abandoned to an experience of crucifixion.

As this example illustrates, the collapse of adaptive, vertically split aspects of the personality may lead to the emergence of less well-adapted aspects of the patient. Psychosis in the psychiatric sense, for example, schizophrenia or affective conditions such as depression or hypermania may emerge. Alternatively, but rarely, bizarre or grossly violent acts may result. Again the analyst may be placed at risk or the risk may be displaced.

In a group run by a male therapist, one of the male members became increasingly hostile to another male member, whom he contended was making sexual overtures to him, which he did not like. His increasingly angry outbursts came to dominate the group. Finally the man came to a group session to say that a (male) driver had 'cut me up' in traffic. Driving dangerously he had used his car to block the man's path. He had then taken a sledgehammer, which he used in his work, from the boot of his car and set about the other driver's vehicle. Fortunately the driver of the car had the good sense to run away and leave the matter to the police. On being arrested the man broke down, attempted suicide and required compulsory detention in hospital.

Psychotic

For some patients, early failures of containment reprised in the present transference relationship, lead to the re-emergence into consciousness of split-off anxieties about annihilation, which are felt to be unbearable. In contrast to borderline patients, for whom the emergence of psychotic anxieties are both precipitated by and mediated by the sense that their objects are unreliable, frankly psychotic patients resort to increasingly bizarre, projective and disintegrative defences in the face of a sense of the relatively complete absence of containing objects.

Events in the environment, personal setback or developmental tasks that the individual is not equipped to negotiate, lead to the deployment of defensive phantasies of omniscient and omnipotent possession of the object, as a defence against catastrophic anxieties about separation which have as a sequel, uncontained aggression which gives rise to violence. Young people developing schizophrenia at the point at which they are faced with leaving their parental home, is one such example; women who experience the birth of a child as the collapse of their idealizations or omnipotence, suffering post-natal 'depression' as a consequence, another.

These phantasies of omnipotence are a contributing factor to the repetitions that may be observed in such people's behaviour, in the way of invariant elements.

> *Concern is felt by supervising psychiatric staff, when a man released from prison on 'Life Licence' for killing his wife in a psychotic rage, appears to be repeating the pattern of their relationship with a woman to whom he becomes engaged. They are sufficiently concerned about both the behaviour and his apparent resistance to accepting the parallels, for them to arrange for his forcible recall to prison.*

The compulsions of sexual offenders, if it is understood that anxieties of a psychotic kind underlie these, is another example. In a suitable setting it may be possible to address these issues with offenders. Analytic understanding may then have some therapeutic value as opposed to being limited to helping to more accurately assess the risk that such people pose. In an appropriate setting the projective and identificatory aspects of the transference/countertransference may then be explored in order to see how far the patient's evacuatory defences operate in an intractable, destructive way and how far the patient is able to make use of the understanding and containment provided by the interpretation of the transference relationship.

With offending, dangerous or seriously anti-social patients they may be taken into treatment with a view to achieving psychological change or merely as a way of achieving some relief from their suffering, without falling into the kind of splitting that sets to one side the suffering that the patient has caused and may be capable of causing in the future. Perhaps it goes without saying that recognizing that there may be a part of the person that is seeking health should not deflect from the strong possibility that this aspiration is poorly founded and that the patient remains a person with dangerous or destructive potential.

In the transference related to psychotic patients or the psychotic aspects of the patients, it is the fixity and intensity with which the projections are maintained that is both the prevailing characteristic and the biggest problem for treatment. This is complicated by the extent to which the psychotic aspect of the patient may be partial or global. The psychotic functioning may have an impact across the patient's ability to function or may be quite discrete; patients may be clearly deluded or they may apparently be without any obvious sign of being delusional. Alternatively their delusion may be circumscribed.

An elderly woman was admitted to a psychiatric hospital from a general hospital to which she had been admitted with a physical condition. The staff had become concerned that she had an 'odd idea'. It transpired that she was a rather sharp, critical, not to say an angry woman, who emphatically insisted that she could see a baby out of the corner of her eye. The baby cried constantly, she claimed, which was a source of both irritation and outrage to her because nobody was attending to it. 'Why doesn't somebody do something about that wretched child?' she would demand. The delusion had been with her for many years and had not apparently prevented her from a full, if somewhat skewed, work and social life.

No doubt this was a complicated matter but simply put, she seemed to have made a defensive identification with a mother whom she felt to be critical, rejecting and uncaring in relation to her baby self. This was then experienced, in a quite concrete way as external if close by, intrusive and a constant source of irritation. It is of course unclear as to how far this is an accurate representation of her actual mother as opposed to an idea of mother distorted by her own rage at abandonment. The relation between her internal objects in this angry, neglectful way was then repeated in her delusion as well as her relations with objects in the external world, including the exasperated and frequently hurt hospital staff whose help and understanding was inevitably rejected.

There are fluctuations and degrees of intensity with which the unwanted aspects of the patient are projected and the capacity for projection and projective identification, is in any case, dependent upon at least a degree of integrity in the sense of self-reflecting competent internal psychic structures, for the development of a sense of their being internal spaces in the self and other, for there to be a space into which the internal contents can be projected. This is related to the development of a core sense of self (Stern 1985) and a skin (Bick 1968). Faults in the development of a sense of bounded internal spaces either because they have not been established or are damaged in attacks on the internal objects can lead to escalating violence in projective identification as the projections are experienced as disappearing into 'outer space', along with the development of psychotic ideation that characterizes such states.

For the most part the violence in the relations between the internal objects is confined to just that, in any explicit sense. It is, however, likely to be repeated in the transference for example, in the implicit seductions and threats which are brought to bear upon the analyst, in an attempt to preserve a defensive system based on splitting and projective identification. Almost inevitably this will lead to acting-out or acting-in as Sandler, Holder and Dare (1973) have called it and discernment of this can be a way of accessing the patient's internal relations. It may, however, be the case that the sense of violation elicited in the patient, as the projections are withdrawn and the splits brought together, means that the analytic relationship will fail in the task of containing the anxiety. In such circumstances evacuatory, acting out in the form of violence towards the self, the analyst or displaced onto other people becomes a distinct possibility.

> *A woman had blinded herself by removing one of her eyeballs and damaging the other. When a member of hospital staff commented to her that it must have been very painful, the patient commented. 'You might think so, but you do not know what I might see'. Another woman had cut off part of her tongue. When asked why she had done so, she wrote down that voices in her head had told her to do so because of the evil things that she might say.*

Delusional Transference

Delusion means the persistence of an idea in the face of clear evidence to the contrary. In the ordinary run of things it is the illusory quality of transference that prevails. The ideational content of the transference remains open to modification and the sense of being contingent upon the relationship between analyst and patient. Nonetheless some patients do develop convictions which seem to have very little to do with external reality but rather represent an aspect of the patient fixedly projected into the analyst or the analytic relation. The man in the group described above is an example of this. To give a further example,

> *A patient increasingly rejects an analyst's interpretations insisting rather that they were defensive on the part of the analyst. The patient declared herself in love with the analyst and demanded that the analyst should set aside his professional position, as it is a 'sham' and a way of trying to disavow the analyst's reciprocal love for the patient. When the analyst retains his analytic position, the patient breaks off treatment, only to begin stalking, finally attacking him and causing serious injury. Even after arrest the patient continues to proclaim both her own love for the analyst and the analyst's love for her, denied by him only because of convention and pressure brought to bear by the analyst's professional body, his wife and society at large.*

The development of a delusional transference is always something to be concerned about in therapy or analysis and the extent to which aggression can be contained within the analytic work will be an important consideration when thinking about whether or not a treatment should be commenced, continued or terminated. An important question will be about the 'suitability' *of* treatment and not just the suitability of the patient *for* treatment and this will depend upon the extent to which it can be judged whether or not the patient's disturbance can be managed internally by the patient, and by the analyst within the therapeutic relationship. Analytic work that undermines defences against split-off aggression disintegrated as a consequence of poorly developed ego structures is always in danger of precipitating uncontrolled, uncontained violence.

It is important to hold in mind the fact that gross splits against unbearable anxiety about aggression in early infancy form a defence against affective experiences which are feared to be annihilatory in the present, and in the absence of ego structure may be used to provide mental structures of a fragile kind.

> *A man has a history of minor sexual offences. In his absence, a search of his home by the police investigating offences of which he is not the author, uncovers his collection of (as it later transpires legal) pornographic videos. These are, however, removed by the police for examination. Deprived of them, immediately after their removal, the man commits a serious sexual assault upon a woman.*

Negative Therapeutic Reactions

In psychotic areas of functioning the intimacy created by the therapist's understanding may be experienced not as a relief or as a containing experience, but instead elicit destructive attacks upon the analysis and the analyst. This situation may be a surprise to the analyst (and indeed consciously to the patient) and seem inexplicable, for example, arising in the wake of a period of apparently productive and useful analytic work. In such circumstances it may, however, be the very fact that the patient has established a dependent relationship with an object outside of the patient's omnipotence that is felt to be intolerable. Such a relationship is felt to carry with it the possibility of being let down, dropped or annihilated as a consequence of rejection or absorption by the object and this is defended against by attacking the dependent relationship.

Transference phenomena of these sorts, which we have already touched on above, have been discussed as 'negative therapeutic reactions', including more generally patients' attacks upon the good work of the analyst. Freud first noted the way that some patients seem to become more disturbed, even when the analytic work was proceeding in a way that is to all other intents and purposes satisfactory, proposing that such a phenomenon might perhaps be an expression of the operation of an excess of the death instinct. Klein elaborated upon this, introducing her concept of envy, in relation to the analyst and the analyst's creative work. Rosenfeld has also widened the use of the concept to include patients' reactions to errors in the analyst's understanding of the patient or the patient's reaction to defensive evasion of him or her by the analyst (Rosenfeld 1987).

Envy is no doubt a potent element in those situations in which the growth of intimacy and dependency in the analytic relationship leads to increasingly violent attacks upon the integrity and worth of the analyst and the analytic work, as noted, usually along the lines of the analyst being dirty, dishonest, incompetent, sadistic, mentally disturbed or ill. There may, however, be other components, such as those suggested by Glasser, in his theory of the 'Core Complex' (Glasser 1979). The core complex refers to those situations in which the patient's capacity for bearing feelings about separation lead to the patient seeking refuge in a phantasy or fantasy of becoming merged with the object. Such a solution evokes anxieties of its own, however, particularly the anxiety of loss of identity or even of annihilated as a consequence of the merging. This gives rise either to periods of 'stable' fixity in the pattern of relations with objects in that they are never allowed to get either too far away nor too close or to the emotional swings associated with dissociated states such as schizophrenia. Violence of one sort or another may result from the panicky states of mind contingent on either attempts to break free from fused states or desperate attempts to hang on to the rejecting object.

Projective identificatory mechanisms are clearly important in this and their elucidation and understanding in the transference, countertransference relationship the means by which their operation and contents can become known. Anxiety about the reliability of the object upon whom the patient depends can feature also. The greater the dependence, the greater the fear of what will happen if the patient comes to feel that the analyst is either unavailable or unreliable. Such situations can lead to the patient attacking the goodness of what the analyst provides and the resurgence of the do-it-yourself, self-care systems (Kalshed 1996) that have previously held the patient together. Such systems may be erected to preserve a sense of 'being-together' in the patient, even if this 'integrity' is illusory and based upon the splitting off and projection of what are felt to be the 'bad' parts of the analyst and the patient (Fordham 1974). Clinically, the paradox here will be the way in which the patient will have a subjective, if fragile, sense of mental integrity based upon splitting and projection; they live, as it were, only in one part of themselves. As they come to be more aware of their state of disintegration with less recourse to splitting and projection, the increase in real integrity involves recognition of the extent to which they are split. Often this is experienced as a falling apart or going to pieces and 'getting themselves together' is felt to be a worsening of their condition often with angry protests from the patient about the analyst's incompetence, malevolence or madness. Such situations make considerable demands upon the analyst's abilities to discriminate between those elements which are really destructive of the patient's integrity and those which augment this, but are anxiety provoking and painful.

8 Aggression, Violence and the Analyst's Experience of the Patient

This brings us to the emotional effects of exposure to aggression and violence; this is not to say that the effects of exposure to aggression and violence are limited to emotion and feeling. On the contrary the effects may be wide ranging, including, for example, distortions in perception, in the capacity to think and in the ability to link thinking and feeling. These effects are, however, secondary to the emotional, and in particular the unconscious, emotional effects of such exposure.

There are of course fairly obvious ways in which exposure to aggression and especially to violence, affects us even if this includes allowing room for personal variation. At a basic level, aggression and violence may evoke fear, the wish to create a distance, even to flee from the aggressive or violent person; indeed this is likely to be part of its purpose. Somatically, aggression and violence may be experienced as something concretely noxious or toxic; it may induce nausea or the urge to vomit, urinate or defecate. It is this visceral quality of violence in particular that links it closely to bodily experience although as we have contended, this can obscure its essential, psychological qualities.

At the very least it is likely to be an uncomfortable experience to be in the presence of somebody who is aggressive. With exceptions, which we will talk about later, it is frightening to be in the presence of violence. The degree of discomfort or fear will be related to the degree of threat that we feel the aggression or violence faces us with. This is compounded by the degree to which the sense of threat of violence evokes our own aggression and perhaps capacity for violence. Exposure to aggression or violence may be accompanied by feelings of fear or anger. The quality of the anxiety evoked may be that of terror or horror.

At a distance, aggression and violence may stir excitement, which in some circumstances is defensively sexualized. Alternatively the impulse to retaliate, to fight, might be provoked. At a more differentiated level, feelings of disgust, repugnance and outrage may be experienced. At a more differentiated level still matters of context increasingly feature and these may mitigate raw and undifferentiated experience so that compassion or concern may enter the picture. Such a response might occur where the vulnerability of the aggressive or violent person is immediately apparent. It is outside of the remit of this book, but children who murder or commit serious assaults, exemplify the particularly complex responses provoked, with the tendency to either emphasize the vulnerability and set aside the violence or emphasize the violence and ignore the vulnerability (Morrison 1997; Alvarez 1997). With adults, more usually the vulnerability will not be immediately apparent in that violence or the threat of violence (which can itself be a sort of violence) are intended to disguise an overwhelming sense of vulnerability.

A patient with a history of assault was referred to a therapist for assessment in a clinic. He arrived dressed entirely in leather that was covered in motifs that advertised his membership of a motorcycle gang. He adopted a belligerent and implicitly threatening attitude towards the therapist. As the interview proceeded, he boasted about how he rode his motorcycle in a reckless manner at high speed. This elicited feelings of anger, then alarm and finally concern in the therapist, as he became increasingly aware of the disparity between the 'tough' exterior expressed by the man's manner and leather attire, and his desperate attempts to triumph over his actual, thin-skinned vulnerability enacted in the high speed, high risk, motor cycle riding. When the therapist commented upon this the man went on to describe a childhood history of neglect and systematic humiliation at the hands of his father.

We have described at length the ways in which aggression and violence are often conflated with each other. Human beings may be filled with guilt, doubt or confusion regarding the legitimacy or otherwise of their aggressive feelings and actions. This has the effect of making exposure to aggression and violence, both internally and externally a disorientating experience. The prominence of denial, splitting, identificatory and projective processes may have the effect of eroding a sense of boundary so that it may be difficult to identify the location of the aggression or violence in self or other. Violence presents particular difficulties in that it is the very antithesis of mental containment.

In particular we have seen how the processes of projection, introjection and identification are important in the way that aggression and violence are manifested in the therapeutic relationship and the ways that therapists comes to make identifications with the patient and become the repository of the patient's projections. This has come to be thought about as 'countertransference'. This is somewhat at odds with Freud's original concept, however, which has been changed and extended considerably over time to the point that important aspects of his original idea have been lost and this has led to a good deal of confusion.

This has particular implications for therapists and the ways in which they are likely to encounter and experience aggression and violence in therapeutic relationships with two main aspects. The first is the ubiquity of patients' aggression and the prevalence of violent elements. The second is the therapist's aggression and violence, or at least capacity for violence, and the part that these play in the therapeutic encounter.

The Concept of Countertransference

If we are concerned here with the totality of the ways in which therapists experience aggression and violence in relation to patients, it becomes important to consider how far this is identical to or differs from, the ways in which the word 'countertransference', has commonly come to be used.

Originally Freud conceived of countertransference, as the analyst's own neurotic transference to the patient stating that it is,

> ... a result of the patient's influence on [the physician's] *unconscious* feelings   (authors' italics, Freud 1910b, p. 144).

In this definition of countertransference Freud was referring to the potential for an analyst to relate to the patient on the basis of repressed, unconscious and infantile elements and initially considered it to be an impediment to the analyst in conducting an analysis. It was on this basis that Jung, then the president of the International Psycho-analytic Association, introduced the requirement that student analysts must have an extended period of personal analysis as part of their training (McLynn 1996). This, it was hoped, would facilitate a more dispassionate and objective relation to the patient on the part of the analyst, by means of reducing the analyst's 'countertransference'.

Over time it became clear, however, that the operation of projective, introjective and identificatory processes were likely to give rise to affective experiences in the analyst, evoked by the patient, which were only in part the analyst's own or were predominantly evoked by the patient. The aspects of the analyst's affective experience that were intimately related to the psychological working of the patient came to be emphasized therefore, as a valuable means of apprehending and, following reflection upon the experience, understanding the patient.

Between the 1920s and the 1960s a number of authors explored and elaborated upon the processes of projection, coupled with introjection and identification including Racker (1968) and Searles (1979). Racker attempted to systematically consider and define the nature of the analyst's affective experiences, for example, the extent to which the analyst's affective experience might be syntonic with the patient's emotional states or alternatively dystonic (but complementary) and representing split off or unconscious elements in a patient's psyche. Searles, working with psychotic patients considered the intense affective experiences that are evoked by primitive modes of psychological functioning. His often painfully honest accounts of his experience, including erotic feelings when with patients, helped to make way for a mental and theoretical space in analysts' minds in which guilt and shame-filled affective experiences could be thought about clinically and used as a means of understanding patient's experience.

Elsewhere, Klein and her followers (Klein 1946; Heimann 1950; Money-Kyrle 1978) explored the implications of her concept of projective identification and the operation of projective identificatory processes in the patient/analyst relationship. Heimann in particular arrived at the conclusion that countertransference included the totality of the feelings which the analyst has towards the patient (Heimann 1950). In consequence, in time, some analysts began to treat all of the analyst's affective experience as though it originated in the patient and although both terms continued to be used, it began to be difficult to see how the concept of projective identification was different in quality, from that of countertransference.

As a result, the term countertransference has come to be used in divergent, sometimes contradictory ways but often implicitly containing the idea that the entirety of the therapist's affective experience, when with the patient, is a consequence of the projective processes employed by the patient.

It may or may not be true that in any given situation or at any given time a patient's projections might affect the therapist and that this is a matter both to be allowed for and considered carefully; the operation of primitive modes of communication and evacuation by means of projective identification will, in this area of work, make particular demands upon the therapist's capacity for tolerating painful and disturbing states of mind (Carpy 1989). However, the aggregation of the affective states of both patient and therapist in the mind of the therapist sets aside the complexity of the nuances and influences at play and especially the interplay between patient and therapist. For patients in states of confusion and especially in confusional states a particularly important function of the therapist is to tolerate the uncertainty, from the point of view of both intensity and ambiguity, without making defensive and premature attempts to introduce pseudo-clarity. This is important for patient's struggling to give meaning to, make sense of and make distinctions about their raw and poorly differentiated affective experiences. Patients may be unable to distinguish the constructive and destructive aspects of their aggression and the therapist may be uncertain about this also. The task of the therapist will be to contain his or her affective response to the patient during the period in which its significance remains unclear, until it becomes clear and available for return to the patient as a clarification or as part of an interpretation.

There is, however, a caveat to be added at this point, which concerns patients' capacity for being able to bear painful and violating affective experiences. Analysts have to make considered judgements about patients' capacity to tolerate their affective states. A violent patient may resort to violence in the face of affective experiences, which they are unable to tolerate. At one end of the spectrum this may be expressed in a violent rejection of the analyst's interpretation or by acting-in in ways that invalidate the psychic reality of the analyst's interpretation. At the other end of the spectrum it may lead to violent assault upon the analyst, either directly or displaced onto others or onto the patient's self. In assessing the appropriateness or otherwise of interpreting the patient's violating affective experiences, it will be the analyst's own affective responses to the patient that will give the best guide to the patient's capacities. These can be considered critically; for example, whether they are syntonic or dystonic with the patient's affective state and whether the need of the patient is for the therapist's, at least for the moment, silent containment of the material, or elaborative articulation. It might be important, for example, to make distinctions about the origins of say, an analyst's feeling of fear; how far is this related to anxieties experienced in the analyst which are not to do with the patient? Is it to do with the analyst projecting his or her own aggression into the patient? How much is the fear a consequence of the analyst's realistic appreciation of the threat to self or others that the patient currently poses or how far is the feeling of fear a consequence the patient's projections or projective identifications? These matters will of course interrelate and the capacity for processing and considering these matters will be a matter borne upon by among other things, the experience and personal capacities of the analyst as well as the context in which the patient is being seen; one might feel more able to contain the emergence of a murderer's fragile sense of his masculinity on a locked ward or prison, than in a private consulting room!

The extended, and we might say over-extended, definition of countertransference, at odds with the original concept, tends to obscure the unconscious aspects of the therapist's relation to the patient and this is of particular importance, where the unconscious pressure is towards disavowal or splitting which is particularly likely in relation to aggression and violence. It may be worthwhile therefore to consider briefly the therapist's affective experience in the presence of the patient, which may have a number of component parts. These might include:

1. *The therapist's transference to the patient, where the patient is obscured by the fixed projection of an object in the therapist's internal world.* This may be repressed,

unconscious, infantile and therefore neurotic and the patient's actual qualities may be obscured by the therapist's projections. It is in this sense that the term 'countertransference' was originally used by Freud (1910b); literally countertransference.

Alternatively the patient may represent or come to represent a potential or quality within the therapist, which has yet to be realized, but may or may not be an actual characteristic of the patient. If this is so, in the latter case this will not relate to a figure in the therapist's past, but rather their future. This latter sense is controversial, because it is at odds with the idea that the transference consists only of figures from the past, which are repeated in the transference relation. It is widely accepted now, however, that psychological development cannot be considered to be complete with the resolution of the Oedipus complex.

In both cases the therapist's internalization of their own analysis and capacity for continuing self-analysis is important in effecting a withdrawal of the projection(s) so that the therapist can discern what is truly a psychic quality that belongs to the patient as opposed to being a projection of his or her own or is a characteristic distorted by his or her own projection. This state of affairs might be characterized as a therapist's 'over-identification' with the patient. In practice, such situations are probably inevitable and even desirable (Bollas 1987) and the important factor is likely to be the fixity with which an over-identification is held to. If there is fluidity between states of partial identification and over-identification this may facilitate a fuller appreciation of the patient by the therapist.

2. *The therapist's empathic appreciation of the patient's material.* This is usually viewed as being a relatively superficial, conscious or preconscious matter, based on a partial identification with the patient. Its usefulness, clinically, is likely to be dependent upon the therapist's capacity for self-analysis. These identifications are likely to be 'realistic' in the sense of the therapist retaining a clear sense of him or her self even when he or she has a

profound and accurate sense of appreciating the psychic state that the patient is in. Complications arise, however, where the analyst's apprehension of the patient's affective state is not syntonic but dystonic. Racker (1968), for example, has distinguished between complementary and concordant countertransferences, the former where the analyst carries a split-off part of the patient, the latter where the analyst's experience is similar to the patient's.

3. *Those affects elicited in the therapist as a consequence of the patient's projective identifications.* Bion extended the understanding of projective identification when he showed the ways in which it is used not only as a defence but also as an ordinary, if developmentally early, means of communication ('normal projective identification'). Bion (1987), by way of example, describes how a mother might be seized by the conviction that her baby is going to die. The effect is to get the mother to attend to the baby and the mother is understood by Bion to be the recipient of a primitive communication by her baby of the unbearable fear of death. Importantly the identificatory aspect of the projection takes the form of the *mother* fearing the baby will die as opposed to being aware that the *baby* is afraid that it will die. The latter may also be a matter of projection but by the by, this is an example of the way in which important distinctions are lost, if all projective processes are aggregated under the rubric of 'projective identification' (Spillius 1983; Hinshelwood 1989).

These processes also operate within the patient/therapist relationship as both defence and a 'normal' means of communicating undifferentiated, primitive affective states.

Clinically, an important part of the work of the therapist will be to consider the origins of his or her affective response to the patient.

A patient evokes feelings of intense hatred in the analyst. After a while these feelings abate somewhat as the analyst recognizes the extent to which the patient embodies qualities, which the analyst dislikes in himself and are associated with his own father.

Another patient evokes intense feelings of hatred. The analyst comes to understand that the patient is projecting his intense feelings of hatred towards his father into the analyst, who in the patient's mind is identified with the father. The analyst understands this as a syntonic or concordant countertransference.

A third patient evokes intense feelings of fear in the analyst. In this case the analyst also comes to understand that the patient is projecting his intense feelings of hatred towards his father into the analyst, who in the patient's mind is identified in with the father. The analyst understands this as a complementary countertransference.

Resistance in the Therapist and Patient

Fordham (1996) has noted the tendency to use the term 'countertransference' to cover all the affective responses by the analyst, which are not necessarily transferred and so are not necessarily illusions. The aggregating of the affective experience of the therapist within the concept of 'countertransference' exacerbates the tendency towards unconsciousness and lack of differentiation in both patient and therapist. This can be systemic and in particular areas may effectively be a collusion set to deny matters that are painful for both parties either separately or together. Even in the absence of this it seems to us to be desirable to be able to make a range of subtle distinctions about the origins and effects of the affective elements that make themselves felt in the clinical situation. We are of the view that the term 'countertransference' makes most sense when it is used to refer to the illusory aspect of the relationship between the patient and the therapist and to have a way of distinguishing this from other aspects of the therapeutic relationship as well as paying attention to the subtleties and nuances of the affective ebb and flow.

Without this it can become difficult to make distinctions about the origins of the feelings that inform the analyst's understanding of their patient. A patient may, for example, feel particularly hopeless about finding a way of having their aggression met and understood. A sense of hopelessness with consequent lack of motivation is a common experience faced by analysts when making assessments of patients who are not manifestly aggressive or violent but who have difficulties in this area. Some patients who present in a very cut-off way may be defending themselves against serious mental disturbance, with the potential for acting out violently if the disturbance is prematurely gone into and in some cases gone into at all. Often, however, with obsessional or borderline patients, analysts are inclined to accept the patient's hopelessness at face value or even feel hopeless about the patient himself or herself. They may then conclude that the patient is unsuitable for therapy. This may be a correct decision based on an assessment of the patient's likely ability to use the therapy or for the therapy to be helpful rather than stirring up rage or violence, which cannot be contained within the parameters of a therapy or analysis. But there is also the possibility that the analyst is unconsciously colluding with the patient in order to deny the underlying rage. A strong sense of hopelessness along with fear, menace or nihilism, evoked in the assessor may be a consequence of the patient resorting to projective identification in order to convey something to the analyst about their internal world. The rejection for treatment will then be an enactment of the identificatory aspect of the projective identification, rather than a considered assessment of the patient's suitability.

Whether or not this can be taken up in an assessment or indeed any other clinical situation, will be dependent upon the clinician's ability to consider their experience and how far it is a consequence of primitive defences or means of communication and how far it is related to the therapist's limitations in terms of ability, experience, personal emotional vulnerability or setting (which are, however, also important considerations regarding whether or not a therapy should be embarked upon or continued with).

These factors are frequently exacerbated by the painful and harrowing ways in which aggression and violence come to be enacted.

> *A policewoman and a social worker were interviewing a small girl whom, it was alleged, had been sexually abused. The girl played throughout the interview with a doll and a dolls house. The professionals asked her numerous questions about what had happened to her. She did not respond directly to the questions, but her play consisted of a story in which*

a burglar broke into the house, overwhelmed the doll and systematically stole or destroyed its contents. When the policewoman and the social worker left, another social worker, who had been watching through a one-way screen asked if she had said anything about the abuse. They replied 'No, nothing. She was just playing with her doll'.

In an example more confined to the affective experience itself, Casement (1985) gives an example of a therapist saying to a patient expressing her feeling that her situation was a hopeless one, that if she (the therapist) felt that way, she would not be there. The conscious communication was intended to be one of hope, and solidarity with the patient. What she unconsciously conveyed was that if the patient really managed to convey the depth of her despair to the therapist, the therapist would not be able to bear it.

Often resistance to the emergence of painful feeling states is talked about as though it is confined to the patient; in reality it is to be found in the therapist also. The therapist will need to be on the lookout for such resistances, not only with a view to realizing that the resistance is taking place and impairing the therapist's understanding, but because the resistance might itself be saying something about that which the resistance is protecting against. Especially when working with people who are violent or potentially violent, resistances and defences are often in place to protect the person from affective experiences, which they are unable to contain and which uncontained, may lead to acts of violence or other states of mental disintegration. For this reason, an analyst encountering resistances in himself or herself needs to give careful thought to the origin of this and whether the anxiety that underlies the resistance is a realistic one or an expression of a patient's exaggerated fear. Careful exploration of fantasies and the underlying unconscious phantasy, especially through the analyst's affective experience of the patient will be important for making such distinction. Where a patient has a history of impulsiveness, violence, 'accidents' or expresses concerns about their capacity for violence, a watching brief is to be recommended until the meaning of such material becomes clear; 'fools rush in where angels fear to tread'. However, if it is true that there are dangers in premature interventions or interventions based on poor understanding it is also true that patients are deprived of a therapeutic help when interventions are withheld out of anxiety or a lack of patience by an analyst or therapist unwilling or unable to allocate enough time for the necessary groundwork.

> *An intelligent, well-educated but rather isolated teenager telephoned an analyst in panic. He had found a psychotherapist in the 'Yellow Pages' and had met with her on a number of occasions. He had understood the therapist as having exhorted him to 'say how you really feel'. In a rather dramatic way the young man had then started to shout and rage against the adult world. To the patient's surprise the therapist had then slapped him around the face and told him to leave or she would call the police because of his aggressive behaviour!*

It is difficult at a remove to know exactly what was going on in this situation even if it is clear that there were considerable confusions about boundaries and the origins and location of strong feelings. But this is a good example of the ways in which a lack of analysis and poor training leave a therapist poorly equipped to deal with a patient's aggression and quite likely leave patients vulnerable to the therapist's projected own. In this case the man used his initiative in seeking further help (by going to a library and finding a name in a psychotherapy register) helped by his sense that the aggression was at least, not just his. One can easily imagine that a less resourceful patient or one with less in the way of ego strength might have been reluctant to seek further help or that the incident may have reinforced his original anxieties.

In this case the patient's difficulties with aggression are neurotic in that subsequent analytic exploration revealed the patient's exaggerated sense of the destructiveness in his aggressive feelings. This may not always be the case as in the example of a young, socially isolated woman with two small children. She sought help, because she was tormented by impulses to smother them while they slept. She was offered regular but infrequent 'supportive' interviews as well as some practical help. The woman later killed the children. Here the therapist failed to register that the woman's anxieties were being considerably underplayed. Of course many people have such ideas or feelings, which are often a sources of considerable anxiety, not to say distress. In the main these are not likely to lead to murderous or violent acts but in this case the 'bluntedness' of her emotional responses, a result of psychotic defence mechanisms, seem to have led the professionals involved to underestimate the degree of her disturbance.

Aggression, Violence and the Manifestation of the Countertransference in the Therapeutic Relationship

In Chapter 4 we suggested the analogy of a 'paint box', to describe the ways in which affects colour experience. There is a range of affects, a range of colours and infinite variation according to tone and subtlety of hue. Aggression and its derivatives are only one colour but with a good deal of room for variation as a consequence of the ways in which aggression combines with and is influenced by the colours of other affective states. Some writers have talked about this in terms of the quality of attachment, a term which evokes a misconception. This is to the effect that the instinctive goal (in which affect is a driving force) is '… always some form of attachment to an object' (Galway 1996, p. 159) and the work of Bowlby (1971), for example, is couched in these terms. A more accurate description, however, might be that the goal is to find a relation to the object. Affectivity is a principal element in determining any particular relation but this makes for a highly complex picture affectively speaking; some clinical material from an analysis may illustrate this.

A patient arrives for an analytic session. The analyst opens the door and the patient steps rapidly forward, bringing his body into close physical proximity to the analyst, at the same time apparently seeking eye contact. The analyst experiences this as an invasion of his personal space and of being intruded upon. The analyst feels very irritated. The analyst does not return the direct look, but is aware that he has either to step rapidly aside for the patient to pass or stand his ground, which will lead to abrupt physical contact. The analyst feels placed in a position in which he must choose between taking an action, which he expects will be interpreted as capitulation by the patient and that in standing his ground he will be taking up a position that will be experienced as a confrontation. The analyst takes the former course, stepping back and, noting a feeling of defeat. The patient, having entered the room, moves towards the couch. Stepping up to it he bends, then pummels the cushion at its head for some moments, finally rotating it before lying down on the couch, places his head upon the cushion. The patient then contracts, bringing his knees up to his stomach, dropping his shoulders and stretching his arms downwards. This is accompanied by straining, groaning sounds. Finally the patient relaxes, lying horizontal and flat upon the couch and begins to talk.

The analyst has observed and experienced this small drama being played out five times a week for a number of years. He has refrained from commenting upon it. It is experienced as being rather unpleasant, but the analyst has observed that there are a number of variations. There is the degree of rapidity with which the patient passes through the door and in so doing passes into the analyst's personal space. There are also variations in the avidity with which the patient seeks eye contact. These variations are accompanied by changes in the analyst's feeling, which range from feeling 'blank' through to irritation, and on occasion to feeling furious. Other variations in the patient's behaviour are noted. On occasion the patient merely smoothes the cushion, while at other times it is picked up, beaten and is sometimes reversed, so that its front face is turned down and its reverse face is turned up.

The analyst understands this drama as in part expressing the patient's anxiety about his wish to get close to the analyst and a consequent desire to defensively evoke a phantasy of omnipotent control over the analyst, which in this case involves the phantasy of getting inside of him. The patient must either dominate the analyst or feel himself to be subject to the analyst's domination and then be at risk of being rejected and in this case, humiliated by the analyst. This seems to be related, among other things, to jealousy and envy. The analyst infers (although it has never been directly stated) that the patient's preoccupation with the cushion concerns the fact that other people use it.

The patient has said that he feels that it might be dirty and that he might become infected or contaminated by placing his own head upon it. The 'dirt' seems to consist of the fragments of the patient's jealousy and envy that the patient is very frightened will get inside of him and make him ill or even kill him. The analyst has had the thought that the couch stands for the analyst's body, the pillow for the analyst's breast (or to be more accurate that the patient experiences it *as* if it were the analyst's breast). The pummelling of the cushion is thought about as the patient taking possession of the analyst's breast; 'whipping it into shape' and in so doing, the patient makes the breast his own. The patient's straining evokes an association in the analyst of forced defecation and this seems to be his strenuous attempt to eliminate those aggressive aspects of himself, which he feels are a threat to his relationship with the alternately idealized and denigrated analyst.

As with the patient in Chapter 4, this sort of interchange is the everyday stuff of analysis and it can be understood in a variety of ways. Fonagy (1993) conceptualizes the difficulty in terms of the patient's failure to develop an accurate and in some cases any sense of other people having a separate or different mind. At best the patient might assume asymmetry between their own and the therapist's mind (Matte Blanco 1975), which in such circumstances gives rise to considerable paranoia. There are of course variations in the matter of degree; in Fonagy's view, a psychopath, for example, might be somebody who has not had the sort of parenting experiences, which enabled them to develop either an accurate sense of the meaning of their own experience or perhaps as importantly a sense of other people as having thoughts, feelings or motivations of their own. Consequently other people are experienced as merely frustrating or gratifying of more or less urgent wishes, with little capacity for allowing for other people's needs or motivation or for the deferment of gratification. From this perspective, where possible, the therapist's role is to as accurately as possible empathize with the patient's states of mind, and the therapist's affective experience of the patient is seen as crucial for being able to do this. The therapist's capacity for identification and attunement with the patient and ability to articulate this in the form of comments designed to convey understanding is envisaged as increasingly allowing the patient to develop and to make sense of their experience relative to other people, initially the therapist.

Such an approach might be contrasted with the one that sees the problem less in terms of failure to develop a capacity for feeling but rather the development of defensive strategies in the face of overwhelming emotions or unbearably painful feelings. Feelings are seen as being systematically repressed or split off from and projected. This model would emphasize not a lack of feeling, but rather, by means of projective and splitting mechanisms, the emptying out of the self into the other of the unbearable experience. This approach in relation to aggression was outlined originally by Freud in *A Child is being Beaten* (1919) in his description of the ways in which splitting and projection are brought to bear in the genesis of masochism, and this was subsequently developed by Klein and her followers. This approach requires the analyst to consider their experience in terms of affects that the patient cannot currently bear. The analyst, however, has to find a way of doing so. The analyst's affective experience is reflected upon in order to ascertain what it is in the patient's experience that cannot be borne and is being evacuated into the analyst. This may give the impression of a calm and relatively distanced position *vis-a-vis* the patient. In the area of aggression and violence as with other raw and passionate affective states in reality this may be more a matter of trying to retain or even find a capacity to think in the face of affective storms. These may be disorganized and undirected or alternatively blitzes directed towards the analyst's thinking capacity, which is somewhere perceived by the patient (and perhaps by the analyst) as a means by which psychological and emotional links might be made in a way that will bring about dreaded and forcefully rejected mental realizations in the patient. Bion talked about the capacity to maintain an analytic attitude in such situation as opposed to being drawn into acting out as the capacity to 'think under fire' (Bion 1970).

Looked at from this point of view the psychopath's apparent coldness is less a consequence of their lack of feeling and more a consequence of the ways in which they systematically evoke powerful feelings (not least through their anti-social and provocative actions) in the people around them as a way of engendering the omnipotent fantasy and subjective experience, that they do not have such feelings in themselves. As we saw in

Chapter 3, this is of course a matter of degree with such processes present in all people, but with a varying degree to which projective, splitting and projective identificatory mechanisms are involved.

Both approaches value the analyst's feelings as a means of empathizing with and understanding the patient's experience. Both see this as more than a superficial matter but one which involves the processing and transformation of raw undifferentiated experience, into a form that makes it available for containment, thinking, management and use by the patient. As we saw in Chapter 4, these processes both in infancy and in the therapeutic situation have a neurological substrate, in which the parent or later the therapist's accurate attunement and identifications with the patient play an important part in enabling the growth of that part of the brain responsible for managing affective states. This is not, however, simply a matter of the therapist or analyst being the parent that the infant did not have and of the so-called 'corrective emotional experience' (Alexander et al. 1946). The adult in therapy, or indeed the child in child therapy, is not simply having an experience of parenting, although often, psychotherapists have a tendency to talk about it in these terms. Such an idea ignores the reality of the patient's adult status (or with a child the development which has already taken place), which carries with it the patient's capacity to consider, reflect and attend to him or her self. It also makes no allowance for the defences and resistances, which have developed in the patient's psyche as a means of self-protection.

In all patients, aggression and less often violence or violent elements are important elements in the patient's preoccupations, mind and material. Over time it may become possible to elucidate the development and relationships between the sensual, affective and cognitive elements of the session and their significance for the patient. In the session described above the patient 'patiently' rehearses the matter, with variations, over a long period of time presumably to give the analyst plenty of time to get hold of the elements and undertake the slow work of untangling what of the aggression belongs to the patient and what to the analyst. What in the aggression is in the service of differentiation and development and what is destructive and an attack of the patient's mind and sense of reality? Some of this may be fairly easily discerned from our description and comments, but much remains deeply ambiguous and remains so, until such time as its nature becomes clearer in the analytic work.

Bateman (1999) has talked about the extent to which patients who have particular difficulties with aggression and violence may be open to therapeutic interventions at those points in their lives and in therapy where there is a change in their defensive structure from a 'thick-skinned' to a 'thin-skinned' narcissistic (Rosenfeld 1987) organization or vice versa. This can be thought about in a similar way, in terms of the cusp between aggression and violence; it is at this point that the patient having come up against the reality of their aggression, is poised between having the potential for integrating it or in the absence of being able to see a place for it inside of their mind, opt for defensive repression or splitting, depending on the quality of the anxiety.

Some Idiosyncratic Aspects of Countertransference in Relation to Violence

So far we have considered some of the more ordinary aspects of the therapist's affective experience and some of the component parts of this, and aggression is not essentially different from other affects in this regard. Violence does, however, have a tendency to generate particular affective responses, especially the tendency towards states of dissociation or denial. We gave the example of the sexually abused little girl above and in Chapter 4 we described the case of a woman, who said that she would be missing a number of sessions, which the analyst misunderstood and failed to interpret and which nearly led to the end of the analysis.

In a moving paper, Valerie Sinason (1986) has described her experience of denying the fact of sexual abuse, to a child with whom she was working in order to explicitly address his having been abused. It is very easy in such situations to then be overwhelmed by guilt or to try to defensively evade the sense of guilt. Sinason manages to convey to the child that her shocking denial of the obvious is only momentary, but is a measure of how unbearably painful the reality of the abuse is to the child and that he has conveyed to her what this feels like.

Professionals apparently oblivious to violence, despite the fact that addressing it is an explicit and central part of their job is regularly characterized in the media and by the various enquiries, set up to investigate 'failures' in the procedures and organizations whose task it is to care for and protect children and other vulnerable groups as a matter of personal or organizational inadequacies, lack of ability or training or worse. The evidence offered often makes it hard not to conclude that incompetence is widespread and that there is a lamentable inability among child care professionals to fulfil a reasonable minimum requirement for the practice of this work. In our professional life we will know of such instances; it will be noted that this will almost certainly be in the conduct of *other* people.

Another possibility, however, is that there is a particular quality of violence which has as its corollary a tendency for the person to in one way or another cut off. Symington (1996), for example, describes interviewing a child murderer and the overwhelming feeling of sleepiness that overtook him when he addressed the offence with the prisoner. Symington identifies guilt, and in particular guilt about destructive attacks on the capacity to think as the origin of violence. As we noted in Chapter 4, while we agree that guilt may play a causal role, any unbearable affect may be felt to be uncontainable and therefore have a violating quality. So shame or erotic feelings or any other affect of sufficient intensity, uncontained may also lead to violence. It is the evocation of aggressive affects compounding this that is crucial.

This is certainly not to argue for the throwing aside of expectations of vigilance, probity and professional competence, quite the contrary. Only that in the presence of these qualities as well as the presence of a failure, it may be helpful to consider whether the 'absence' is a function and characteristic of violence rather than a lack in the analyst, therapist or other professional. Excessive guilt is likely to hinder the consideration of such a possibility and again this may be part of its purpose as an attack upon people's capacity to think. In this circumstance, then the wish to scapegoat may be a further expression of the violence, which fails to find a container.

9 Relationships between Sex and Violence

Aggression and violence are routinely and as a matter of course, associated with sex; in ordinary relations, the extent to which aggression enters into sexual relations and how aggression in the form of violence, characterizes sexual perversion.

Over the last three or four decades western society has gone through successive confrontations with the social manifestations of violence in its various forms: at times these have acquired the characteristics of 'moral panic' (Cohen 1972). In the 1970s and 1980s emerged the issue of non-accidental injury to children, with society having to assimilate the painful possibility of parental violence towards their own children. Denial, often by those daily presented with evidence, such as doctors, nurses and social workers, alternated with anxiety about excessive or inappropriate state intervention. Over time this has settled into a unsatisfactory alternation, mostly played out in the media, between condemnation of the 'authorities' for their failure to act to protect injured or murdered children, with castigation for 'excessive' zeal or unwarranted accusation, leading to the break-up of innocent families. More recently a similar pattern has emerged in relation to violence between spouses, particularly violence by husbands towards wives and in a more high profile manner, child sexual abuse.

Recent fears about paedophiles are an extension of this development, as concern has moved on from the immediate realities of sexual abuse, to anxious searching for those people who are doing the abusing. Part of the fear stems from an increasing realization of the damage that childhood sexual abuse does. These fears, however, have at times taken on an exaggerated, even hysterical tone and this phenomenon may be linked to the nature of perversion as a psychic mechanism.

Aggression is an integral part of human sexuality. Sexuality involves dependence upon external objects, both part and whole, concretely and symbolically, at various levels of psychic functioning, in a way that inevitably generates anxieties about loss. Sexuality brings together loving and hating feelings in ways that generate anxieties about preserving and enhancing the object as well as denigrating and damaging it. We have discussed at some length the ways in which human development involves the integration of affective and other psychological elements and this in large part consists of managing and integrating the confluences of these affective elements. It is the ephemeral qualities and delicate balances that are involved, which are at the root of both human creativity and human destructiveness. While integration of emotional states enriches, opportunities for disintegration, destructiveness and emotional poverty are ample. As we have seen, the psychic work that is involved in separation and making distinctions between aggression and violence is onerous and problematical.

So, for example, sexual dysfunction may have at its root anxieties about aggression in relation to sexuality. Failure to achieve or maintain penile erection may have as a cause, anxiety either about aggressive wishes in relation to a partner or ideas about real or imagined aggression towards him by the partner. This could have various aspects to it, associated with various phantasies about bodily functions. A man may feel that the act of penetration is an inherently violent act or that it might be experienced as such by his partner; that ejaculant is soiling or dirtying or is intended to spoil or dirty. Vaginismus may have as a cause anxieties about being hurt or dirtied or anxiety about an aggressive wish to acquire a penis in order to possess it or enviously deprive the man of it. There are of course myriad possible combinations of phantasies between partners. As we have repeatedly noted, clinically the significance of a particular symptom, needs carefully elucidating and identical physical manifestations may have numerous possible causes. Often the anxiety will be less to do with the aggressive wishes, in relation to a partner *per se*, so much as anxiety about being able to distinguish the aggressive wish from one that is violent. So the wish to retain separateness during sexual relations, which requires aggression as a component part, may be feared to be indistinguishable from a wish to hurt the partner. It is only in the presence of a conscious or unconscious wish to hurt the other that the combination of sex and aggression can be truly called perverse and only where this has the character of a psychic structure that it can be defined as a perversion.

If perversion is characterized as the wish to hurt, disguised as sexual or loving relations then it has as a function the channelling of violence into a sexual activity in a way that has a manic, anti-depressant function while at the same time serving to obscure an essentially violent intention. This is to be carefully distinguished, especially clinically, from those manifestations of aggression within sexual relations, which are in the service of separation, differentiation, trust and intimacy. Some of the high-profile paedophile exposures have been of otherwise upstanding members of the community apparently above suspicion, placed in positions of trust in school or local authority childcare situations. When disclosure takes place, there is a sense of shock that extends beyond the normal response to hearing of a sad tragedy of offender and victim. The shock is that no one would have known. The perpetrator paid his taxes, was apparently happily married and sat on the local council. The perpetrator did not have a chaotic lifestyle of drugs and violence; he did not have 'hate' tattooed across his knuckles, he was not easily identified and distinguished. He was 'one of us'.

Some of the public debate is directly related to this issue. The demand for the publication of the addresses of convicted paedophiles, the legitimacy of the so-called 'naming and shaming', the registration and tracking by the authorities; all of these issues are to increase the visibility of the hidden 'pervert' in society's midst. Even though such measures are unlikely to be effective as a child protection measure and indeed may be counterproductive the wish to make visible, what is hidden becomes overriding.

Definitions and Concepts

The ambiguity and hidden/private nature of sexuality makes the defining of perversion difficult, in a culture with changing mores. The pressure will often be to arrive at definitions, which relate to behaviour because it is this that can be most easily described, defined and controlled. We have discussed the extent to which behaviour along with all other judgements made on appearance, provides unreliable evidence of actual worth or meaning; indeed it is likely to mislead. Behaviour, which in one historical period is defined as perverse, may in another merely be a matter of sexual diversity. Often this is cyclic; what is morally prohibited and branded as perverse by one generation is adopted by its teenage youth as part of their adolescent rebellion, to become normal and everyday. Arguably, the 'perversions' of the 1940s and 1950s included fellatio, cunnilingus and voyeurism in the form of pornography have now obtained varying degrees of acceptability, within the general culture, which would have been unthinkable 50 years ago, but may have found common currency in other cultures or during other historical periods.

A further problem in defining perversions is to draw a distinction between perversion as a psychic mechanism and perversion as a pathological symptom. If perversion is an aspect of sexual behaviour or fantasy that articulates aggressive impulses, it becomes pathological psychiatrically only when the expression of the perversion becomes more important than the expression of the loving aspects of the relationship within which it is practised. If aggression is an essential element, which needs to be accommodated within a relationship, then a degree of perversion inevitably enters in. Freud talked about this in terms of 'infantile polymorphous perversity' (Freud 1905; Meltzer 1973) in which the 'perverse element has the quality of "foreplay"', but retaining heterosexual vaginal intercourse as a culmination of the sexual act. Although the normative quality of Freud's original definition may be questioned, the psychological and emotional qualities of the relationship and the ascendancy of love over hate remains.

A man was anxious about the extent to which his wife wearing high-heeled shoes when they had sexual intercourse, heightened his sexual excitement.

Technically, the point at which perversity becomes a perversion proper is when the stilettos become more important than the wife; the point at which the man sustains a sexual relationship with his wife in order to indulge his fetish, rather than as a manifestation of his love for her. A partner in such a relationship may have the curious but distinct feeling of being somehow after the fact; a clotheshorse rather than an individual and of the engagement going past her rather than engaging her. The perversion consists of the man treating his partner as the means of enacting the fetish, rather than the sexual relationship being an end in itself.

This definition of pathological perversion takes as its central point an enactment, which is more important than the relationship with the partner as a separate person and this definition holds even for the more extreme manifestations of sexual perversity such as paedophilia or necrophilia. For example, by engaging in sexual activity with a child, the paedophilic individual is putting his or her sexual excitement ahead of the interests of the child, who will always be damaged in the encounter both by the exposure to enactments and affective states, which they are insufficiently psychologically (or indeed physically) mature to manage or integrate, and by the confusion generated by that which is nominally close and loving, in reality being distant and suffused with hate. For the perpetrator, power and control over the sexual object takes the place of equality and interchange; for the immature victim of the encounter, the result is the confusion, in varying degrees, of merger, power and control, with difference, equality and mutuality.

A further difficulty in discussing perversion arises out of confusion about the concept more generally. The term 'perverse' has a wider and more common usage than in the sexual realm and this links perversion and psychic mechanisms with a wider meaning. The central quality of the perversion is the expression of hatred via media usually associated with loving and creativity so that lovemaking becomes an assault or rape. The opposite of that which is expected, is expressed. A man, who while on a reducing diet in the interests of his health, takes up smoking to manage his craving for sweet things, is acting perversely. Both overeating and smoking can be self-destructive actions. While eating and nourishment is a creative activity, overindulgence is a vehicle for the expression of aggression. The fat man closing down this perverse relationship to food by going on a diet might seek an alternative mechanism to manage his aggression namely smoking. This incidentally illustrates a common problem in the treatment of perversions because despite the disappearance of the 'symptoms' the underlying problem may not be touched by treatment but is merely expressed through a different medium. Even though the original symptoms are apparently alleviated, the destructiveness may come to be expressed in some other hidden way. In this way the apparent help that a patient gains from the therapy and the analyst, is belied by the continuation of the perverse mode of relating in some other behavioural form. In the transference the perversion comes to be expressed in the way that the analyst is made a 'fool of', thinking that the patient has been helped, when in fact this is a sham.

So if a well-known marathon runner is an acclaimed icon of healthy living, how does one conceive of a person whose motivation to train for a marathon, is hatred of his or her partner and children and the wish to be away from them as much as possible, with training being a perfect and unimpeachable excuse? Clinically the question would be about whether the motivation for a 'punishing training schedule' is a punishment, rather than training.

A young man develops an interest in Thai history and language, which he studies at university. His friends and family financially and materially support his studies and his visits to the country, but once there, he spends all of his time in the red light districts as a sex tourist, having sex with under age boys. When this is discovered he implies that it is his studies that have led him to a country where, in moments of weakness and loneliness, he succumbs to the seductions of paederastic sex that is easily available. This assertion also carries the subtle implication that it is his family that is responsible for his plight; that their support was in reality a careless abandonment of him, which left him exposed to unexpected hazards he was ill-equipped to deal with. In therapy it becomes clear, however, that this is not true. In reality he was well aware of the opportunities for illegal sexual activities long before going to Thailand. His trips abroad had been with the primary purpose of engaging in these, were something that he had carefully planned for, and which he had made practically possible and 'legitimized' by his academic and cultural activities.

Such long-term attempts to realize perverse ambitions, disguised as socially acceptable, even laudable activities, are a regular feature of perverse psychological states, and add a further twist to the way in which other people are drawn into the experience of hate disguised as love or destruction disguised as creativity. This is one of the reasons that the perverse aspects of a person may for a long time be effectively denied, or where this is no longer possible, subject to intense hatred, often disproportionate to the offence. The sense of betrayal that perversion engenders may easily be felt to be unbearable and this is as true in the analytic, transference/countertransference situation as it is in society generally.

Hatred and Fear of Damage to the Self

One consequence of the confusion surrounding perversity is that a number of different understandings of the phenomenon have been proposed. Each contribution has added to the analytic understanding of the subject and following this, we will attempt to synthesize some of the analytic accounts, starting by describing each in turn.

The first model derives from Stoller's work. Stoller refers to the perversions as 'the erotic form of hatred' (1975). Stoller has described the commercialization of sex, associated with the 'sexual revolution' of the 1960s and 1970s, for example, strip clubs and the much wider availability of pornography, approaching the issue from the perspective of an observing clinician and psychoanalyst, describing the themes related to covert aggression behind the explicit sexualization.

As we have seen during our exploration of the metapsychology of aggression and violence, Freud arrived at the idea of a dualism of instincts, life and death, via a route that included the phenomenon of masochism in the form of an unconscious sense of guilt. In later hypotheses, he proposed that the two instincts, on the one hand creative and loving and on the other the destructive and hateful were balanced and in opposition. Within this theory, perversion could be defined as an expression of thanatotic, destructive drives through the normal channels of the libidinal instincts, the expression of hatred and destructiveness erotically. Freud proposed some incident or trauma that had taken place at an early developmental stage partially fusing the two creative and destructive instincts. Within this 'hydraulic' model this fusion creates a structural conduit in the psyche for aggressive instincts to be expressed erotically, rather like a congenital cardiac defect that can result in the mixture of venous and arterial blood. Stoller envisages a mixing of destructive and creative drives to comprise the structure of a perversion.

Many paedophiles in psychodynamic psychotherapy have a history of themselves being abused as children. In analytic treatment, they often identify a central element contributing to the excitement of the perversion. Analytic exploration reveals this to be, at least symbolically, the moment at which they themselves were corrupted as a child. As abusers it is the moment at which the corruption becomes manifest; the moment at which they, as the 'sugar daddy' become an abuser; the dawning realization on the face of the child they abuse, along with the trauma it engenders, as the sexual expectation becomes real. On exploration, this can often be linked back to their own experiences of abuse, and the moment that was most traumatic for them, the very same moment that they experienced the revelation of betrayal and of the confusion of love and hate.

There is a cogent argument that proposes that the societal hatred of and moral panic about paedophiles, is driven in large part by widespread childhood traumatic childhood experiences. This is especially clear in prison environments, where sex offenders are segregated for their own protection from enraged and murderous inmates who have themselves usually been victims of some sort of childhood sexual exploitation. One hypothesis is that the paedophile has the same experiences, but the expression of his murderous rage does not take the form of attacking other paedophiles. Instead his violence is sexualized, and he attacks children. The hatred is focussed and refined, and turns into a longer game of grooming and seduction with the final aim of corruption; of killing the innocence of the child victim; of corrupting and destroying the sexual naivety in the child that was destroyed for them as a child.

The paedophile's hatred of childhood innocence, or hatred of his or her own abusers, being converted into a perverse sexual enactment is a particular example of a very general mechanism. Scratch the surface of a promiscuous Casanova type man who avows that he 'loves women', and often one finds a deep hatred, contempt and fear of them. Frequently the pursuit and conquest of the woman followed by the consummation is engaged in as a battle of hunter and prey. Once the woman has been, as one man put it, 'bagged and shagged', she is of no consequence, other than as a notch on the bedpost. Underlying this may be a fear of femininity making the man vulnerable, with rage at this potential vulnerability, leading to a compulsive need to overpower, seduce control and ultimately humiliate a series of women.

The second model of perversion might be termed the classical model. In Freud's paper on *Fetishism* (1927), he explores the phenomenon of the woman adorned by a particular object that attracts the fetishist's excitement, for example, the stiletto heels described above. Other examples might include cross-dressing, rubber, women smoking cigars and body piercing. Freud suggested that the fetish item symbolized the penis, and that the core excitement of the woman adorned with the fetish item was that they represented a woman with a penis. Freud proposed that the excitement could be traced back to the initial castration anxiety felt by young boys when they discover that women do not have a penis. In the perversion this discovery leads to a fear that his own penis might be lost and this is never fully resolved. The fetish allows a repetition compulsion of this trauma, which at the same time is denied in the phantasy of the woman 'regaining' her penis, under the control of the man.

In popular culture, phallic, powerful women from Joan of Arc through to the female 'James Bond' villains onto contemporary, female captains of industry, have been the focus of excited male preoccupation. As we have noted such ideas are to a degree ubiquitous but the point at which a fetish moves from expressing a man's preference in his wife's choice of clothing or a woman's preferences for a man's clothing, peccadilloes enjoyed by both partners, but become pathological at the point when the relation becomes less important than the item of clothing. In explaining this dynamic, Stoller's account emphasizes the extent to which a wife or a husband, as an individual, is aggressively traduced in the pursuit of the fetish. The pursuit of the fetish becomes an erotic form of hatred against the partner. The reality of the other person, with individual wishes, desires and interests is destroyed, by being subsumed within the fetish.

A Defence Against Psychosis

A third model of perversion, which proposes perversion as a defence against psychosis, requires a brief excursion into the metapsychology of Lacan (2001). Lacanian theory rests heavily on the continental, philosophical, existential tradition in which the individual is essentially alone in the world, other than for some degree of illusory and unsatisfactory contact with the Other. Lacan constructs three reactions to this situation, one neurotic, one perverse and one psychotic. The neurotic denies reality (where denial is a relatively healthy and developed defence); the perverse person disavows reality (which is a much more rigid structure), and the psychotic creates a delusional world. This model neatly places perversions in between the neurotic defences on the one hand, and the psychotic on the other, and chimes with other writers' formulation of the core pathology as something stronger than denial but weaker than delusion, such as Steiner's account of perversion involving the 'turning of a blind eye' to a potential painful, psychological reality, for example, death (Steiner 1993). From this perspective masturbatory use of pornography involves violence, in the extent to which it both denigrates the object and acts to do away with dependency along with the passing of time and the concomitant reality of death.

The clinical usefulness of this model is three fold. Firstly, it explains how perversion manages to contain extreme disturbance. How clinically, people who might be psychotic as a result of their experiences (for example, men who have been seduced by their mothers) can contain the trauma with a perversion (for example, violent rape fantasies). Secondly, it explains how those with quite a high degree of perverse psychopathology, indicating quite severe disturbance, can function relatively well in everyday life.

A vicar abused in childhood by a member of the clergy was generally felt to be good in all aspects of his job, and a respected member of the community. Secretly, however, he engaged a sequence of pre-pubescent choirboys in mutual masturbation.

In this instance the perversity operated as a kind of 'sink' in which to pour all the unarticulated frustrations and irritations of his work, and to bury the significance and pain of his own experiences by evoking it in the boys. When exposed, the chaos and dismay both in the vicar and his congregation contained both the sense of madness and bewilderment of the vicar and the dismay of his congregation. For both, the turning of a 'blind eye' into the full glare of realization and disclosure recapitulates what is experienced as traumatic.

Clinically, the analytic exploration and treatment of perversion is not straightforward because of the extent to which it can serve as a defence against other, more disintegrated states of mind. The patient who has been seduced by his mother, who in analysis is disturbed by his ideas of committing rape, may initially deny that there is any link between the two. The memory of the maternal seduction will either be denied as a memory, or the emotions attached will dissociate by means of flimsy, but effective rationalizations that mother was being kind or loving. This may mirror the rationalizations of the abuser.

In therapy, a woman had mentioned on a number of occasions anxiety about her young son suffering from intestinal worms. In particular the need to take prophylactic measures, for example, applying creams and emoluments of one sort or another to his rectum. Only after some time did the analyst understand that she was describing the way in which she anally penetrated and masturbated the child and that her compulsion to do so both appalled and excited her and that she was trying to tell the analyst about this.

In an abused abuser, the origins of violence might at first be obscure. During analytic treatment, rape fantasies might be explored, for example, as an expression of generalized violent wishes towards women or violence towards a particular woman. This may later lead to the idea that the woman to whom violence is felt to relate is to the mother, at which point the patient is likely to become very disturbed indeed, and possibly violent to the current maternal transference object, the therapist or a displacement. In such circumstances the patient is suddenly faced with the dilemma that the rape fantasy perversion has been shielded from them all along; murderous rage towards the primary caregiver set against the dependency; a wish to kill the abusive mother balanced against the attachment to her. In such circumstances the undefended confrontation with the conflict and perhaps its repetition in the transference situation may lead to a depressive or other form of psychotic breakdown. Alternatively, the abscess may simply be closed over again, with a further fantasy about or enactment of a rape, again sealing the dynamic dilemma into the perversion.

In the early stages of Freud's work, there was a simplistic notion that traumata could be conceived of as psychic abscesses that caused neurotic symptoms. Symptom formation heralds the pointing of the abscess and the process of exploration of this might lead to discharge of the contents and resolution. In the realm of abscess pathology, some diseases can create 'cold abscesses' – where the pathogen (such as tuberculosis) reduces the body's immune response in order to hide the severity of the infection. If a neurosis can be conceived of as an asymptomatic abscess, then a perversion is a cold abscess. It is very much more serious, silent and stable. It can remain stable, but present for years or a lifetime if undisturbed. The disturbance of the perverse cold abscess during treatment or with a disclosure ('outing') disrupts the stability of the containing structure, with a clear potential for psychotic breakdown.

Another way of understanding the stability and longevity of such perverse solutions is via the process of horizontal splitting of the ego. As we have seen, Klein and her followers describe the psychological process whereby the object, for example the mother, cannot be conceived of as a mixed bag or a curate's egg, with good aspects and bad ones. Instead, the mother is 'split' into a good part and a bad one. This leaves the infant free to attack and bite the bad breast and love the good one. An extension of this process can be turned on the self, such that the self becomes split into a good and a bad part (Fairbarn 1952). Where a bad, attacking part of the self is perceived, for example, in relation to both the good and bad breasts, attached to the same mother, what had previously been viewed as a righteous attack on the bad breast is apprehended as hurting the good enough, whole mother. In the circumstances which facilitate integration, recognition arises that a mistake has been made and for the infant to become aware of their own destructive potential, to feel guilty and to establish a degree of depressive position functioning. An easier, quicker and less psychically disruptive option for the infant is to disavow the part of the personality that felt justified in attacking the bad breast, 'it wasn't me'. This disavowal of a part of the personality creates a vertical split in the ego, and in the personality, with the creation of a sub-personality.

It seems to be one of the characteristics of being human that while there is a consistency of personality, so that people seem not to have changed at old school reunions, there is also variability, so that the contrite man stopped for speeding is a different creature to the one bragging about the incident in the pub afterwards. Clearly, such disavowed sub-personalities or split-off parts of the ego are ideal for the operation of perverse psychic mechanisms. The vertically split-off part of the ego develops a separate and distinct superego moral code, and a different mechanism for managing unintegrated, impulsive affective states. In this split-off part the perverse solution can become the norm. Over the years that the vicar has befriended and abused boys within this sub-personality it has become a morally neutral norm. In the larger part of his personality, of course, he would abhor such abuse. In the aegis of the personality's smaller satellite, the veto is dissolved.

This mechanism for the management of a perversion is not so much psychotic as dissociative. There is dissociation between the two parts of the personality, where the perversion is active and at rest. The reconnection of these two parts of the mind is a descriptively psychotic experience. Is the vicar deluded that such abuse is wrong, is the vicar deluded that they have been carrying out such activity? Are the congregation deluded that the vicar is a man of upstanding ethical principles, and so on.

Crystallizing and Sexualizing Object Relations

The fourth broad approach to the perversions is that they are a translation of developmental patterns of object relating or trauma; that if, to quote Freud's seminal paper, you were a 'child being beaten' (Freud 1919), there is a possibility in adult life that this will become manifest as a masochistic perversion.

To explore this model of perversion, a developmental context needs to be rehearsed. In brief, it can be argued that a perversion cannot be diagnosed before the age of 18. During development, libidinal interest is pluripotential; the infantile polymorphous perversity to which we have already referred and can alight on all sorts of different apparently perverse subjects. For example, the oedipal wish for union with the parent of the opposite sex (albeit within a child's understanding) is a normal aspect of development, whereas sexual fantasies by a parent for the child of the opposite sex might reasonably be identified as perverse. Likewise, in later life, excessive orality or anality might have a perverse aetiology, but such fixations are a normal aspect of childhood development.

If the developmental path of sexuality and libido passes through the Freudian stages of oral, anal and phallic, prior to being sublimated into latency non-sexual creative activities (Freud 1905), then the return of sexual interest from about ten onwards, accompanying puberty, leads to a more specific development of a sexual fantasy life, accompanied by masturbation.

This teenage period of masturbatory fantasy and experiment scrolls through the different manifestations of sexuality, oral, anal, genital, aggressive, submissive, fetishistic, same sex, opposite sex. During adolescence, it is safe to do this, because the exploratory, sexual experimentation is taking place in fantasy, rather than being more riskily tried out in reality. Indeed, it is essential that these teenage excursions into the perverse do take place in fantasy; one of the traumas of sexual abuse is the premature concretization of such sexual fantasy by actual sexual activity and experimentation with adults exploiting the child's growing adult interest combined with their residual submission to the adult's authority. The young person needs the freedom to fantasize widely, and freely to establish a preferred sexuality.

By age 18, sexual focus will have settled on one predominant sexual fantasy, the 'central masturbatory fantasy' (Laufer & Laufer 1995). This central masturbatory fantasy is important in two respects. Firstly, it contains within it the person's core object relationship; their characteristic way of relating to other people. This core relationship is encoded as a sexual scenario, but can be decoded in the analytic setting. Secondly, within the central masturbatory fantasy will be a degree of fusion of loving and aggressive feelings. The content of this central masturbatory fantasy will be more or less perverse, and this degree of perversion will subsequently be manifest in relationships throughout life.

One way of understanding the paraphillic or perverse elements that contribute to the central masturbatory fantasy is the way that they symbolize aspects of aggression or violence that are characteristic of the individual's core object relation. During development, people learn a characteristic way of relating to other people, a sort of template that they bring to each new encounter or relationship. Often, this core object relation or relational template, is heavily based on the characteristic relationship with the parents or primary care giver and contains the pattern of affective relations that characterized that relationship. So someone who had critical parents will assume criticism in future relationships; someone with loving parents might assume love, someone with idealizing parents will assume that they will be idealized by their partner.

Some difficulties in relationships in general can be understood in terms of the goodness of fit between the real relationship, and the one expected by the template. Someone who is used to being idealized might get a bit of a shock in a relationship where this is not continued, and is more likely to gravitate towards a partner who will provide this. Extended into the central masturbatory fantasy, such an idealizing core object relation might manifest itself as a fantasy of the partner being in awe of the penis. A critical core object relationship might manifest itself as some form of subjugation or masochistic fantasy and so on.

For example, a woman seduced by a step-father, when she was aged 12 will most likely have experienced this as traumatic, which will include a considerable degree of hatred about the incident. If the step-father was an unsavoury, leery character, and the abuse was carried out under the pretence of normal family life, these elements will be incorporated into the central masturbatory fantasy. For example, the woman may develop a 'normal family life' sexuality, with a partner, but have occasions when she is both shocked and excited by something leery, boozy and smutty. It may even be that during intercourse with her clean-cut husband, in order to reach orgasm, she flashes into her mind some aspect of his or another man who captures the dirty and hidden aspect of sexuality. She may find interesting programmes about the type of men that use prostitutes and pornography in a shocked sort of way, and remember the television programme when next engaged in an intercourse.

The fact that the woman re-enacts the childhood abusive trauma in her own sexual fantasy in no way indicates that the abusive experience was ego-syntonic. The woman does not approve of what her step-father did, even though aspects of it have become part of her habitual masturbatory fantasy. The extreme nature of the trauma amplified by the experience of precocious excitement has meant that the issue has not been able to be dealt with and worked through. It remains as a psychological cold abscess through adolescence 'scrolling through' the possible perversions in masturbatory fantasy. Eventually, one of the perversions is found that sticks, because it captures an aspect of the trauma. The perversion that is alighted upon will in some way capture an essential aspect of the trauma.

By rehearsing the trauma in sexualized form in masturbatory fantasy, the woman has command over it. She has not been able to deal with it in the real world (by killing her step-father as she might feel like doing, although of course it is possible too that she might), but instead, she can be in control of a fantasy situation that contains the kernel of the trauma via a masturbatory fantasy. The psychological mechanism underlying this process is essentially the same as Freud's formulation of the repetition compulsion, where an unresolved trauma is symbolized in a symptom, and then endlessly repeated.

One of Stoller's findings was to compare the fascination and unquenchable thirst for erotic or pornographic material of the aficionado of a particular perversion, as compared to the total boredom of the non-aficionado for the same material. He describes his own experience of reading cross-dressing novelettes, noting the same narrative. The manly man in a situation encounters a powerful woman; is forced to don some female clothing on some pretext, is initially disgusted by this, but then grows to like it, and becomes excited, followed by some form of sexual denouement. Each time the structure of the story is essentially the same, with only the detail of characters and settings changing.

The specificity of the perversion and the fact that a particular perversion exactly meets the sexual fantasy of a particular person highlights a specificity that is explained by the role that the perversion plays in recreating in the sexual realm the essence of the core object relationship. The individual had no control over the traumas that shaped the core object relationship as a child, but they do have control over choosing to rehearse the perverse fantasy. This small degree of control is felt to be better than nothing.

This account can be linked with the classical account of the perversions. In Freud's understanding of the significance of the fetish, he proposed that the central trauma was the realization by the boy of the possibility of castration, evidenced by seeing his mother without a penis. The sexualization of this trauma involves giving his mother a substitute penis, the fetish, high heels, a feather boa, whatever. During the sexual act, the fetish item may be removed, re-enacting the castration; or may not be, with the maintenance of the threat of removal. Either way, the central trauma is sexualized and rehearsed in fantasy.

In summary, the perversion can be seen as a sexualized crystallization of developmental object relations, in which unintegrated aggression or violence is a dominant part. This is a two-stage process where the trauma from a core relationship is first sexualized and secondly, omnipotently repeated as a way of mastering the anxiety.

Pseudo-Creativity

Within the field of the perversions may be found the complex set of disorders surrounding cross-gender behaviour. For most people, their gender (their social masculinity or femininity as distinguished from their physical sex) is pretty much determined by their physical sex. Gender identity is a complex but stable combination of physical sex and physique, masculine and feminine psychological attitudes and sexual object choice. Gender disorders vary from on the one hand a degree of inconsistency around the gender penumbra, such as sexual passivity in males or activity in women; such as 'lads' cross-dressing and women who never wear skirts. Such mild inconsistencies are often contained via compromises in partner selection. Women with more masculine gender aspects might find a more passive male partner, for example.

Alternatively, difficulty integrating aspects of gender can be captured as a perversion. For example, a male, assertive captain of industry may regularly visit a prostitute to be spanked and mildly humiliated, adopting a passive role. For others, gender disorder challenges can be symbolized in the form of cross-dressing. Such behaviour will usually take the form of a sexually exciting fantasy (for a man) of dressing in female clothes accompanied by masturbation. Such activity comprises one end of a spectrum of gender disorders that has at its other extreme a clear and unshakable conviction of being the wrong sex, in a wrongly sexed body. For these more primary transsexuals, such a conviction will have been stable and troublesome since the first awareness during development of a physical distinction between the sexes. In between these two extremes are a large group of secondary trans-sexuals for whom the sexual frisson of cross-dressing has waned, and a gradually developing conviction of cross-gender identity, or transsexualism, is developing.

Aggression may be a central factor in such situations.

A man describes how he is confused by the fact that it is only when he wears woman's clothes that he can get an erection. Exploration of this reveals that apparently paradoxically this is related to him feeling more 'manly' when he is wearing a woman's dress. The type of dress is later found to be associated with his mother and a narrative emerges in which his masculinity is felt to be fragile and crumbles in the face of feeling abandoned by his mother. His sense of being able to hang onto his mother is felt to be too tenuous to invest in an actual external object and so, as a solution, he has attempted to actually become her. His object choice is a heterosexual one, but he can only feel manly when in control and possession of his mother and free from the fear of abandonment. This he achieves by 'becoming her'.

The reason for this exposition of the basic pathologies of cross-gender behaviours is to introduce the notion of perverse creativity.

In the assessment of gender-disordered individuals, an important diagnostic indicator is the degree to which the gender disorder is still an active perversion. For example, a biological man who masturbates while cross-dressed still has more perverse functioning associated with his gender than someone who simply wears female clothes. Likewise, of two biological males living full time in the female role, the one who works as a 'pre-op transsexual' prostitute and advertises in telephone kiosks has more perverse functioning than the one who works in Marks and Spencer's.

The notion of the 'Perverse Universe' derives from the work of Chasseguet-Smigel (1984). In brief, she proposes a distinction between genuine creativity and perverse creativity. In biological terms, real creativity can be associated with the genital tract, the vagina and the womb, where babies can be made. Perverse creativity can be associated with a nearby tract, the anus, where something is also created, namely faeces. Perverse or pseudo-creativity can be understood as the creations of the anus, mistaken as creations of the vagina. With the help of the perverse mechanisms of disavowal and 'turning a blind eye', perverse creativity can be mistaken for real, rather like the fairy tale of the emperor's new clothes.

Chasseguet-Smirgel also proposes that the notion of the 'ideal' is perverse. Accompanying real creativity is a sense of doubt and problems. Children being born is a difficult process, there are always problems and difficulties associated that need to be worked through. The same is not true for a perverse creation; in an illusory manner it can be born perfect. For the more perverse transgendered patients, their image of themselves as women is not a normal everyday one, but is an idealized one, for example, in the fantasy of being a supermodel. Life after the sex change is seen as ideal in a way that no normal life could really be.

The distinction between real creativity and pseudo can be extended into psychoanalytic metapsychology. Simply stated, an idea is born out of the combination of two pre-existing ideas coming together in the same way that a man and a woman do to create a baby. New ideas are born of struggle and doubt, as the two contradictory ideas jostle and compete prior to being able to combine. Pseudo-creativity, on the other hand, is not derived from this combination of difference to create anew. Pseudo-creativity is simply a rehash of what has gone before, produced without the struggle to incorporate something different.

Each new masturbatory cross-dressing novelette that Stoller read during his research was substantially the same as the last, and yet was new and exciting to its avid readership. These novels illustrate the nature of pseudo-creativity in that the same old stuff is being churned around (like the peristaltic churning of faeces in the colon) so that it looks a bit different, but is essentially the same. Critically, it is perceived by a particular group as being new and fresh, illustrating the perverse mechanism.

Chasseguet-Smirgel's work and the notion of perverse creativity provides a descriptive account of an important aspect of perversion; the libraries of particular sexual peccadilloes that are available for the aficionado should they chose to go looking, and the repetition compulsion aspect of the perverse activity.

Narcissistic Sexuality

The Portman Clinic in London has produced a number of theorists, two of whose understanding of the perversions can loosely be categorized under the rubric of narcissism. Glasser's core complex model has been briefly described earlier (Glasser 1979), and provides a framework to understand both violence and the perversions. Briefly, he argues that the enactment of the violent or perverse act constitutes a sort of intimacy so that, for example, when giving or receiving violence, there is a momentary close and intimate relation.

In the same way when a prostitute consents to the enactment of a sadomasochistic perversion, this involves a flooding moment of extreme closeness for the client. The fetishist who enjoys being forcibly dressed in female clothing, if they find a partner to enact the fantasy, derives a sense of engagement with the person that has the quality of being total for the duration of the enactment. For the violent or perverse person, however, at the end of the enactment of violence or the perversion, they will feel lonely, isolated and alone; estranged from the intimacy of the act. Other than during the enactment of the perversion, they are likely to find relationships unsatisfying, and to remain aloof, distant and emotionally uninvolved.

Glasser described this oscillation between extreme closeness and intimacy during the act, and subsequent isolation the 'core complex'. The individual enthralled to the core complex is unable to exist in a normal relatedness to the object, but instead oscillates wildly between a phantasy of extreme intimacy, which involves getting inside the object, and being at a vast distance. During the excited enactment with the prostitute, tied up and flagellated say, there was intimacy; subsequently he may denigrate and dismiss her contemptuously, contemptuous even of her for agreeing to participate and enact the fantasy itself and in this way distance himself from her.

Glasser's model describes better the sadistic perversions, when the fetish involves the control of the object and cruelty to it. This mild form may be found in bedroom practices of bondage, say handcuffing of one or the other partner to the bed with its central phantasy of total surrender on the one side or of total domination and control on the other. More extreme are the fetishists and prostitutes who own purpose-built dungeons to cater for the demand. At the very extreme end are sex offenders who imprison their victim and prior to killing them, enact sexual assaults. In these extreme cases, the killing often takes place after the sexual assault, precipitated by the perpetrators need to escape from the act or the victim. Having enacted the Glasserian close/fused part of the perversion, the urge to distance the object is just as extreme, and the victim needs to be 'dispatched' sometimes by being killed.

In these cases, the perverse intimacy is to be found in the fantasy of total control of the object. The perversion is that the object has to be totally at the mercy of the 'top. In sadomasochistic community parlance, the 'top' is the one in control or sadist, and the 'bottom' is the masochist. Paradoxically, this has its largely unconscious reverse embodied in the evacuatory projective identificatory mechanism that characterizes these phenomena so that in the sadomasochistic literature, part of the excitement of the 'bottom' is the phantasy that in reality they are not helpless but are in complete control. This may be concretely contained in the 'word' that is agreed by both parties prior to the enactment in order to allow the 'bottom' to stop whatever the torture is or may be only implicit in the complex projective process which allows the perverse and illusory fusion with, and control of the partner.

The other major contribution form the Portman Clinic is Weldon, whose book *Mother, Madonna, Whore; Idealization and Denigration of Motherhood*, explored the nature of perversions in women (1988). Up until this book, with some exceptions (Winnicott 1949) there was a collective belief that perversions were male phenomena and that the sex industry was purely a response to this male disease; that women who went into prostitution were forced into an evil trade that they despised because of sexually abusive men. While clearly in some cases, this is true and that a cycle of sexual victimhood may start with a sexually abusive experience in childhood, Weldon has described a more complex picture both in relation to aetiology and manifestation.

Weldon proposes a fundamental distinction between the expression of perversity between the sexes that can be derived from physical and gender attributes. She proposed that for men, perversion is manifest outside the self. Fetishism is about what the woman wears to become the object of the man's desire; the pornography industry is about looking at other people having sex; visiting prostitutes and promiscuity is about sex with different women. The feminist objectors to pornography argue that it 'objectifies women', and this is true, however, Weldon contends that this is to some extent an innately derived aspect of male sexuality, in its tendency to focus on an external object.

Kleinians, for example, have contended that infants have some awareness of sex difference from before the development of conscious awareness of sex differences; a sense of having something to prod and poke with boys, a sense of an internal space or receptacle for a girl. These primordial senses are of course rudimentary but fundamental and from these core experiences of sex difference may be derived some of the differential manifestations of the perversions between the sexes.

Male perversion is directed at something outside the body, something that can be prodded and poked; something for the penis to target. In this it follows male sexuality, directed to outside the body; aimed at an object. Thus, the 'objectification of women'; as sexuality for men becomes less loving and more perverse, so the sexual target becomes an object, adorned by fantasy or fetish, but less engaged with as an individual.

Following the same reasoning, something can be said about female sexuality and perversion based on the primordial sexual consciousness described above. According to Weldon, female perversion is directed inwards, towards the body, towards this perceived inner space that constitutes womanhood. Female perversion is manifest as an enactment directed at the self or focussed on the self. In the same way as for male perversion, fetishism can be conceived as an exemplar, for female perversion, prostitution seems to be the classic manifestation.

The reframing of prostitution as a female perversion captures a variety of aspects of the phenomenon. It captures the woman's masochistic risk-taking, as she opens up her body and makes herself vulnerable to a series of unknown men. It provides a passive vehicle for promiscuity, and for a passive acquiescence to the variety of male perversions that are more available on the open market than in stable relationships. The Stollerian element of hatred in the interaction is present in the contempt the prostitute has both for her 'punters' or 'tricks', and also, at some level, for herself for plying her trade, for example, treating her body as though it is a 'thing' to be exploited, for material gain rather than essentially personal.

The final piece of the jigsaw regarding female perversion for Weldon concerns children and childcare. In brief, mothering can become perverse via forms of child abuse. To understand how this happens requires a brief recapitulation. Part of the frustration for the partner, the long-suffering wife wearing an ill-fitting nurse's uniform, for example, is that the individual is actually not interested in the wife for herself, but rather he becomes consumed with desire for his own fantasy, as embodied by his wife in the nurse's uniform. The fantasy that includes a nurse's uniform is a creation of the man's mind. The man is having sex with a fantasy in his own mind, and not with his wife. The act is essentially perverse.

For the duration of the perverse fantasy, the man is 'narcissistically identified' with the woman. The wife simply embodies an aspect of the man's mind; his nurse's fantasy. During the enactment of the perversion, in reality, the man is having sex with his wife, but somehow she disappears. It is as if she becomes inhabited by his fantasy but ceases to exist in her own right. This is why enacting other people's fantasies can be a bit unpleasant.

For some time, it has been recognized that a degree of narcissistic identification takes place in the process of mothering, and that this can be pathological. The infant gazes into the face of the mother and sees itself. It is a common experience of parents to gaze into their children's faces and to see themselves, but then to correct this. It is this process of correction that is crucial. Infancy and then childhood development is about establishing degrees of independence; about initially establishing a sense of 'me and not me', and then about negotiating 'me' in the world with all the different and demanding 'not me's.

Perverse mothering, involves two stages. In the first stage, the mother's narcissistic correction does not take place. The mother continues to see the infant and child as an extension of herself. In the second stage, the mother 'self-harms'. Women focus their violence and their perversion inwards on themselves via self-cutting and prostitution. If she perceives her child as part of herself, self-harm will include harming her child.

The implication of this is that the varying degrees of abuse of children, provides a sink for parental violence. Such abuse need not be extreme, and may be disguised by secondary gains, for example, the stories of ten- or eleven-year-olds gaining university places, behind which is a story of a strict and regimented parental coaching and harassing them driven by a narcissistic identification.

What is rather chilling about such perverse parenting is that the child's experience is rather like the wife in the nurse's uniform, or the prostitute in a bored way beating the tied up client's buttocks, waiting for the punter to hurry up and climax. Like the wife and the prostitute, the child is not being perceived as an individual, but simply as an embodiment of a fantasy. For the 11-year-old studying all the time, the parental fantasy is of knowledge and wisdom. Often the projected parental phantasy is much more unpleasant, of stupidity, of naughtiness, manipulativeness and malevolence; of being the cause of relationship breakup, of strife and poverty. These are aspects of the parents' minds that are frequently projected onto children, and for which they are attacked.

Weldon proposes that because children are the fruit of the mother's womb, and because of the maternal preoccupation with attacking the self rather than prodding and attacking the other, women might be more inclined towards the perversion of parenting than men. Whereas there are massive industries catering for male perversion, partly staffed by aspects of female perversion, it may be that the majority of female perversion goes largely unnoticed, because it is manifest within this relationship with their children.

Clearly, Weldon's account of perverse mothering contains at its core a narcissistic pathology. The Chasseguet-Smirgel pseudo-creative perverse universe could be understood as entirely narcissistic. It is 'pseudo' because it is self-referential, obsessional and anal rather than open to and engaging of something 'not me', outside and different; it is a self-produced product. It is the safe, self-referential and sterile recapitulation of a personal fantasy rather than the risky engagement of a part of another person that might create something entirely new, for example, a baby.

A significant question about the nature of the perverse intimacy of the 'close' phase of Glasser's core complex concerns whether the violent act is committed towards the real other person, or whether it is against a phantasy projected into that person at that time. So if a man gets a prostitute to tie him up and cane him, in the process experiencing a flood of closeness, does he feel close to the prostitute as a woman in her own right, or is it a 'closeness' to his own fantasy? Does he, as it were, climb into his own phantasy? Psychiatrists describe a 'delusional mood', when a schizophrenic patient is psychotic, but cannot quite work out what is wrong. Such a delusional mood proceeds the crystallization of a delusion; the 'ah ha' moment, when the schizophrenic person realizes that the problem is that the CIA are tracking him and reading his mind and it is this that accounts for the curious experiences and feelings he is having. A Glasserian enactment of a perversion sounds similar to this phenomenon. A 'moment of madness', where the real world momentarily disappears, and narcissistic phantasy takes over. Little wonder that following this, as the individual returns to the real world, that there is withdrawal from the object, the distant phase of the core complex.

In the debate about the nature of narcissism, psychoanalysts of the more classical tradition see it as a fund of self-esteem; a benign illusion of infantile fusion with an omnipotent mother. Researches into infant development have not supported this on the one hand; the Kleinian school on the other has come to think more in terms of narcissism being the principal vehicle for the expression of rage and destructiveness. Instinct and affect drive the individual to create links and relationships with the outside world elaborated in fantasy as a prelude to engagement; in the opposite direction, narcissistic withdrawal pull the individual away from this into the world of omnipotent fantasy as a substitute for engagement. These narcissistic impulses are anti-libidinal, anti-relationship and depending on one's theoretical orientation either an expression of the death drive or complex patterns of splitting and projection.

Conclusions

One of the difficult issues clinically, when dealing with perverse patients is trying to dig through the thick layer of guilt and associated disavowal to be able to start to talk about and understand the pathology itself. For a period, there was a view that the clinical problem with the perversions was that there was no guilt.

On the surface, there may not be; so paedophiles using the internet to view child pornography feel that they are prosecuted for a 'victimless crime'. Psychoanalytically, however, a significant and important element in the perversion is doing something for which one can hate one's self; something one can be ashamed of. In turn, this unconscious sense of guilt powerfully entrenches denial and disavowal to maintain its integrity.

A narcissistic account of perversion sheds light on this guilt. Narcissistic, perverse sexuality uses the partner as a projection screen on which to manifest sexual fantasies. The partner, the wife dressed as a nurse, the prostitute beating client's buttocks, is a means to access the fantasy, not an end in themselves.

It may be that one of the difficulties in discussing perversion is that perversion, abhorrent though we all think it is, is part of normal psychic functioning to a greater or lesser degree. There are no 'perverts' and 'normals' in the world, rather people with more or less perverse levels of functioning. In the same way as aggression is a normal part of everyday life, a degree of aggression expressed sexually is normal. If this is the case, it is not going to attract any less guilt simply because it is widespread. Instead, it is likely to be disavowed by the majority (itself a perverse solution) and create an environment rife with moral panics about perversion.

Perversions may be a way of getting 'close' to people without actually engaging. A perverse relationship may not be an object relation proper, but may be an imitation of it. The husband having sex with his wife dressed in a nurse's uniform is not having sex with his wife, but he is engaged in a fantasy of intimacy with another person, and he is engaging in this fantasy with another person. It could be worse. He could believe that he is a nurse. He could believe that his wife is an identical double of him in a Capgras delusion. In other words, he could be psychotic. The perversions may represent severe psychopathology, but they are not the most severe psychopathology. Perversions contain phantasies of object relating carried out with other people and this can be conceived of as a step close to sanity than a purely psychotic withdrawal. Like the definition of hypocrisy, that it is the 'homage vice pays to virtue', the perversions might represent efforts towards object relations by those who are unable to sustain them.

10 Aggression and Violence against the Self

Attitudes to Suicide and Self-Harm

Suicide and self-harm evoke a variety of emotional responses ranging from sympathy to antipathy; for the most part, however, they are disapproved of even if, in exceptional circumstances they are considered acceptable and even occasionally praiseworthy. Responses will depend heavily upon context and there are degrees of cultural variation in relation to this. In some societies and in some circumstances in Western society it may be deemed to be the least dishonourable thing to commit suicide; the Second World War Imperial Japanese soldier, the 'suicide' bomber, the businessman embezzler 'doing the decent thing'. Every human society has views on the matter from a variety of different perspectives: philosophical, religious, psychological and ethical. Some have proposed that suicide is *the* philosophical question. Camus states 'There is only one serious philosophical consideration which is whether or not to commit suicide' (Camus 2000), meaning that not death, but life is problematical. Despite these exceptions, however, self-harm and suicide are characteristically considered to be unethical. Most religions, for example, relate it to the sin of loss of faith; philosophy with a loss of meaning. Historically the latter has led to the paradoxical position in some jurisdictions, of para suicide (suicide attempt survived) being a capital offence.

Exemption from the proscription against suicide and self-harm is always equivocal and contingent upon special circumstance, for example, suicide in the face of terminal or painful disease or profound disability. Some societies in recent years have come to allow limited recourse to so called 'assisted suicide' in such circumstances; the equivocal nature of the act, along with the obvious opportunity that it affords for abuse, have made others reluctant to follow suit. Those organizations such as EXIT, which have advocated the legalization of assisted suicide have tended to take as their point of principle, the idea of suicide as a rational choice based on conscious considerations. As we will see this may be a somewhat simplistic, if not misleading, idea which neglects the existence and operation of unconscious ideas and influences.

In modern societies, suicide is considered to be a significant social problem, ranking among the ten most frequent causes of death in European countries (Kreitman 1988). In his influential sociological study, Durkheim (1951) described what he termed anomic or egoistic suicide where a society or an individual has lost touch with or feels themselves to be out of step with cultural norms and values. More recently Gilligan (1992) has, from a more analytic approach, talked about suicide in terms of it being a public health problem. Psychiatric approaches to suicide see it as correlated with various types of psychological disturbance, for example, as an expression of psychotic illness especially when accompanied by frank delusions. In the functional psychoses such as schizophrenia this might include auditory hallucinations commanding the individual to kill him- or herself; in the affective psychoses such as depression the individual might feel that the world and their loved ones would be better off without them. In the absence of such clear loss of contact with generally agreed norms about the nature of reality, where there is no psychiatric illness or where there is more room for equivocation there has been considerable debate about whether people have the right to end their own lives, without being branded as mad and restrained and medically treated against their will.

Statistically, incidents of self-harm far outweigh suicide. Diagnostically among those people who survive a 'suicide attempt', one has to distinguish those whose intention was not to kill but to hurt themselves, from those who have failed in their intention to die. People who have failed in a suicide attempt are those who have clearly planned to die, but have not done so, because they have been found by an unexpected visitor or because of some unexpected fault in their method; the actual as opposed to the assumed effects of medication used for overdose, for example. Benzodiazepine sleeping tablets are often expected to be fatal in moderate overdose, for example, which they are not. In reality of course any individual is likely to be more or less ambivalent about their own demise for a variety of reasons; some to do with method, some to do with outcome. Many who complete suicide attempts, along with other people who self-harm, will meet their deaths unintentionally; the person who inadvertently cuts a major artery, bleeding to death or who mistakenly believes that a drug such as paracetamol is not dangerous in moderate overdose, when in reality it is. This again reiterates the point that we have emphasized throughout this book; that the act itself may be deceptive or misleading; that identical acts in the physical sense may have different meanings. The dead person's overdose may not necessarily be understood as an expression of their wish to die nor another person's survival as an unequivocal expression of their wish to live.

This is of course of the greatest importance in clinical work with suicidal patients, patients who become suicidal or self-harming or the suicidal or self-destructive tendencies in all patients.

Aggression Towards the Self in Normal Development

In earlier chapters, we considered the ways in which consciousness may be viewed not as homogenous, but more accurately as having a tendency towards homogeneity in the face of heterogeneity. Walt Whitman said 'Do I contradict myself? Very well then I contradict myself, (I am large, I contain multitudes.)' (Whitman 1998). This can be understood in part as a consequence of the way in which human beings are able to self-reflect upon aspects of themselves. Damasio's conception of the ways in which both the immediate and the enduring sense of self originate, which includes the acquisition of images of states of self in its relation to objects which may then be related to as external objects (see Chapter 6). This provides the basis both for the elaboration of states of self and for splitting in pathology. States of self can then be related to as consistent with or at odds with prevailing enduring states of self. Just as other objects in the environment are related to with reference to the affective states that they evoke, so do these internal images, which we might imagine, in elaborated and relatively complex form as constituting internal objects and the relations between internal object. Aggression then plays its part, modulating the enduring or present states of the self's relationship with these images. Put crudely, aggression may have a role in internal processes which modify or contain impulses or enactments. Aggression is required in order to mange the self. For example, this can be personified in terms of something like, the part of the self which gets my self out of bed in the morning, in the face of that part of the self, which would prefer to stay in bed. Colloquially we might call this self-discipline or commitment. Or in oversimplistic terms, say an internal parent that manages an internal child. We might refer to this as a 'superego' function or in excess (or as we have proposed where cruder and more broadly splitting and projective forms of psychological structures are resorted to), we might refer to a punitive or ego destructive superego. Failures in this area might be where the 'bad' parts of the self are dominant leading to the establishment of 'gang' or 'mafia' type internal organization (Rosenfeld 1987; Meltzer 1973). Aggression as a relationship between internal objects is a necessary one and where integrated plays the crucial role in relation to containment especially where it touches upon impulsive aspects or aspects which, if acted upon would be against the longer term interests of the self, whatever the attractions of acting upon the immediate impulse.

Aggression is an inevitable aspect of this internal interplay necessary for the regulation of the self in relation to its environment and to preserve it against injury or death. Where this protection breaks down, aggression is also an important aspect of a person's response; a large part of the pain associated with an accidental injury will be the anger that is felt by the person towards him- or herself. This can of course be conceptualized as something like rage with the mother that fails to protect.

Freud and Self-Destruction

In Chapter 2, we described how Freud increasingly needed to account for aggression in his metapsychology; in particular, the existence of excessive guilt, the punitive persecuting superego, and the phenomena of sadism and masochism. He was struck too by the extent to which some patients destroyed the good work that had been done in analysis, rejecting the analyst in favour of clinging to destructive and self-destructive psychological attitudes. This led Freud to reluctantly posit the concept of the 'Death Instinct', 'Thanatos' the destructive counterpoint to the life instinct, 'Eros'.

Freud conceived of the death instinct as being essentially directed towards the self and the expression of each individual's drive towards a return to an unanimated undifferentiated state, which he considered to be primary. Aggression towards objects in the environment was the defensive turning outwards of this innate self-destructiveness; as we have noted this notion of inherent self-destructiveness was an important contributing factor to the pessimism that characterizes much of his later writings (Freud 1930).

Freud's concept of the death instinct especially as elaborated by Klein is an attractive one in the extent to which it offers an explanation for some of the most frustrating and painful clinical experiences with which analysts and therapists are faced. Not only the ruining of solid, conscientiously and hard found gains in understanding, but also the destructive force which attaches to some forms of psychological organization. The patient, who is found to be secretly acting out in ways that make a mockery of the apparent growth in the capacity for self-containment and ability to relate; the impulsive act of self-destruction that threatens the continuing viability of a therapy or analysis. The notion of the death instinct gives meaning to what may be felt to be inexplicable, especially in the light of our limitations in understanding the more obscure aspects of human destructiveness, either in principle or in practice.

There have, however, been a number of critics of Freud and Klein's concepts of the death instinct, for example, Rycroft (1967) (Hinshelwood 1989), who have pointed out that the idea seems to go against most of what is known about biological processes and flies in the face of the powerful imperative for survival. Freud (1917) conceptualized suicide in terms of the splitting of the ego and the attack by one part of the ego, on the other, which was identified with a lost object.

The clinical problems that Freud and Klein were trying to account for remain, however, and the problem is of how to account for them.

Splitting and Projection

If aggression, or more accurately the aggressions, constitute an ordinary instinctual endowment, then we suggest that violence is

a consequence of a failure to process or integrate this, necessi-
tating patterns of splitting and projection (among other things);
this seems to be particularly relevant when we come to considering the question of aggression and violence against the self.

A central implication of Damasio's concept of the sense of self
(1999), is that it is possible for human beings to be self-reflective
because of their capacity to treat images (in Damasio's sense of
the word, but see also Bion) of their own states of self as though
they are external objects. In circumstances in which those images
involve the apprehension of affective states that are felt to be
unbearable, then resorting to splitting and especially projective
identification allows it to be possible to treat aspects of the self
as though they are either external objects or even characteristics
of another object. From this perspective of aggression, if it is
about modulating the relation with objects and creating a sense
of separateness or distance, it may be brought to bear by the self,
in relation to aspects of the self. Where integrated this is the basis
of self-reflection, insight and the very stuff of psychic structures.
Where it is not possible to integrate the experience, the tendency
is towards splitting and projection and the treating of aspects of
the self as external objects, including threatening external objects
to be attacked, driven away, killed or annihilated.

There is a good understanding of these processes of splitting
and projective identification in analytic theory and practice (even
if the mechanisms have not been well understood), but these
processes are particularly important when it comes to considering
suicide and self-harm. In particular the paradox of the person
who seeks their own injury or demise, in the face of the array of
imperatives for self-survival with which people are more obviously endowed, not the least of which is the fear of death in its
various forms and intensities. This is achieved by the action of the
splitting and projection so that the self-harming person in important ways, is operating on the basis of the illusion (or delusion)
that they are attacking not themselves, but rather a threatening
other. In reality of course the attack will be on themselves but is
undertaken on the basis of a phantasy that it will be the 'other'
(that is, the other into whom an unwanted part of themselves has
been projected) that is harmed; they will not be harmed and
indeed, paradoxically, may believe that they will be preserved
from harm by the action. An example here might be the hero or

indeed the villain in the film, who either accepts death or commits suicide as a way of 'evading' his enemies. The fixity with which such pathological patterns of splitting and projection are clung to is commensurate with the strength of the anxiety which they defend against. We have considered already the differences between neurotic as opposed to psychotic anxieties. The quality of the anxiety may be obscure and this constitutes an important problem for diagnosis and prognosis, with particular implications for the treatment of suicidal and self-harming patients. An understanding of the processes of splitting and projection are also of importance when it comes to understanding the apparent intractability of many self-harming states and their resistance to therapeutic interventions and of the technical problems that such cases involve.

Commonly it is understood that suicide and self-harm are an attack upon the self instead of an attack upon the world; less frequently the attack upon the self may be understood *as* an attack upon the world and the people in it, although such a state of play intuitively felt, may be in part responsible for the antipathy with which many para-suicides or people, who self-harm evoke in professionals who treat them, even if this is largely rationalized in terms of such patients 'depriving' other 'deserving' patients of treatment, because of 'attention seeking behaviour'. This disparity will seem less paradoxical when the fantasy and phantasy aspects are taken into consideration and we will turn to this shortly.

> ... an attack on another person may be driven by an impulse to destroy something inside oneself. Contrastingly a suicide or act of self-mutilation may occur if the self or the body becomes identified with a hated other   (Bateman 1999, p. 111).

The murderousness implicit in suicide was, as we have noted, reflected in the past by the treatment of attempted suicide as a capital crime, for which one could be hanged. This is consistent with the extent to which suicide is recognized to be violence directed towards the self, as a displacement for an attack directed outwards. The question can then be asked, for example, by Bell, 'who is being murdered?' (Bell 2001). The reflection by Menninger that the form that the violence against the self takes and, for example, the part of the body or bodily function against which it is directed, will be of significance in a symbolic sense when understanding its meaning and the aspect of the other, to which the violence is directed.

> *A 22-year-old single mother has taken three overdoses of paracetamol, the most recent of which resulted in some liver damage as a result of the toxic effects. The circumstances of each suicide attempt had emerged following the end of a romantic relationship. In counselling, it is clear that at the moment when the tablets are being taken, she is in a blind rage, most recently, having just put the phone down on a friend who had confirmed that her boyfriend was being unfaithful. The patient entirely disavows that there might be an aggressive motivation in her self-harm, seeing her self as overwhelmed by self-pity and sadness, to the irritation of the counsellor. The counsellor proposes to the woman that at the moment of taking the tablets she might have wanted to murder her boyfriend's girlfriend. Thinking the counsellor is referring to the woman with whom the boyfriend has been unfaithful, she agrees. The counsellor further suggests that in her blind rage not only did she wish to murder herself, as the boyfriend's girlfriend, but also she wished to murder her young daughter's mother. The woman is enraged in the session, feeling betrayed and attacked by the counsellor but accepts the point that is being made, leading the therapist to be concerned that the self-harm might be repeated after the session.*

While there are similarities between suicide and those attacks upon the body, which do not lead to death, there are also important distinctions to be made. Whereas the aim of suicide is the death of the object, with self-harm, the aim is not death, but an attack upon a part of the body, which is affectively invested in phantasy, with an aspect of the object. These differences will be important in considering how far a para-suicide is a failed suicide as opposed to an example of self-harm. The differences between the two may be best illustrated by examples.

> *A 16-year-old woman is engaging in her first sexual relationship. Following intercourse, she remembers the details of the*

sexual abuse that occurred between her and a friend of her father between the ages of 7 and 11. She is intensely disturbed by this, driven to inconsolable tears. In an argument with her boyfriend, during which she accuses him of not caring, she rushes into the kitchen and dramatically and impulsively picks up the bread knife, cuts into her forearms and makes a jagged wound that immediately bleeds freely. Seeing the blood, she is immediately calm. Her horrified boyfriend finds her later, sitting in the chair watching the blood drip and the knife still in one hand. She is quiet and acquiescent as she is taken to casualty and the wound is dressed. In the subsequent few years, a pattern emerges where a difficulty is responded to with cutting the forearm, followed by a period of calmness.

A 42-year-old divorced man with grown-up children with whom he has no contact is facing problems in his work, with the possibility of redundancy and has recently been diagnosed as having prostate cancer. While the cancer is treatable, and is at an early stage, he concludes that he has little to live for, and decides after some thought to kill himself. He finds out about and joins a voluntary euthanasia society, learns about methods of suicide, and opts for drinking a bottle of spirits and tying a large plastic bag over his head. He decides on a date several months ahead, the anniversary of his wedding, and puts his affairs in order, rewrites his will, cancels his magazine subscriptions and leaving a note for the milkman. In the event, he is successful, with police being alerted several months after his disappearance by neighbours, who have become concerned about a smell from the flat.

In the case of the successful suicide, the intent is to ablate what is felt to be the source of the mental pain. Self-murder may disguise the rage felt by the person towards a persecuting or attacking world, or objects in it. These objects may include aspects of the person's own body, felt at a basic level to be 'bad' and representative of the link between the bad, persecuting mother and the bad part of the self. This may be compared to the self-situation where the attack is not to ablate but to punish and take revenge.

This gives rise to the way in which the destruction of the self may be misleading; if it is intended that the bad part of the self and the bad part of the object is destroyed, so the phantasy goes, there is the extent to which in phantasy it is intended that the good part of the self and of the object should be preserved.

> *A middle-aged man had come to feel angry and disillusioned about his life and filled with disappointment that his personal relationships and career had fallen short of the expectations that he had as a younger man. An assault upon him had left him feeling impotent and humiliated and frighteningly conscious of his own mortality. Standing by a river at night, he looked into the water and was full of a fantasy that if he threw himself in he would be enveloped by its 'velvety blackness' and imagined himself drifting away from the pain of his life into a warm dark cocoon. In consequence, he jumped in. The reality proved rather different. The water was cold, and inhaling it hurt his lungs; the water stank and the beautiful dream gave way to a frightening reality. By luck he was able to get himself to the shore and pull himself across the mud and out of the water.*

As a powerful and central psychic event, plans for or thoughts of suicide are likely to become the nexus of diverse strands of thought and fantasy. Perhaps the most invidious of these has been identified by Cambell and Hale (1991) who note that many suicidal people have a fantasy of life continuing after their death. This does not refer to a religious belief of an after-life, but rather the fantasies that people have about the reactions of others to the news of their death, or fantasies of what their funeral will be like and so on. In the example of the man given above, the enactment explored in a therapy, made it possible to bring together the splitting in a way that explicated the under-lying dynamic and brought the split-off hate and aggression back into the picture. The basic phantasy is a common one among unhappy adolescents fantasizing about their own death. In the fantasy they imagine themselves present at their own funeral, observing the distress of their loving regretful parents now 'good' having lost their loved, beautiful and 'good' child, in contrast to the 'bad' unappreciative parents, apparently only conscious of the extent to which their bad child fails to fulfil their expectations. Mostly, fortunately, these ubiquitous fan-tasies are not enacted in gross ways. Where they are, there is usually a serious gap in the person's capacity to manage or process their affective experience.

A 37-year-old woman, having dowsed herself in petrol, set herself to fire. Her fantasy was that this would afford a great release, the flames somehow giving vent to the indefinable but ineffable and dreadful tension that filled her daily existence but that she could find no means of expressing.

Another person might have sufficiently developed mental structures, say ego strength, to be able to give this experience mental representation in a way that means it is available for mitigation and management; one might be able to say about her that she was 'angry', for example, (although crucially not that she *felt* angry). This woman did not feel angry even if objectively one might be able to say that this woman's actions were her expressions of her anger. The immediate and then the enduring pain of the terrible burns that she suffered were a long way from what she imagined would be the wished for sense of release from what she endured. Of the same sort are the situations staff working in casualty departments of hospitals find themselves dealing with when a patient, having intentionally overdosed with prescription drugs such as paracetamol recovers from the initial effects and decide that they do not want to die, only to do so after a little while in anguish, because of the liver damage that they have sustained.

All of the theoretical structures that underpin the different psychoanalytic and psychotherapeutic schools allocate a central psychic role to anxiety about preparation for or denial of the fact of death. Both the act and the fantasy of suicide are omnipotent attempts to deny this reality; that it is inevitable and that all human beings are powerless to avoid it. A woman whose family had a long and well-established tradition, associated with the ownership of a particular family estate conceived of her life in terms of her 'family', meaning the many generations of her family. The reality of the limited time span of her own life was effectively denied by her cultivating the sense that the family and the family estate were 'immortal'. The cost of this was that she consistently felt that it was impossible to have any life, identity or children of her own; all were sacrificed for dynastic purposes. Another patient spoke of killing himself in terms of wanting to 'destroy the whole world and everyone in it'; this was an attempt to deny his feelings of powerlessness about the inescapable reality of death by making himself death's author; although he could not destroy the world, killing himself he would fully destroy his own version of the world. Thus the reality of death may be inverted; life is full of threat while the *tabular rasa* that death affords, offers a canvas upon which attractive fantasies may be painted.

> *A 40-year-old woman with two teenage children, began therapy as a consequence of marital difficulties and depression. In her youth, she had taken several overdoses, and was again preoccupied with taking an overdose. Having worked as a nurse, she was now knowledgeable about lethal doses of drugs, contemptuous of her suicidal attempts as a teenager and expressed the idea that this time she would 'get it right'. She stored coproxamol tablets (potentially lethal) that had been prescribed for other ailments, and kept a large quantity of them together with an unopened bottle of vodka and a carton of orange juice 'to make it all palatable' in a rucksack hidden in the cloakroom. In her therapy, she teased and terrorized the therapist with the knowledge of this suicide kit, enjoying his concern and helplessness in the situation. Once this dynamic has been looked at, in a more reflective session, she talked about how she saw the ruck sack as her 'parachute'.*

In another session, she spoke about the effect that her suicide might have on her family. It emerged that she had quite detailed fantasies about the reactions of the different members. While each of these fantasies was dressed up as concern, underlying them seemed to be a deep sense of resentment at each of her two children ('the boys') and her husband. With her husband it was for an affair he had had two years previously; this was reasonably accessible for analytic exploration. In relation to 'the boys' it was much more hidden, and was related to fundamental ambivalences about being a mother, and having to put up with the inevitable attacks made by children growing up.

The therapist became preoccupied with why the contents of the rucksack were 'the parachute', thinking to himself that the contents were more like a suicide bomb that would blow her to pieces, and rip apart the lives of her husband and children.

Eventually he was able to formulate in terms of her need for the parachute to take her safely out of something dangerous, and that perhaps she had a fantasy that it was not her own death that she anticipated, but the getting away from those elements in her life that she felt threatened by, to a place of safety.

By obscuring the reality of death by the drama of suicide and grieving relatives, the patient can remain oblivious to its lethal nature. This obliviousness potentiates the possibility of the individual carrying the plan out. Last minute, second thoughts are quelled by the satisfaction of the fantasy of the life after they have gone, seen in the reactions of others to their death. The patients are fantasizing themselves as an observer to these reactions; fantasizing themselves as an observer of their own funeral, and thus fantasizing for themselves a role, an existence after their death. In such a state of mind, suicide is undertaken without an acknowledgement of the reality of death and oblivion that will result.

Some writers have identified the 'paradisiacal' or ideal fantasy/unconscious phantasy that often seems to accompany suicidal acts, for example a fantasy of an ideal fusion with mother (Schachter 1999; Campbell 1999; Bateman 1999). The man described above, who jumped into the river, prior to his leap, imagined the river to be warm, holding and velvety; in his mind associated with a return to the womb. The origin of such commonly described and even more widely implied fusion states have been much debated and we have touched on this in Chapters 2 and 9. Freud, for example, imagined such 'oceanic' states to be a regression to a state of 'primary narcissism'. (1914); others have disputed this seeing the phantasy as a defensive one produced by resort to excessive projective identification or have talked about normal states of symbiosis (Rosenfeld 1987). There is some agreement, however, that the absence or effective absence of a father may be of importance in development of suicidal tendencies, both from the point of view of anxiety about being trapped inside a bad mother (Meltzer 1992) with suicide as an attempt to escape, and suicide as a means to enact phantasies about fusion with an ideal mother as a defence against separation anxiety. Additionally Fonagy and Target (1999) have suggested that an absent father, may significantly undermine the capacity of men to have an internal mental model of themselves '… "less contaminated" by the ambivalence which affects the maternal image ...' (p. 65). Along the same lines, Campbell identifies the absence of a father as leading to the depriving of the individual of a 'third' position, thus impairing the process of separation from mother along with diminished capacity for thinking and mentalization.

Freud originally thought about this in terms of splitting and projection (1917), but it is the concept of violent or excessive projective identification, which has been used to describe the psychological mechanism by which painful realities, including painful feeling or sensations contingent upon bodily injury, can be evacuated and located outside of the self. In the psychiatric setting many of the major mental illnesses, do not seem to be painful to patients in an acute sense. After recovery patients who have been in regressed and especially withdrawn, psychotic states often describe these more in terms of being blank or numb. It is the staff or relatives who often find the patient's state unbearably painful or anxiety provoking; much overzealous treatment of such patient people can be linked to the staff's need for relief rather than the patient's.

A man was admitted to hospital in a state of schizophrenic, catatonic, withdrawal. Such a state is characterized by so-called 'waxy flexibility'. A patient's limb, an arm, for example, raised into the air by a third party, will be left there by the patient indefinitely. When asked about this at a later date when he had somewhat recovered, the patient explained that he had felt as though he had been flayed alive. He was aware of every single environmental influence, all of which were exquisitely painful to him if they touched him. He meant by this, both physical and mental events. In his 'skinless' state he was able to avoid the pain, however, by remaining absolutely motionless.

Such processes of projection and dissociation allow people to inflict terrible and painful injuries upon themselves, apparently without compunction. This may involve gross confusion of internal and external realities, for example, the woman who we talked about in Chapter 7 who blinded herself saying, 'you might think so [that it was painful], but *you* do not know what I might see'.

The picture may be more complicated still. One consequence of the kinds of evacuatory processes that we have described is that patients may become increasingly tormented by their resultant sense of emptiness. This may be of varying degrees and qualities. They may feel that they lack substance; one patient repeatedly dreamed that she became flat and one dimensional, another that she was incontinent of every orifice. Alternatively they may feel that they lack any sense of internal orientation, patients who resort to adhesive identification, for example, and habitually defer to others. Such people are often 'put upon' or are compulsive 'helpers'. One young woman broke down when she went to university, feeling she could not do the work despite gaining many 'A' levels at school. In analysis she came to realize that what she had been good at was answering other people's questions, but was more or less unable to think for herself and it was this latter ability that was required of her at the university.

Bulimic patients can gorge themselves in an attempt to obtain a sense of fullness and compensate for the profound sense of emptiness that they have engendered in themselves. The 'stuffing' may be an attempt to offset the sense of lacking feeling that the projective identification may have given rise to. Vomiting and forced bowel evacuations may be the concrete expression of the pattern of psychological emptying and filling. William Faulkner has a character in one of his novels say that if given a choice between 'nothing' and 'grief', 'I'll take grief'. The unconscious choice that suicidal and self-harming patients have made is for 'nothing'. In reality this 'nothing' is not without consequence in that the evocation of 'nothing', like Banquo's murder, leaves 'ghosts' of the objects which have been violently got rid of, returning in persecutory or depressive form, which in the long run may become intolerable.

> In analysis, a woman dreamed that she was swimming across a shallow lake. At the bottom of the lake was a deep bed of fine, but noxious silt. If her arm and leg movements were vigorous enough to give her both buoyancy and forward motion, the silt was stirred up and she would be engulfed and choked by it.

In this may be seen, both the anxiety that the evacuatory processes evoke as well as the characteristic cyclical form, as attempts to evacuate and recover may become expressed in ever more serious and painful self-mutilations or ever increasing self-destructive acts which culminate in a suicide attempt or suicide. Balint (1968) has pointed out that the significance of these suicidal/self-destructive acts is that they are a way of life rather than a means of death.

For such patient's acts of self-destruction including parasuicide or self-harm may be ways of trying to break out of this situation. In serious cases people resort to an increasingly vicious circle of cutting themselves in order to try to 'find pain' and with it a sense of being real and alive. The pain is felt to hold out hope of recovering themselves and the attention of others. The complexities of the projective and evacuatory mechanisms may make it very difficult to offer analytic help however.

Clinical Issues and Issues of Technique

If suicide is a way of life rather than a way of death in therapy or analysis it will be in less overt forms than the pattern of self-destructiveness becomes apparently. There is of course a continuum; no individual will be without some such traits in their character. There will, however, be people who will disguise such tendencies not least because of the over-determination of the psychological situation. So we differentiated between the 'punishing training regime' of the marathon runner and the training regime as punishment, aimed principally at his wife and children illustrating the secondary gains that may accrue as a consequence of the 'success' that the 'dedication' to training might bring. The punishing-ness of the training has the effect of being both an outlet for rage or sadism at the same time as effectively punishing the man who is training, in order to neutralize his sense of guilt. Perversely the situation may arise where the man can angrily (and falsely) reject the idea that he is behaving in an angry or punishing way, by pointing out the material benefits and honours that have accrued, not only to the man but also to his family. Thus the man's violence may be denied by him and self-righteously and falsely attributed to the wife or family.

It seems likely that much chronic illness, which is a consequence of factors at least notionally in the control of the individual such as overeating, smoking, excessive recourse to alcohol, excessive work and so on, have their roots in this kind of set up and may be viewed as varieties of self-harm or suicide even where there is a strong passive component or the self-destructiveness is attenuated or protracted over many years.

The refractory nature of these conditions requires comment; we have already commented on the idea that Freud and Klein's concept of the death instinct had its roots in the difficulty that these patients present, with their insistence either that the analyst is no good or that the analysis is going well only because of the analyst's ability to get better. In the analytic encounter it may be impossible and will frequently be almost impossible for the analyst to, as it were, 'get out from under' the patient's projection of their neediness, dependency, distress and anger. Characteristically such patients will be endlessly accommodating and helpful with the 'analyst's problem' or alternatively angry, hurt and resentful at the analyst's failure to appreciate the patient's attempts to help the analyst, with the analyst's difficulty. Only with the greatest difficulty will the patient be able to begin to identify the neediness, rage or destructiveness, along with the wish for help *for him- or herself* in them.

An important consequence of the splitting and projection is the extent to which the patient may seem to be oblivious to the reality of or consequences of their self-harming or destructive actions. In the transference this is likely to be expressed in the subtle sense that any need for change or for concern about consequences, resides not in the mind of the patient but rather in the mind of the analyst; the patient may appear to be concerned only in passing or not at all about injurious or fatal consequences of their action being effectively split off from these realities as something that may intimately involve them. An atmosphere of *faux* cooperation may evolve within the therapy or analysis in which the patient will apparently be concerned to address the issue of the self-destructiveness, but in reality this will be on the basis that this is out of a wish to cooperate or comply with the wishes or alleviate the concerns of the therapist. The patient is not anxious about him- or herself; they are preoccupied with the therapist or analyst and it is as if the situation is reversed so that the analyst is the person who is in difficulty.

The splitting aspect of such situations is from time to time painfully and tragically revealed. Occasionally the revelation may enable the work to take place or develop. Cambell and

Hale (1985), for example, has discussed the ways in which it might be important to interview para-suicidal patients, following a suicidal act, before they have a night's sleep and the capacity to dream. Hale contends that the suicidal act, may have the quality of a breakdown, in which the split-off aspect of the self, which is usually unavailable comes to the fore. Sleep and dreams may have the effect of restoring the previous spurious integrity of the personality so that the murderous/enraged suicidal part of the personality is once again lost. In the case of the man who jumped into the river it was possible to do just this and the breakdown could then be considered as something closer to a breakthrough. This is a hazardous proposition, however, and not to be precipitated. It is a common tragedy in Accident and Emergency hospital departments that the suicidal act, enacted on the basis of the split phantasy/fantasy becomes something different in reality. The woman who immolated herself and indeed subsequently died of the effects of her burns is an example of this, as are the people who take paracetamol overdoses, recover from the immediate effects, realize the split-off aspects of their situation but nevertheless die shortly afterwards as a consequence of the toxic effects of the drug upon their liver.

In therapy or analysis it may be possible to allow the breakdown in the defensive pattern of splitting and projection in a more controlled way. This is not without its hazards also. Interpretation of the way in which the patient systematically and often subtly shifts the emphasis in their psychological situation to locate the wish for change or the knowledge of the difficulties in the therapist, is likely to result in an increasing awareness of the feelings of rage and consequent guilt, which have been habitually split off from. The accusation will be made that the analyst is no good or is making the patient worse, either because of their incompetence, malignance or because of serious psychological difficulties of their own. Practitioners treating such patients must be prepared and experienced enough to wear such storms and also to resist external pressures from outside of them, including friends or other professionals in order to see the thing through. Sooner or later the patient must make their own decision as to whether they want to live or die, if they are to escape from the illusory sense that this is essentially a matter for others and they are unaffected. Such a position may be difficult for the analyst or therapist to hold in the face of the risk that the patient, given such a choice, may kill him- or herself. As one patient explained to the analyst, 'What I really want to do is to tie you up and then kill myself here on the couch in front of you when there is nothing that you can do'. Disguised under this may be the essence of an aspect of the underlying phantasy that drives many patients. In terms of professional responsibility, the guilt that such patients evoke along with its uncontained nature may mean that therapists are unfairly held responsible by family or authorities, for the suicide or suicide attempt, when they themselves feel guilty that the patient is dead or injured. This is an important consideration when approaching the treatment of patients who constitute a real risk to themselves; even if accusations are not made, the anxiety engendered may lead to the practitioners fatally 'pulling their punches' or entering into sadomasochistic collusions in order to avoid the anticipated sense of guilt or culpability.

The pressure to take up a collusive position is complicated by common humanity and the knowledge that patients may become temporarily gripped by destructive states of mind, so that they require temporary restraint. Forceful interventions made to restrain suicidal and self-harming patients, however unintentionally, may have the effect of reinforcing patients' wishes to locate anxiety outside of themselves. The danger is that such interventions may, and indeed may be intended to, reinforce the fantasy that the anger/concern/anxiety resides in the outside world and not in the patient. In therapy the pressure on the therapist will be to identify with the identificatory aspect of the projective identification. Such a situation may produce an illusory 'therapeutic alliance' but essentially be a sadomasochistic collusion ruled over by the murderous part of the patient, making implicit murderous threats. One such patient responded to each interpretation about such matters with 'don't go down that road!'.

A patient, who abused drugs and regularly placed himself in hazardous situations, was ostensibly concerned about this. Indeed at one level he was clearly terrified of his self-destructive capacity. Nonetheless the analyst noticed that the patient subtly changed the analyst's interpretation of the needy part of him into a matter of a more abstract notion of 'what was good for him' or even 'you think that I should ...'. In this way the part of him that could experience his desire or need- iness as an immediate reality was denied and displaced.

Many suicidal or self-harming patients may be contained with- in the analytic relationship; acting out may be avoided in its more dangerous forms if the self-destructive elements can be drawn into the transference and contained in the analytic relationship. Certainly this is true of the self-destructive and self-harming ele- ments which feature in all patients and all therapeutic work. The potential for acting out that more seriously disturbed patients present with, may mean that the therapist or analyst will have to give serious consideration as to how the patient will be managed in the event of the self-harming elements threatening to become uncontained. As we have noted the involvement of other parties may need to be taken into account either in an unwelcome way or where arrangements need to be made for additional help from other professionals, for example, from a General Practitioner or a psychiatrist, where there is a serious risk to the patient. This is true even where the therapist is, for example, a psychiatrist, because as we noted the pressure upon the therapist to act in order to escape from emerging, painful, affective states, rather than to think may be considerable. Such situations necessitate the separation of the roles of analyst or psychotherapist from the role of therapist in its more general sense; such separations need, how- ever, to be carefully considered in terms of their implications and to avoid the therapy being fatally undermined.

11 Aggression, Violence, Institutions and Groups

The Containment of Violence in Institutions

Over the last decade, the vogue for organizational 'mission statements' has been adopted by a number of police forces; one force, for example, states that it will 'protect people from violence, disorder and fear'. While such copy may be dismissed as PR posturing, it does reflect a truth about the function of the police as an organization whose core business includes the management of violence. If the police manage violence in the community, then the courts are the bureaucracy that oversees it, the prison service warehouses those too violent to be allowed freedom and the armed forces managing violence at the level of the nation state; politicians are their bureaucratic executives. Hobbes argued that in a state of nature, the life of man consists of

> no arts; no letters; no society; and which is worse of all continual fear and danger of violent death; and life of man solitary, poor, nasty, brutish and short   (Hobbes 1651, Part 1, Chapter 13).

The creation of a society governed by social structures and organizations, in his view, limited the licence of the individual, but was a way of ending 'the war of each against all'. The organizations of the criminal justice system, police, courts and prisons, keep the peace within a society by force if necessary. In this way, people are protected from a nasty, 'brutish and short' life by organizations. There are of course versions of mankind's inherent nature, other than Hobbes, which are less pessimistic in their assumptions. Nonetheless, there is broad agreement that it is individuals, using the authority delegated by organizations, that have the task of containing the social expression of aggression and violence. In this chapter, we examine some of the psychodynamics that can emerge in these organizations as a result of their function of containing and dealing with violence although it will become clear that there is considerable room for crossover with the issues that we discussed in Chapter 9.

Conversely organizations may perpetrate violence; there is violence committed by an invading army or by an organized criminal gang. There are, however, other ways that organizations do violence. As well as the intended acts of aggression that may be the task of an organization, there are other apparently unintended acts of violence for which organizations can be responsible. Sociologists in the 1960s such as Goffman described a process of entry into organizations such as the army or a psychiatric hospital, where the identity and personal individuality of a newcomer has to be extinguished, and in which they have to be re-born in a new manufactured and conforming identity. Wearing the organization's uniform and regulation haircut associated with the adoption of a set of conformist ideas, facilitates the individual being subsumed within the organization (Goffman 1961). Then there are the ways in which organizations can neutralize the humanity or sanity of their members. The question of how the workers in the Second World War concentration camps were able as individuals to carry out their cruel work; the development of the 'lynch mob' mentality, where a group of people become organized to do something that individually, they would eschew.

At the other end of the scale, some organizations actively commission, create and carry out aggressive action; the aggressive use of force of an invading army, which may so easily become violent or provide the cover for individual acts of violence; the violence of an organized criminal or terrorist gang. The difference between aggression and violence as actions of organizations is in whether the aim is the reduction or containment of violence or the creation and development of it. The organization is relevant because the means by which this task is carried out is facilitated by the benefits of coordinating the activities of a number of people towards the same end.

In this chapter, a number of issues that contribute to these phenomena will be explored, looking briefly at issues of structure and culture, then some of the psychodynamic understandings of group and organizational function. The discussion will be illustrated with reference to a particular set of organizations namely prisons, who have a clear task of containing and processing violence.

Organizational Structure and Culture

Organizational structure is usually demonstrated by some form of map or chart, with the chief executive at the top with a tier of directors underneath, and the various structures of their departments. The importance of such structures in organisations dealing with violence is clear demonstrated by the ranks in the army, from private through lance corporals, corporals, sergeants, sergeants major and on to the officer grades. In these settings, the concept of an 'order' by a superior ranking officer, where the subordinate is simply required to carry out the command has its origins in combat situations where the superior vision of the officer/managers provides task focus in the chaos of battle.

While the advantages of a command structure in an organization in the confusion of battle are clear, specifically in relation to aggression, there is another aspect. In the commission of aggressive acts by organizations, 'obeying orders'; 'following policy': or 'usual practice' all potentiate the effectiveness of an organization in drawing upon the capacity for aggression and especially aggressive action. Two celebrated studies illustrate this phenomenon. In the Milgram experiment, normal subjects were found to be able to administer quite high levels of pain in the form of electric shocks to people in a separate room. In brief, the subjects were told that the experiment was not about their own behaviour, but rather about the behaviour of a second group in a separate room. The subjects were instructed to ask the second group questions, and to administer increasing levels of electric shock when questions were wrongly answered. The members of the second group purposefully answered questions incorrectly, and simulated pain when 'shocked' and this was heard by the questioners. The observation was that normal subjects are prepared to inflict quite high levels of pain in a setting legitimized by the authority of the researchers in charge (Milgram 1974).

The second experiment demonstrating this phenomenon was Zimbardo's study (Sabini & Silver 1982). A mock prison setting was set up, and subjects were randomly assigned to a prisoner group and a guard group for a residential role-play exercise. The observation was that the 'guard's' cruelty and sadism towards the 'prisoners' became so extreme that the experiment had to be discontinued. The individuals had been arbitrarily assigned to each group, but the structure of the differentiation, potentiated by the authority assigned to the guard group legitimized the use of aggression by the guard group to the prisoner group. Further more, the legitimacy of this seemed to be accepted not only by the 'guard' group, but also by the 'prisoner' group few of whom left, (as they were free to do) forcing the researchers to terminate the study prematurely.

The literature concerning Management struggles to define the nature of organizational culture, understanding this as the 'difficulty of seeing the wind', and concluding that culture is 'the way we do things around here' (Main 1989). From a psychodynamic perspective, the culture of an organization consists of the psychological set in which the task is carried out. The culture of the organization defines the nature of the task; the definition of the task and the ideological perspective of the organization that say, places a car bomb, determines designation as either terrorist or freedom fighter. A vignette may illustrate this.

A 37-year-old man attacks a prison officer, punching him in the face one morning when his cell is unlocked. The staff notes that the prisoner has had a poor relation with this officer in the past, that in general he is oppositional and concludes that he has consciously attacked the officer in malice. They are suspicious that he is enjoying the violence and that he will attack other officers, and so they dress in riot gear to take him down to the segregation unit. He violently resists, and the officers feel relieved that they were prepared for the trouble. He is seen by the doctor on duty, who asks why he attacked this particular officer, and a story emerges of how the officer is putting thoughts into his mind, and that the officer comes back in the middle of the night and speaks to him through the cell door, telling him he is a homosexual. The doctor concludes that he is actively psychotic and hallucinated, deluded that he is receiving telepathic messages from the officer. He transfers him to the prison healthcare wing, where he is no longer a security risk and cooperates with the regime.

In the normal prison wing, the task of managing the prisoner is defined as the control of an aggressive, violent and unpredictable prisoner. In the healthcare unit, he is a patient with an acute psychosis. In the first setting, he is likely to react more violently than in the second, thus confirming the erroneous assumption of the staff group. The man is likely to react entirely differently in the two settings. The only real difference between them is the way that the task of containing him is defined, either as the control of a dangerous and unpredictable man or as a paranoid and psychotic patient with a propensity to violence to be cared for. Elsewhere the many studies that have been undertaken into the emotional attitude of the carers of schizophrenic patients clearly demonstrates that whether the attitude is critical or concerned, has a large impact upon relapse rates (Leff & Vaughn 1985). The High Expressed Emotion research demonstrates the extent to which encouraging benign attitudes and discouraging the malign may have considerable impact on prognosis.

Jimmy is a fiercely proud, independent and violent 32-year-old man serving a ten-year sentence for robbery. Violently abused while in care, he is highly distrustful of all authority, and especially of prison officers and governors. For the four years since he was convicted, he has, in his own words, 'fought the system', taking every opportunity to break rules, to get into confrontations and fights with prison officers or with other prisoners, or where possible to otherwise disrupt the smooth running of the prison.

At times, he has become angry at 'the screws winding me up', accusing them of 'playing mind games', with him to provoke him. For example, he is convinced that they keep back letters that have arrived for him, on purpose, just to get a reaction. He has decided that this is a good strategy and has started 'winding up' the screws in return. Usually housed in relatively well-staffed segregation units because of his behaviour, he spends his time listening to the sotto-voce discussions between the prison officers, learning who is married, who has children, what their individual crises are, then uses this information with which to attack them subsequently. One officer's wife is ill. Jimmy takes to shouting through the edge of the door in his cell in a sing song voice, 'Officer Jones, she's dying, she's going soon, and its all your fault. Its because of your filthy perversions, you fucking nonce'. Clearly audible, these words echo around the bare walls of the segregation unit, leading to peals of laughter from other inmates, some of whom join in.

Officer Jones, in spite of a culture among the officers of a mild macho bravado, is clearly shaken and upset, especially because he is genuinely concerned about his wife's health, and because her ailment is gynaecological. The rest of the staff team in the segregation unit is angry and annoyed at Jimmy's attacks. The managing governor of the unit realizes that there is a difficult potential in the situation. He meets Officer Jones to discuss how to proceed, Jones feels that it would not be appropriate to be removed from the unit, as this would represent a 'scalp' for Jimmy, however, he is moved back to being less in contact with him. Next, the governor meets with the staff group for three reasons; to identify a management strategy for Jimmy to include an adjudication and punishment for this behaviour, and to make the staff group aware of the strategy vis-à-vis officer Jones. But thirdly, and most importantly, the governor frames the task. He acknowledges that Jimmy is being extremely provocative and that as individuals they must want to get back to him for hurting deeply one of their friends (Officer Jones); but he points out that it is for this sort of behaviour that Jimmy is housed in the segregation unit; that as professional prison officers, it is their job to tolerate and manage the provocation and violence of the prisoners. He goes on to recall some of the more colourful characters and incidents that the team have had to manage in the previous few years, commenting that as a team they had got through these testing times, and that they would get through this current problem.

After several days of singing through the gap at the side of his door, Jimmy is disappointed. He expected that something would happen – that he would be 'jumped' by the officers or even moved to a different prison. Instead, he had lost privileges for a week, and that was it. Maybe they are all heartless, he thought. 'I'd be upset if someone said that about my missus'.

This example illustrates several issues, firstly, the task of managing and containing violence that is the work of a prison, and that this violence can be both in the physical and psychological realms. Secondly, it illustrates the potential traps and pitfalls of the work, the temptation to respond in kind to the violence, and the inevitability of there being victims of the violence that is being contained. Thirdly, it demonstrates the importance of the cultural and ideological environment in which the work is carried out. The manager frames the work as containing the violence without responding in kind.

For many organizations that deal in violence, there is a power differential; the organization's task is legitimized legally, such that the individual can feel, and in reality is, relatively powerless. This power differential is predicated on the fact that the organization will not violently manage the violence, but will do so professionally and with a minimum of force. The task in our terms is to respond to violence with aggression, in integrated appropriate ways. The building of prisons, the locking of doors, the confinement of trouble makers and the use of force to restrain where this is needed, in order to protect the interests and safety of society, other inmates, staff and the inmate him- or herself, without resort to violence. The problem is the corrupting influence of power and of maintaining the differentiation between the use of aggression, including forceful action and the use of violence. There is always a temptation to use the power differential to settle the score. Maintaining a professional culture is absolutely crucial in the safe operation of such settings where there can be extreme provocation and violence, and where there is overwhelming power on one side.

The Organization as a Group

From a psychodynamic perspective, organizations are groups of people, and so their functioning is subject to group dynamics. The organization as a whole is a large group, and the subgroups within it can be understood in terms of small group dynamics. These two will be explored in turn, using material to illustrate some of the organizational dilemmas that emerge.

So called 'large group dynamics' have a particular flavour. Kreeger (1971) identified a number of these characteristics of large groups. In particular, he argues that being in a large group has the effect of dissolving individual identity. The effect of this dissolution of identity is to create quasi-psychotic phenomena; the fantasy of being persecuted or of the hostility of the group; the fantasy of thinking with the same mind and so on. A person in a large group can easily disavow their own views and values, surrendering them to the collective mentality.

> *Simon, a 25-year-old unemployed physics graduate is in prison on remand, charged with GBH and affray, having been involved in a football supporter-related scuffle outside a pub. Sitting in his cell he is incredulous that his usual Saturday ritual of supporting his local team had gone so wrong. He had ended up with a large group of lads that a friend of his knew. After the match (which they lost) they had gone to a pub to drown their sorrows and get something to eat. He had stayed on because the 'crack' was good, some of the lads in the group were quite funny, he had liked their team loyalty, and the pub was full of disconsolate supporters. But their colours had been seen through the window by the 'away' supporters who had started jeering. Things had moved very fast; the group he was in were suddenly very angry, as was everyone in the pub. His group had gone out and attacked the jeering opposition. Simon had never been in a football fight before and he did not know what had come over him. The police had arrived suddenly, and he had been bundled into a van. His lawyer had told him that several of the other lads in the group he had been in, had long histories of such violence.*

The ability of a large group setting to dissolve individual identity is the reason why large groups can be swayed by charismatic rhetoric. Searching for some stable identity, the individual seeks something to identify with, a value set to be able to adopt, and finds it in the oration of the leader.

In an organization, aspects of identity within the structure come from the sub-group and the specific tasks one is assigned. Nevertheless, at one level, the organization is still functioning as a large group. Arranged into organizations or not, large groups of people are powerful, and there is a constant risk that this power can be abused. The combination of this power and the dissolution of individual values, and therefore the moral compasses of individuals can result in ordinary people doing extraordinary things.

The direction of a large group such as the Nazi camp staff to carry out repugnant and violent acts utilizes the power of the large group on the one hand, and its vulnerability to dissolving the moral compass of the individuals that comprise it on the other.

At a more micro level, organizations are divided into smaller sub-groups. Wilfred Bion, had the experience early in his career, of running a ward for shell-shocked soldiers, following which he wrote *Experiences in Groups* (Bion 1968) which hypothesized a number of characteristic unconscious processes that are take place. The interaction of these smaller sub-groups that make up organizations, each with their avowed task, and their unconscious dynamics creates a complex mix. In organizations dealing with violence, the potential for these dynamics to become very severe is high. Violence being contained by an organization adds volatility to the dynamics. Working all day with people who have actually killed their bosses, wives or associates or who have actually done them violence adds piquancy to the normal aggressive fantasies that group members have towards each other, and that different groups have towards each other.

The governing board of an organization for example, may as a group exhibit the sorts of psychodynamics that emerge in these settings. The mechanism whereby the larger organization functions as a group is based on the theory of systems. The larger organization consists of a number of groups with differing tasks, but with clear lines of connection and communication between them.

Grendon Prison is a 240 bed therapeutic community prison divided into six relatively autonomous therapeutic community units, five treatment communities where residents stay between eighteen months and three years and one assessment/preparation unit. Each therapeutic community is run by a multidisciplinary team that comprises a psychotherapist, who is the clinical lead; a forensic psychologist, a probation officer, twelve officers, two of whom are group therapy specialists and two senior officer-managers.

These community multidisciplinary teams are strong and coherent, meeting seven or eights times per week to carry on the everyday work of managing the therapeutic community, and the clinical progress and crises of the client group as they struggle with and re-enact in the clinical setting their personality difficulties. The prison is managed by a 'senior management group' with a multidisciplinary membership that echoes the disciplines available to the individual therapeutic communities with therapy, forensic psychology, probation and prison managers, led by the prison's governor. Unlike the therapeutic community teams, the senior team has the other organizational functions represented, personnel, finance and so on. Working for this management team are two other committees, one overseeing the operational functioning of the prison and the other overseeing its therapeutic function.

The structure of the organization therefore mainly consists of two tiers of groups – the senior multidisciplinary team and the community teams. However, there is an additional dimension structurally, via the different disciplines. There are strong and coherent discipline groups through the prison, with the therapists' group comprising the collection of therapists; the forensic psychologists' group who have an additional task of leading on research and development; the probation team, the senior officers' group and so on. Thus, there is a matrix of different groupings, each with their interrelations.

In this example, the organization comprises a series of interlocking and interrelated groups, each of which are subject to the group dynamic processes descried by Bion. Bion's 'basic assumption' model of group dynamics distinguishes between the manifest task of the group, the task of the senior group in the example being to lead and steer the prison, and a latent task, one that is unconscious. He names the unconscious task of the group the 'basic assumption', and proposes some characteristic preoccupations of groups. Firstly, Bion argues that groups gathered together may tend to feel that they are dependent on a leader, and that they are followers, basic assumption one, 'dependency'.

Some of the Grendon small groups are facilitated by part-time therapists who spend the majority of their time in practice outside. In one group, a new part-time therapist had arrived and taken over. The group itself was in a bad way, the previous facilitator (a probation officer) had been well loved, and a very long-standing member of staff, although one who was seen as hard and unyielding. As a result issues were frequently brought from the group to the community meeting about things he had said or refused to do. In spite of this he was seen as fair, and it became clear when he left that his group had been quite attached to him; because although the fact of this man's impending departure had been discussed, the group was still very disgruntled, with one or two members acting out and becoming quite a concern.

> *The new therapist in the group settled in over a period of several weeks. After a while, it was noted in the community that the regular complaints about their therapist had disappeared; the group members declared themselves happy with their new (part time) therapist.*
>
> *In supervision, a different picture emerged. The new therapist was being run ragged by being asked to do things, and instead of interpreting, was trying to carry them out. He had been in touch with group member's probation officers, liasing with other members of staff and art therapy and psychodrama and over various issues and so on. Somehow, the culture of the group had changed from one where understanding emerged from the discussion in the group, to one where understanding emerged from the mind and the experience of the therapist. After six weeks, he was completely exhausted and depleted.*
>
> *As an experienced therapist, he could quickly see how he had acted into a dependency dynamic, and with further discussion could see that, while experienced otherwise, his lack of experience with Grendon type patients had left him vulnerable. It was as if in the first few sessions of the group, he had been mugged and his wallet taken, and that this had become a pattern so that he felt initially extorted into giving, helping and doing the understanding himself, and latterly, this dependency on him in the group became the norm.*

In criminal justice structures there is a confusion about who does the punishing of criminals. Is it the prison officer, the prison governor, the judge or the politician who makes the laws? This confusion might be an example of a dependency dynamic. The workers in prison settings can avoid taking responsibility for the fact that the client group is being punished by appealing to the higher authority of the judge. Prison culture, as an example, is quasi-militaristic, being a 'disciplined' service, where commands and instructions are issued by senior staff, with an expectation that they will be obeyed and carried out. If they are not, this can be conceived of as a disciplinary offence. The risk of such structures is that they can foster a 'dependency' mind set, so that if a prisoner escapes, its not the problem of the officer on the landing, it is the governor's fault.

A second Bion basic assumption dynamic is that the task of the group is to fight about an issue – a basic assumption 'fight/flight' group. Arguments break out, and seem to become the reason for the group's existence.

> *On one of the Grendon therapeutic communities, there had been a confrontation with a prisoner who had been challenged over strong suspicions that he had been bringing in and dealing in drugs. In the meeting, the prisoner had got very angry, and had threatened the therapist that he had friends outside who would find out where he lived and come after him and his family. The prisoner was known to have gang connections outside, and this was seen as no idle threat.*
>
> *In the subsequent staff meetings, there were bitter recriminations between staff, some feeling that the prisoner had been pushed too far, such that he had been forced into making a threat, others felt he had not been pushed far enough in his treatment so far, such that the confrontation had been necessary. Each side in this argument was angry and fearful of the situation. Privately, afterwards, a number of staff firmed up their resolve to apply for transfers and look for other jobs.*

Internecine disputes and arguments between different members of multidisciplinary teams either stemming from clashing personalities or from the fundamentally different ideological bases of the different disciplines, are part of everyday life working in multidisciplinary teams. Working with violent patients, however, the possibility of teams breaking down into such fight/flight dynamics is much greater. In the example above, the prisoner is challenged because this is the work of the day; that individuals are challenged about aspects of their psychopathology, in this case bringing in drugs to the prison. The man's reaction to this was threatening and importantly he was known to be capable of carrying out such threats. The fact that the violent patient actually is violent and actually does cross the boundary between verbal aggression and physical violence means that violent clinical exchanges always have the potential to extend into reality. This fact impacts on the nature of the staff team dynamics for those looking after such patients, such that they are more prone to resort to the fight/flight dynamics described.

The third Bion basic assumption dynamic is that of 'pairing'. Here, the group becomes preoccupied with the idea that two members of the group (either man and woman, or some other creative couple) will get together and create a baby, a messiah that will resolve all the problems of the group.

One of the Grendon small groups had a chronic difficulty, in that two of the members had convictions for violence to sex offenders and one member was serving a sentence for the indecent assault of a minor. The group seemed perpetually about to fall apart, because of the aggression of the two towards the third, such that the latter seemed unable to tell his story and engage effectively in treatment, as he would be shouted down, 'nonced off', or the other two would need to articulate their own difficulties, drowning him out. Unfortunately, the man with the indecent assault conviction was rather used to being victimized, and indeed rather enjoyed it, because it gave him an opportunity to appear willing to work on himself, but unable to do so, because of the two 'big bad bullies'.

The (male) officer in the group who was the group facilitator was joined by a new (female) member of staff, another officer who, it became known, had been involved in the Sex Offender Treatment Programme (SOTP) in her previous job. In the group, she began to comment on the indecent assault man's use of the situation to hide behind. Overall, the sense of impasse in the group disappeared, the lead (male) officer-therapist seemed to become much more effective in his intervention.

This apparent improvement was discussed in the group, and it became clear that firstly there was a fantasy that the new (female) officer was discussing the group at length with the male lead officer-therapist; that her experience of SOTP was influencing the male officer, such that he was managing the group better. Curiously, this discussion of the nature of the interaction between the two staff members preoccupied the group, with increasingly excited discussion, emerging in a joke that they were 'talking about sex' together.

In supervision, the two therapists talked about their discomfort at the assumption in the group that they were having an affair. The supervisor proposed that the apparent improvement in the functioning in the group was not real, but rather the group had been able to come together around a basic assumption dynamic of pairing. That the group had a fantasy that the two officer co-therapists would in some way produce something that would save the group; that there was a pairing fantasy with the expectation that a messiah would emerge to save the group.

A fourth very common group dynamic that emerges is that of 'scapegoating'. The word 'scapegoat' derives from the ritual of animal sacrifice, where the sins and wrongdoing of a group of people were symbolically placed on a goat who was sacrificed. This dynamic is both common and invidious in group settings.

Partly by interpreting the pairing dynamic and partly with the group's increasing familiarity with the new therapist, the pairing dynamic receded. In its place, instead of the battle between the man with the indecent assault conviction and the two 'bullies', there was a more difficult to define sense of uneasiness within the group. It seemed as if, not only did the two bullies prevent the man with the indecent assault conviction exploring his issues, but that the whole group were rather uncomfortable. The issue disappeared in the group for several sessions, until another client in the community was accused of 'selling [his] arse', i.e., having homosexual sex for material gain, contravening the 'no sex' rule of the community.

The small group was electrified by the discussion of this event, in particular there was a strong view raised and shared that sex offenders should not be treated with prisoners with violent crimes. The charge was that they were not able to explore their issues, being intimidated by the more violent inmates. In the group, the indecent assault man was in agreement with this, complaining that he was not able to be treated for this reason, and that he had been let down. The whole group concluded that indeed, a mistake had been made in the allocation of the indecent assault man to the group, and indeed the community, and a formal request was made by him to the staff to be transferred.

The issue was discussed in the staff group. The officer-therapists in the group were inclined to agree with the request, and the debate turned into a much more general discussion of the disadvantages of mixing sex and violent offenders in the group. This discussion was stopped by the senior officer, a man in his 50s with decades of experience. One of the two 'bullies' he knew well, and he remembered a discussion some years before where sexual experiences had been discussed. This 'bully's' most exciting experience had been a group sex incident with a prostitute and four of his friends that had taken place in the euphoria following a successful bank robbery. Significantly, it had emerged that the prostitute was under the impression that she was visiting an individual, and that the group sex incident had actually been closer to a rape. With money to spare, she had been paid well, and had not complained to the police, but at the time, the four friends did not have her consent. She had actually been coerced and intimidated into participating so that she had had no choice. Compared to this, the indecent assault man's conviction was for a string of incidents where he had groped women's breasts or under their skirts in the street; his long sentence being because he had previous convictions for similar behaviour.

The senior officer proposed that everybody in the group had groped a woman without their consent, that everyone in the group had probably committed a sex offence, whether they had been convicted or not. He asserted that everyone in the group was guilty of some sort of violence within their sexual relationships. There was an uproar, with some angrily denouncing the senior officer, and threateningly challenging him, 'are you calling me a nonce?'. The indignation spilled out into the community meeting the next day, with angry denunciations of the senior officer who was 'noncing off' people in the community with no evidence 'what evidence do you have', came the angry challenge. Eventually, the bank robber in the original group shouted down the melee and spoke, describing the incident with the prostitute that had nearly been a rape. This led to a debate about whether this could have constituted a sex offence, 'she was paid, wasn't she'; 'she didn't complain, did she?' 'what's the problem ...?'. Others spoke about similar incidents of near coercion within sexual relations, and how they had never thought that this might be constituted as sexual offending before. The community meeting ended with mutterings in various quarters, and subsequently, the issue was discussed further, but the plan to move the sex offender seemed to evaporate.

Thus, the scapegoat had the sexual anxieties of the group projected onto him exclusively, and there was then a wish to exclude him because of their unbearable nature.

A similar mechanism was identified by Menzies-Lyth in her well-known study of nursing in hospital (Menzies-Lyth 1961), although in this case the splitting is less in relation to the individual within the group, but rather by the group in relation to the individual. Menzies-Lyth describes the ways in which the difficulty experienced by nurses in managing their affective experience in relation to the patient, particularly the aggressive and sexual feelings that patients arouse, is dealt with by, as it were, dividing the patients up. So the patient becomes defined by their condition, 'the appendicitis in the second bed' rather than by themselves as individuals. This has some pay-off for the patient too, who may be placed in a passive position, which involves the idealization of the doctors, nurses and hospital setting. This makes it much easier to accept the medicines and surgical procedures, which in other circumstances might be poisons or assaults. The competence and benevolence, if not the omnipotence and omniscience of the staff can be assumed without the deep and overwhelming fears, which are their unconscious counterpart. Medical failures are often responded to in the light of the collapse of the idealization and the emergence of the intense suspicion and fear that is, in the usual course of things denied. Within the psychiatric hospital or the secure unit, there may be a tendency to want to consciously view the patient entirely in passive terms, as the victim of their psychiatric syndrome and to treat them accordingly. As we have noted with the High Expressed Emotion research there are advantages to this both therapeutically and in terms of the ease with patients can be managed. There are, however, costs, not least in the tendency then to split off from hateful or destructive and aggressive aspects of the patient, which can then not be either addressed or allowed for and which may be expressed as perverse or corrupt relationships within the organization.

Alternatively stereotyped or conventional attitudes may then prevail at the expense of actual understanding.

A man who had killed his mother was eligible for release under supervision, but the authorities as a condition of this, required sincere expressions of regret. Over time the man made statements to this effect and in due course he was released. More careful exploration of this with the man revealed something different, however. The man did not really understand what the staff meant about regret. In fact in his view his mother had let him down; it had been her responsibility to take and to continue to take his murderous attacks and she had clearly failed him by dying. If anybody should be sorry it was she.

A woman was distraught when her youngest child was removed from her by social workers, following the death of her first child who had been killed by her boyfriend. When talked to about her distress, the woman blamed the first child for her predicament, complaining that she would not be in this position if her murdered child had not had asked for his father. If he had not done this, the boyfriend would not have got angry and jealous, he would not have killed him and she would not have lost both her sons and her boyfriend.

Both within individual staff members and within the organization there may be considerable pressure against actual contact with patients; abstract ideas about patients, stereotypes or diagnostic or symptomatic features may replace actual contact. In the examples given, assumptions about the significance of the patients' words and actions owe more to the (understandable) prejudices of staff than their actual meaning. Organizational defences against aggression and the painfully arrived at distinctions that need to be made between aggression and violence, may easily come to hold sway at the cost of being able to respond accurately and effectively.

Violence in Organizations

The broad hypothesis pursued in this chapter is that violence in an organization is not a static thing that is repelled like the projectile that bounces off the riot policeman's shield, or the waves that crash against, and are deflected back from a well-designed sea wall. The underlying assumption here is that violence in an organization sets up a dynamic response with reverberations and echoes that can be observed. The reason for this dynamic theory of violence in organizations is that organizations are fundamentally collections of people, and that violence creates an emotional reaction within those people.

One of Freud's earlier theories on the instincts was the 'hydraulic' theory; libido was like water, with a pressure that if blocked in its normal course would find an alternative way of leaking out; the symptom. Drawing on this analogy, the organization can be likened to a pool, and the violent energy that it is containing, likened to the energy contained in the wave patterns and currents within it.

If the organization is the pool and the violence is the stone thrown into it, then the effect within the organization of a violent assault delivered to it will be the concentric wave pattern emanating from the splash. The pattern of the ripples produced by the initial splash will be affected by a number of different variables. Firstly, where the stone lands in the pool, in the middle or at the edge – in the shallow or the deep – will affect the resulting pattern. An assault by a prisoner on a fellow prisoner will have a different effect on the prison than the assault of a prison officer, of one of the governors or of a visiting dignitary. A frontal assault on an army battalion will have a different effect to a bomb in the command and control centre.

Secondly, the structure of the pool will affect the wave pattern. There may be a walled off harbour area that the ripples do not penetrate, so that the turbulence is not evenly spread. The structure of the organization referred to above in terms of different groups will have an effect on the way the dynamic impact of the violence reverberates round the organization. In many organizations, the management is walled off from the immediate effects of violence as it impacts upon the organization as a whole. In the example of the provocative segregated prisoner described above, an important factor was the communication of the impact of the violence from the immediate staff group to the management group. The manager being appraised of the true impact was better able to mitigate the impact.

Thirdly, the waves will be affected by the nature of the fluid in the pool – water will react differently to custard. The cultural attitude and values of the organization and its staff can completely change the nature perception and interpretation of the violent act.

We have drawn here extensively upon the experience of violence in a particular sort of setting, a prison and the ways in which aggression needs to be drawn upon in order to address and manage issues of violence. The distinction between what we have defined as aggression, as opposed to violence is important in maintaining the integrity of the staff group charged with management or treatment.

12 Some Incomplete Reflections upon Aggression and Violence

In Western society at least, people have striven to become increasingly distant from and independent of the painful realities of their body and its temporal existence. This gives rise to guilty, affective states and anxieties of both depressive and persecutory kinds. The wish to escape from the resulting struggle with these anxieties has become a shadow aspect of creative developments in contemporary society. To take an example; without for one moment devaluing the progress made by the 'work group' activities of medical training, research and practice, fight-flight assumptions have not been banished. It is these that have been a significant driving force in the development of a system of modern medicine that holds out the hope of, even if it fails to deliver, the setting aside of illness and the putting off, of death. The temptation is to try to deny mortality and the vulnerability of corporeal reality not least as a source of guilt inducing affects such as aggression, especially in the realm of omnipotent phantasy. The illusion has been created that illness and death are 'exotic' rather than part and parcel of life and hospitals may come to be organized and used by society, in part, to insulate the depredations and debilitations of serious illness and death; it is nowadays uncommon for people to have close contact with the painful progress of terminal and chronic illness or to see the dead body of even their closest relatives. As we saw in Chapter 11, even the staff of hospitals or prisons whose ostensible task is to address the causes and effects of serious illness or of violence, tend to adopt defensive distancing strategies to protect themselves from the present, painful anxieties to which they are exposed (Menzies-Lyth 1961; Hinshelwood 1987).

In the same way the mechanics of producing the staples of human existence, food, shelter, transport and power, may come to be undertaken in a way that hides people from knowledge and experience of the dirty and even bloody realities of production, along with the aggression and destruction that they involve. Guilt about this aggression and destruction is very potent and the marketing of foodstuffs, consumer goods and the creation of society's infrastructure may all be undertaken in ways that are intended to disguise the extent to which these activities involve aggression and destructive acts accompanied by painful, guilt-laden affective states. 'Constructive' or 'advantageous' aspects come to be advanced and emphasized in ways that serve to deny feelings of guilt and especially the depressive and persecutory anxieties that are evoked in consequence. 'Good' marketing is often based on creating the illusion that whatever is being offered has little cost relative to the gain, not only financially but also in terms of the depressive or persecutory anxieties that possession entails. By means of splitting, and through recourse to projective identification, people may divest themselves of the responsibility that they have for the aggression and destructiveness that is an inevitable consequence of existence, locating it instead in some other individual or group of individuals. This universal tendency unchecked is an important component part of sectarianism and racism and a serious disruptive force in individual, social and especially political development.

As a corollary of this tendency towards the reification and disavowal of aggression the destructive aspects of aggression have increasingly come to be emphasized; as we have noted aggression is often treated as though it were synonymous with destruction. The more 'out there' aggression and violence become, the more menacing they are felt to be. But even destruction must be set in context. Meltzer's ruined columns, referred to in Chapter 7 (Meltzer 1986), would not have been made in the first place without destruction of the vegetation on the temple site or the virgin marble hewn from the rock matrix. Destruction is an integral part of construction and so too is aggression part of human growth and development. The painful work of taking responsibility for aggression, for its integration and for true reparation, as opposed to manic denial is, as Klein demonstrated, a fundamental building block of human, psychological growth and development, even if this is a lifelong task rather than a 'developmental stage'.

So, following our excursion into aggression and violence, what conclusions can be drawn? We proposed at the beginning that our exploration would be incomplete, and this seems to have been borne out, and it is on this basis that we make some final general comments, and propose some thoughts about the relevance of these to analytic thinking and practice.

Firstly, if our distinction between aggression and violence is a useful and meaningful one, then clinically their differentiation is critical but also very difficult. Most analysts and therapists will be familiar with gross confusions, for example, as encountered in the perversions, of the 'fair is foul and foul is fair' kind, or in horizontal splitting exemplified by Rosenfeld's case cited in Chapter 8 (Rosenfeld 1987). These are difficult and often shocking when come across; the apparently satisfactory progression of an analysis, which ends in the fortunately infrequent, sudden, unannounced, unexpected and unexplained departure of the patient. More difficult still, however, is the everyday work of considering patient's material in order to apprehend the qualities of the patient's mental states of mind. Important distinctions need to be discerned about the interplay of developmentally constructive and destructive elements; in particular distinguishing the development and elaboration of qualities of mind and relations from those that that are mutilating, amputating suicidal or killing; making distinctions between infantile polymorphous perversity as opposed to perversion proper, for example.

Secondly, an important sub-text in this book, has concerned the development of mind, the operation of anti-mind forces and the ways in which aggression, for example, gives rise both to behaviour and to mental phenomena, constructive and destructive. Where integrated, aggression is an important component part of unconscious autonomic action but is also a precondition for properly psychological states. Where disintegrated, it gives rise to violence, again expressed either as behaviour or in states of mind.

Thirdly, we have commented upon the tendency to conflate behavioural and psychological phenomena. A further central task in analytic work is to distinguish behaviour from mentality and this can only be done by means of understanding the meaning of behaviour rather than trying to infer meaning *from* behaviour. In any analytic work, context is everything. Unfortunately the words 'constructive', 'creative' and 'destructive' are used in analysis and analytic theory too casually or in order to mislead. In either case in a way that implies that the value or meaning of a given subject is self-evident. In reality it may do nothing more than signify the approval or disapproval of an analyst or therapist with a particular part of the patient's personality. At best this may be an expression of the analyst or therapist's intuitive understanding of the matter's developmental significance for a patient. Just as often, however, it will express the analyst's failure to discern the meaning and value of the matter, replacing the analytic relationship with a set of conventions or generalizations derived from stock basic assumptions, theoretic abstractions or social mores. A central aspect of our book, therefore, has been an attempt to approach aggression and related phenomena from a position, which does not prejudge its significance or value, but seeks to understand and evaluate it in terms of the patient's psychological development. Most often this will be achieved through an understanding of the transference/countertransference relationship, by which means the qualities of the relations between the patient's internal objects can be discerned, for example, whether they are internal objects are in a relation that augments or damages.

Fourthly, the tendency towards prejudice in human beings is not to be underestimated. We correlate pleasurable with good and painful with bad. If it is sweet we like it, if it is sour we are less likely to. If it is beautiful it is good, if it is ugly it is bad. Truth is beauty, ugliness a sin. If it is eloquent it is valuable, if it is badly or hesitatingly stated it lacks interest. If it is melodious it elevates us, if it is dissonant we tend to withdraw. All of this is rubbish of course. Articulacy is no measure of veracity and without pain we are lost. But the aversive power of that which is unpleasurable is in-built. The discomfort caused by the occlusion of a baby's nose during feeding is four times more lasting in terms of the baby's expectations than a feed, which is experienced, as pleasurable (Stern 1985). There are more neurological connections made with greater rapidity during painful experiences compared with pleasurable experiences (Damasio 2003). Such a state of affairs can easily be seen to carry important evolutionary advantages and maturity in large part consists of the learned ability to develop discrimination.

Fifthly, disintegrative aggression is employed in the projection of aggression as well as being that which is disavowed; as we have noted, aggression is not only the essence of the destructive act but also what is brought to bear upon the felt, implications of the act. Lady Macbeth states it thus in Act 1 Scene 5, of Macbeth,

Come you spirits that tend on mortal thoughts! Unsex me here.
And fill me from the crown to toe top full
Of direst cruelty; Make thick my blood.
Stop up the access and passage to remorse,
That no compunctious visitings of nature
Shake my fell purpose, nor keep peace between
The effect of it.

(Shakespeare 1606)

As with Lady Macbeth the aggression that is brought to bear in order to effect violence may be disguised in the aggression that is brought forward to justify and rationalize violence. So while the aggression is located in the other, it at the same time is denied in the self, in a 'this will hurt me more than it will hurt you' kind of justification. One consequence of this is the way in which people who recourse to violence seem often to be burdened with a rigid and overwhelming superego. While aggression, unmodified is in phantasy projected, in phantasy too the aggression is felt to menace and define the self. Unavailable for thought or enriched internal and external relations, the tendency is towards critical, rigid and impoverished relations with internal and external objects and brittle, fragile personal relations and psychological integrity. Violent people are often people who are afraid of their aggressive capacities and their capacity for aggression, confusing the aggressive phantasy for violence and ironically resorting to violence in their attempts to distance themselves from their aggression. In consequence a vicious circle is created which has all the characteristics of grabbing a tiger by the tail. Clinically the difficulty is in breaking into the vicious circle.

Finally, we would like to summarize our thoughts about what the relevance of this is for analytic practice. If a central aspect of analysis as a mode of treatment, a method of scientific enquiry and a cultural force is the development, elaboration and explication of mind and the reinstatement and modification of states of mind which have in phantasy been disposed of, then the differentiation of undifferentiated mental elements must be a central aspect of the analytic task. The function of analysis and analytic work is to discern the qualities and meaning of the contents of a patient's mind and in particular affective experience. This may be usefully differentiated from therapeutic approaches to patients based upon the 'benign' reinforcement of splitting, the categorization of patient material or the analysis of material provided by a patient. All of these latter matters are fixed: the contents of the patient's mind are not fixed, however. In the analytic session, affective states ebb and flow, changing from moment to moment and it is not possible to attribute a fixed value or meaning to any material that emerges.

This realization is what differentiated Freud's *Interpretation of Dreams* (Freud 1910a) from the attribution of fixed qualities to dream images, favoured by those people (including it must be said by some people who have trained and identify themselves as analysts) interested in establishing would-be-omnipotent 'parental' systems rather than feeling able to trust the internal parents. These two approaches may be confused, but the messianic and prophetic tone of the former, with appeals to external authority, conviction, suggestion and 'persuasion' (Freud 1910c) may be contrasted with an approach which values patience, uncertainty, autonomy and authority based upon experience (Meltzer 1986). Freud and later analysts' understanding of context enabled them to develop the understanding that meaning has a dynamic quality, which in the analytic situation may only be realized through the transference/countertransference relationship. We considered in Chapter 6 how this is true at all the levels of human functioning from the basic physiological to the abstract mental.

In analysis there may often be an unconscious anti-analytic corollary to the conscious analytic attitude of the analyst, something along the lines that Freud seemed to have in mind with his original concept of countertransference as the analyst's neurotic transference to the patient. In reality, assertions about 'creativity' and 'destructiveness' have no value analytically except descriptively. The creation of a particular artefact or the engagement of a particular type of behaviour, activity or relationship will often attract the sobriquet 'creative' or 'destructive' and this may be accurate, but too often the implied qualities will be deemed to be self-evident when they are not.

The value of analysis is that it allows for the discernment of meaning and value at the level of individual experience and identity rather than masked by conventionality and appeals to social norms. The actual qualities of a given psychological phenomenon can often only be understood in the moment of the ebb and flow of development, regression and anti-developmental elements. We cannot talk about the creativeness or destructiveness of a paintings or play. Where we can discern this at all, it can only be in terms of the confluence of the various elements. It is both analysis' great strength and its weakness that it has such a narrow but greatly magnified focus.

We have considered the way in which historically, analytic models of human psychological growth and development have tended to evolve by extrapolating from psychological processes and mechanisms encountered in clinical work with mentally disordered patients or disordered aspects of patients. Such an approach has reaped great benefits in terms of providing a framework within which it has been possible to organize and begin to understand clinical observations and experience in relation to aggression and violence. This need not, however, lead us to ignore the problems that have arisen as time has gone on. We have contended that the predominance of an approach based from concepts intended to account for pathology has, in important respects, distorted and more importantly limited the usefulness of the conceptual tools that we have at our disposal.

In our exploration of the issues of aggression and violence, we have argued for the development of an analytic model that reframes dynamic developmental processes and mechanisms in terms of normal development. This is not a recent innovation. Bowlby was the first person to systematically approach this and others followed. More recently, analytically orientated theorists such as Stern and Fonagy have augmented and in some respects disputed models based on clinical work and direct observation of mothers and babies, developed originally by Anna Freud, Melanie Klein and their followers. These recent developments have made significant contributions to the understanding of infant development on the basis of empirically derived research as opposed to speculative modelling often, originally arrived at, on the basis of clinical work with adults rather than children.

In our exploration of the issues of aggression and violence, it has seemed as if 'totemic' and 'apostolic' aspects of the development of analytic models has undermined the mainstream of analytic theorizing and a major weakness of the 'normal developmental' approach has been the extent to which behavioural observation has been drawn upon heavily for raw material, when examining both infant development and adult and infant psychopathology. The strength of analytic ideas has been the extent to which they offer a way of penetrating and understanding subjective experience. Inevitably, subjectively derived experience has been relied upon heavily, and this has generated criticism about analytic theory's objective validity in relation to aggression and violence. Although attempts have been made at objective corroboration as a way of attempting to refute criticism and defend analytic ideas against accusations that it is unscientific, subjective, unfalsifiable and so on, these have generally been weakened by the absence of models which integrated objective and subjective aspects.

Theories of aggression and violence that depend too much on behaviour may generate theories that are psychologically superficial. Elsewhere subtle shifts in the argument may be introduced so that observable behaviour may be used, to stand as substitute for psychological elements, where these cannot easily be conceptualized. In the field of aggression and violence there has been a particular tendency to do this as behaviour, which has lend itself to the description 'violent' or has been experienced as violent by the observer, has been used as though it is interchangeable or identical with, 'violent' states of mind. Alternatively violence has been seen as lacking mental correlates and as we have noted, described as 'mindless'. We have commented in Chapter three on Fonagy's work (Fonagy & Target 1999a) in this regard. Violence is often talked about as though it is only behaviour; we have argued that this is not the case. Violence in our view is a psychological phenomenon which *may* have behavioural consequences rather than vice versa.

If those accounts of aggression and violence that attempt to draw upon empirical evidence carry greater conviction from a scientific point of view, they fail to match more mainstream analytic theorizing in their capacity to account for psychological phenomena. Part of the importance of Klein and her followers is that, based upon clinical observations in depth, they have articulated a theory of psychological functioning which transcends superficial assumptions about the correlation between behaviour and mental states and both describes and suggests a model for the complexities and subtleties of mental life which includes its primitive, irrational roots while at the same time connecting this with sophisticated psychological functioning. At the same time it includes a theory of mind and mentation which links the body to behaviour but at the same time is separate from it. In particular the Kleinian explication and exploration of internal worlds and internal objects has allowed for the development of a concept of mind, which is not necessarily hidebound in the way that more polarized theories tend to be. From this perspective, phantasy is the very stuff of mind and all mental activity arising out of it rooted in unconscious phantasy. The distinction then is not between phantasy and reality, but the extent to which unconscious phantasy may be realized in reality and plays the part of precursor to conscious thought (in the way described by Bion in the Grid) or may be used defensively as a way of escaping from affective states, which reality is felt to precipitate.

We have suggested that the reframing of human growth and development and the reconceptualization of psychological processes and mechanisms along the same lines may allow for a fuller integration of models based upon empirical observation with models that privilege the mental world. Pathological mechanisms may then be understood as the employment of normal psychological mechanisms in a defensive way.

In Chapter 6, we considered the ways in which projective identification based upon sympathetic processes of identification at very basic levels of bodily, sensory and affective experience provide prototypical patterns of communication during infant development and for the background to all communication in adult life including, communications made at 'higher' levels, for example, through speech or the production of artefacts. In pathological situations, projective identification is utilized not as a means of communication but as a means of evacuating unbearable affective states or those perceptual or sensory experiences that are feared would lead to unbearable affective states. To give a slightly different sort of example, we have considered too how the limitations imposed by the normal processes of perception can be exploited for defensive purposes; an infant, for example, has initially no perceptual grounds upon which to link an experience of a good feed with another experience of a bad feed even though both feeds may be at the same breast. The pleasurableness or unpleasurableness of the experience is likely to be its defining characteristic. Only over time and after a good deal of psychological development will the infant come to experience both qualities as aspects of the same object. This in our view does not involve splitting. Nonetheless the illusion created by the 'good' feed, of an all-good object is available for exploitation and provides the imaginative basis of active splitting.

With regard to aggression we have described the ways in which aggression initially encountered in unintegrated form, say as part of an emotional experience of the primary object, may be available through the processes of projective and introjective identification, for integration. In the absence of the attunement that allows for projective and introjective identification to take place, the aggression is experienced as overwhelming and a threat to the dependent relationship with the object. It is in this situation that the tendency towards various types of splitting takes place along with evacuatory and destructive projective identification. We have located the origins and mechanisms of violence in the violating unbearable affective experience, which occurs as a consequence of failures of attunement or affective containment and in the projective, evacuatory psychological defences that then arise.

We have proposed that a model based on normal development suggests ways in which psychological mechanisms might operate in ordinary circumstances to develop strong (because integrated and consistent) mental structures, the capacity to tolerate imagination as a basis for thought rather than hallucinatory gratification and the development of increasingly complex characteristics of mind. Development can be seen as proceeding from unintegrated states through to states of relative integration that are relatively stable, albeit proceeding in a dialectical fashion. In pathology, the same processes employed defensively lead to the formation of unstable (because inconsistent) mental structures, the exploitation of imagination to withdraw from reality, polarized and rigid characteristics of mind and the tendency towards psychologically evacuatory action.

Aggression may be said to include raw undifferentiated, unmodulated or mediated unpleasurable subjective mental states which give rise both to automatic behavioural consequences, for example, of a 'flight/fight' kind, which is intended to reorder, say an infant's orientation to its world or to some of the objects in his or her world, and to subjective affective experience. The seeking of pleasure giving as opposed to unpleasure-giving objects is an important component of this. Such situations are likely to be complex and modified by the extent to which they involve not just single affects, but a multiplicity of affects; with aggression, fear or hunger, for example.

Failure to modulate affective experience especially in early infancy results in the failure to develop both physical and mental structures with which to manage affective states; aggression leading to violence, for example. Failure to develop the neurological/psychological structures with which to contain affects like aggression results in the individual having to resort to relatively gross means of managing affective states. Gross splitting and projective identificatory processes are then employed in defence way as a means by which affective states, felt to be overwhelming, can in phantasy be evacuated into an object. Omnipotent control of the outside world, for example, through the provocation and eliciting of painful affects in the other may be used to achieve this. Affects can either give rise to action or alternatively to the generation of a mental world, which includes thought and finally thinking.

It is this 'thinking about feeling' and especially thinking about affective states less differentiated than feeling that forms the backbone of all development, including infant development, learning and analysis. In the former, more problematical are the states that arise in relation to failures of integration, where raw affective states remain relatively undifferentiated and unmodified by the containment provided by the container. Mother and child, teacher and pupil, analyst and patient. Among these it is the analytic relationship, which is structured to both reveal the pattern of sticking and facilitating attempts to unstick it.

This formulation allows us to move away from the idea that the differences between aggression and violence are merely quantitative. Violence has a different quality to aggression, which is merely the 'raw material'. If violence is one of the things that may be done with this raw material so too is the development of mind. Aggression is necessary in order to establish, tolerate and value difference and bring about separation both physical and psychological. Violence is brought to bear in order to attempt to do away with separateness and separation. The delicacy of the balance between aggression and violence is, for example, expressed in the way in which, say cultural or ethnic differences are valued as enriching; but this involves an appreciation of the difference to the self as opposed to guilty defensive over-identification because of an incapacity to bear the aggression which goes with separation or apartheid-type or ethnic-cleansing solutions where all that is hated is located in the 'other'. This may be compared to violence of one sort or another, which may be bought to bear in order to deny or attempt to do away with difference. The polarizing tendency of such splitting to divide along the lines of spurious, but visible differences is of course well known.

What relevance has this for the clinical situation? Does it really matter? Aggression seems to be particularly sensitive to the integration/disintegration polarity that we have outlined. Distinction and differentiation is the basis of analytic work, and it is from this that many therapeutic benefits have been shown to derive (Fonagy, 1999b; Roth & Fonagy 2005). Aggression presents with particular difficulties because it may be the affect, which is disintegrated as well as the force that is brought to bear in order to achieve the disintegration. This includes both in the attempt to elucidate the qualities of the material with which a particular patient is presenting or with difficult, potentially uncontained patients split off from their aggressive affects and despairing about ever having them contained. If the tendency is towards negation of mind then this has implications in the clinical/treatment situation including the tendency between analyst and patient towards collusion to deny the painful reality of aggressive relations.

In this book, we have not sought to propose a comprehensive theory of aggression and violence; we only suggest that some of the assumptions, which have informed thinking and debate in this area might be reconsidered. Our dissatisfaction with many of the conceptual tools in common currency stems in part from what we consider to be the limitations of the concepts and conceptual frameworks available and partly as a consequence of our feeling that these have often been confused, misused and conflated. In order to reconsider matters we have attempted not only to differentiate aggression from violence but also explore the links between them. In the process we have considered not only the function of affects generally, but also the extent to which the disintegration of affects, exemplified in our view by violence, may be seen as opening the way towards an understanding of the origins, nature and function of mind even if this is only possible because of the way in which violence involves the negation of mind.

References

Alexander, F., French, T. M. *et al.* (1946) *Psychoanalytic Therapy: Principles and Application* (New York: Ronald Press).

Alvarez, A. (1997) Response to Morrison, B. 'On violence and childhood: BAP annual lecture', *British Journal of Psychotherapy*, 14 (4).

Astor, J. (2001) 'Is transference the 'total situation?', *Journal of Analytical Psychology*, 46 (3).

Balint, M. (1968) *The Basic Fault: Therapeutic Aspects of Regression* (London: Tavistock).

Bateman, A. (1999) 'Narcissism and its relation to violence and suicide', in *Psychoanalytic Understanding of Violence and Suicide*, R. Perelberg (ed.) (London: Routledge).

Bateman, A. and Fonagy, P. (2004) *Psychotherapy for Borderline Personality Disorder: Mentalization-Based Treatment* (Oxford: Oxford Medical Publications).

Bateman, Fonagy (2003) 'The development of attachment-based treatment program for borderline personality disorder', *Bulletin of the Menninger Clinic*, 67 (3), 187–211.

Bell, D. (2001) 'Who is killing what or whom? Some notes on the internal phenomenology of suicide', *Psychoanalytic Psychotherapy*, 15 (1).

Bick, E. (1968) 'The experience of the skin in early object relations', *International Journal of Psycho-Analysis*, 49, 484–486; republished in (1987), *The Collected Papers of Martha Harris and Esther Bick* (Strath Tay: Clunie Press).

Bion, W. R. (1968) *Experiences in Groups* (London: Tavistock Publications).

Bion, W. R. (1970) *Brazilian Lectures* (London: Karnac Books).

Bion, W. R. (1980) *Bion in New York and Sao Paulo*, F. Bion (ed.) (Strath Tay: Clunie Press).

Bion, W. R. (1984a) *Elements of Psychoanalysis* (London: Karnac Books).

Bion, W. R. (1984b) *Learning from Experience* (London: Karnac Books).

Bion, W. R. (1984c) *Elements of Psychoanalysis* (London: Karnac Books).

Bion, W. R. (1984d) *Attention and Interpretation* (London: Karnac Books).

Bion, W. R. (1987) 'Attacks on linking', in *Second Thoughts* (London: Karnac Books).

Bion, W. R. (1989) *Two Papers: The Grid and the Caesura* (London: Karnac Books).

Bion, W. R. (1992) *Cogitations* (London: Karnac Books).

Blum, H. P. (1994) *Reconstruction in Psychoanalysis; Childhood Revisited and Recreated* (Madison: International Universities Press Inc).

Blum, H. (2003) 'Repression, transference and reconstruction', *International Journal of Psychoanalysis*, 84, 497–502.

Bollas, B. (1987) *The Shadow of the Object* (London: Free Association Books).

Bowlby, J. (1944) 'Forty-four juvenile thieves: Their characters and home life', *International Journal of Psychoanalysis*, 25, 1–57, 207–228.

Bowlby, J. (1971) *Attachment and Loss Volume 1; Attachment* (London: Penguin Books).

Britton, R. (1998) 'Publication anxiety', in *Belief and Imagination* (London: Routledge).

Cambell, D. and Hale, R. (1991) 'Suicidal acts', in J. Holmes (ed.) *Textbook of Psychotherapy in Psychiatric Practice* (London: Churchill Livingstone).

Campbell, D. (1999) 'The role of the father in a pre-suicidal state', in *Psychoanalytic Understanding of Violence and Suicide*, R. Perelberg (ed.) (London: Routledge).

Camus, A. (2000) *The Myth of Sisyphus* (London: Penguin Modern Classics).

Carpy, D. (1989) 'Tolerating the countertransference: A mutative process', *International Journal of Psychoanalysis*, 70, 287.

Cartwright, D. (2002) *Psychoanalysis, Violence and Rage-Type Murder; Murdering Minds* (Hove: Brunner-Routledge).

Carvalho, R. (2002) 'Psychic retreats revisited: Binding primitive destructiveness or securing the object? A matter of emphasis?', *British Journal of Psychotherapy*, 19 (2).

Carvalho, R. (2003) Book Review 'Supervising and being supervised', *Journal of Analytical Psychology*, 48 (5), 719–723.

Casement, P. (1985) *On Learning from the Patient* (London: Tavistock).

Chasseguet-Smirgel, J. (1984) *Creativity and Perversion* (New York: W.W. Norton).

Cleckley, H. (1941) *The Mask of Sanity* (reprinted 1976) (St Louis: CV Mosby).

Cohen, S. (1972) *Folk Devils and Moral Panics* (reprinted 2002) (London: Routledge).

Cordess, C. and Cox, M. (1996). 'Preface: In and out of the mind', in *Forensic Psychotherapy*, C. Cordess & M. Cox (eds) (London: Jessica Kingsley Publications).

Damasio, A. (1999) *The Feeling of What Happens* (London: Vantage).

Damasio, A. (2003) *Looking for Spinoza* (London: Vantage).

De Zulueta, F. (1993) *From Pain to Violence* (London: Wurr Publishers).

Durkheim, E. (1951) *Suicide. A Study in Sociology* (trans/eds) A. Spaulding & G. Simpson (Glencoe: Free Press of Glencoe).

Erickson, E. (1951) *Childhood and Society* (London: Imago).

Fairbairn, R. (1952) *Psycho-analytic Studies of the Personality* (London: Routledge & Kegan Paul).

Fonagy, P. (1991) 'Thinking about thinking: Some clinical and theoretical considerations concerning the treatment of a biorderline patient', *International Journal of Psycho-analysis*, 72, 1–18.

Fonagy, P. (1999) 'Memory and therapeutic action', *International Journal of Psychoanalysis*, 80, 215–225.

Fonagy, P. (2003) 'Rejoinder to Harold Blum', *International Journal of Psychoanalysis*, 84, 503–508.

Fonagy, P., Moran, G.S. and Target, M. (1993) 'Aggression and the psychological self', *International Journal of Psychoanalysis*, 74, 471–485.

Fonagy, P., Steele, M., Steele, H., Moran, G. and Higgins, A. (1991) 'The capacity for understanding mental states: the reflective self in parent and child and its significance for security of attachment', *Infant Mental Health Journal*, 12, 201–218.

Fonagy, P. and Target, M. (1996) 'Personality and sexual development, psychopathy and offending', in *Forensic Psychotherapy*,

C. Cordess & M. Cox (eds) (London: Jessica Kingsley Publications).

Fonagy, P. and Target, M. (1999) 'Towards understanding violence: The use of the body and the role of the father', in *Psychoanalytic Understanding of Violence and Suicide*, R. Perelberg (ed.) (London: Routledge).

Fordham, M. (1957) 'Biological theory and the concept of the archetypes', in *New Developments in Analytical Psychology* (London: Routledge, Kegan Paul).

Fordham, M. (1974) 'Defences of the self', *Journal of Analytical Psychology*, 19 (2).

Fordham, M. (1976) *The Self and Autism* (London: Academic Press).

Fordham, M. (1985a) *Explorations into the Self* (London: Academic Press).

Fordham, M. (1985b) 'Abandonment in infancy', *Chiron*, 2 (1).

Fordham, M. (1988) 'The infant's reach', *Psychological Perspectives*, 21.

Fordham, M. (1995) *The Fenceless Field*, R. Hobdel (ed.) (London: Routledge).

Fordham, M. (1996) *Analyst–Patient Interactions*, S. Shamdasani (ed.) (London: Routledge).

Freud, A. (1963) *The Ego and the Mechanisms of Defence* (London: Tavistock).

Freud, S. (1895) *Project for a Scientific Psychology*, Standard Edn I.

Freud, S. (1905) *Three Essays on Sexuality*, Standard Edn VII.

Freud, S. (1910a) *The Interpretation of Dreams*, Standard Edn XX.

Freud, S. (1910b) *The Future Prospects of Psycho-Analytic Therapy*, Standard Edn XII.

Freud, S. (1910c) *Wild Psycho-Analysis*, Standard Edn XI.

Freud, S. (1914) *On Narcissism: An Introduction*, Standard Edn XIV.

Freud, S. (1915) *Instincts and their Vicissitudes*, Standard Edn XIV.

Freud (1916) *Some Character Types met within Psycho-analytic Work*, Standard Edn XIV.

Freud, S. (1917) *Mourning & Melancholia*, Standard Edn XIV.

Freud, S. (1919) *A Child is being Beaten*, Standard Edn XVII.

Freud, S. (1920) *Beyond the Pleasure Principle*, Standard Edn XVIII.

Freud, S. (1921) *Group Psychology and the Analysis of the Ego*, Standard Edn XVIII.

Freud, S. (1923) *The Ego and the Id*, Standard Edn XIX.

Freud, S. (1927) *Fetishism*, Standard Edn XXI.

Freud, S. (1930) *Civilisation and its Discontents*, Standard Edn XXI.

Freud, S. (1938) *An Outline of Psychoanalysis*, Standard Edn XXIII.

Freud, S. (1939) *Moses & Monotheism*, Standard Edn XXIII.

Freud, S. and Breuer, J. (1895) *Studies in Hysteria*, Standard Edn XX.

Fromm, E. (1997) *The Anatomy of Human Destructiveness* (London: Pimlico Press).

Galway, P. (1996) 'Psychotic and borderline processes', in *Forensic Psychotherapy*, C. Cordess & M. Cox (eds) (London: Jessica Kingsley Publications).

Gilligan, J. (1992) *Violence; Reflections on the Deadliest Epidemic* (London: Jessica Kingsley Publications).

Glasser, M. (1979) 'Some aspects of the role of aggression in the perversions', in I. Rosen (ed.), *Sexual Deviation* (Oxford: Oxford University Press).

Glasser, M. (1994) 'Violence: A psychoanalytic research project', *The Journal of Forensic Psychiatry*, 5, 2.

Glasser, M. (1996), 'The assessment and management of dangerousness: The psycho-analytical contribution', *The Journal of Forensic Psychiatry*, 7, 2, 271–283.

Glasser, M. (1998) 'On violence', *International Journal of Psychoanalysis*, 79.

Goffman, I. (1961) *Asylums* (New York: Anchor Books).

Greenson, R.R. (1965) 'The working alliance and the transference neurosis', *Psycho-analytic Review*, 34, 155–181.

Goffman, I. (1961) *Asylums* (New York: Anchor Books).

Hare, R. (1991) *Manual of the Revised Psychopathy Checklist* (Toronto: Multi Health Systems).

Heimann, P. (1950) 'Countertransference', in M. Tonnesmann (ed.) (1989) *About Children and Children no Longer* (London: Routledge).

Hinshelwood, R. (1987) 'The psychotherapist's role in a large psychiatric institution', *Psychoanalytic Psychotherapy*, 2, 207–215.

Hinshelwood, R. (1989) *A Dictionary of Kleinian Thought* (London: Free Association Books).

Hobbes (1651) *Leviathan* (reprinted 1998) (Oxford: Oxford paperbacks).

Holmes, J. (1993) *John Bowlby and Attachment Theory* (London: Routledge).

Hyatt-Williams, A. (1998) *Cruelty, Violence and Murder* (Northvale New Jersey: Jason Aronson Inc).

Isaacs, S. (1952) 'The nature and function of phantasy', in M. Klein, P. Heimann, S. Isaacs and J. Riviere (eds) (1952) *Developments in Psychoanalysis* (London: Hogarth Press).

Joseph, B. (1985) 'Transference: The total situation', *International Journal of Psychoanalysis*, 66, 447.

Joseph, B. (1997) 'Where there is no vision: From sexualization to sexuality', in D. Bell (ed.) *Reason and Passion: A Celebration of the Work of Hanna Segal* (London: Duckworth).

Jung, C. G. (1916) *The Psychology of the Unconscious*, CW 7 (London: Routledge).

Jung, C. G. (1921) *Psychological Types*, CW 6 (London: Routledge).

Jung, C. G. (1927) *Memorial to J.S*, CW 18 (London: Routledge).

Jung, C. G. (1948) *On the Nature of the Psyche*, CW 8 (London: Routledge).

Jung, C. G. (1963). *Memories, Dreams, Reflections* (London: Collins and Routledge).

Jung. C. G. (1968) *Analytical Psychology; Its Theory and Practice. The Tavistock Lectures* (New York: Pantheon Books).

Kalshed, D. (1996) *The Inner World of Trauma; Archetypal Defences of the Spirit* (London: Routledge).

Kaplan-Solms, K. and Solms, M. (2000) *Clinical Studies in Neuro-psychoanalysis*, (London: Karnac Books).

Khan, M. (1963) *The Privacy of the Self* (London: Karnac Books).

King, P. and Steiner, R. (1991) *The Freud-Klein Controversies 1941–45* (London: Routledge).

Klein, M. (1923) 'The role of the school in the libidinal development of the child', *International Journal of Psychoanalysis*, 5, 312–331.

Klein, M. (1932) *The Psycho-analysis of Children. The Writings of Melanie Klein Vol 2* (London: Hogarth Press).

Klein, M. (1933) 'The early development of conscience in the child', in *Love, guilt and Reparation and Other Works* (1985) (London: Hogarth Press).

Klein, M. (1946) *Notes on some schizoid mechanisms'*, in M. Klein, P. Heimann, S. Isaacs and J. Riviere (eds) (1952) *Developments in Psychoanalysis*, (London: Hogarth Press).

Klein, M. (1952) 'The origins of transference', *International Journal of Psychoanalysis*, 33, 433–438.

Kreeger, L. (ed.) (1971) *The Large Group* (London: Constable).

Lacan, L. (2001) *Ecrits* (London: Routledge).

Laufer, M. and Laufer, M.E. (1995) *Adolecence and Developmental Breakdown: A Psychoanalytic View* (London: Karnac Books).

Leff, J. and Vaughn C. (1985) *Expressed Emotion in Families* (New York: Guilford Press).

Lorenz, K. (1967) *On Aggression* (London: Methuen).

MacDonald, L. (1997) *1915: The Death of Innocence* (London: Penguin Books).

Main, T. (1989). *The Ailment and Other Psychoanalytic Essays* (London: Free Association Books).

Matte Blanco, I. (1975) *The Unconscious as Infinite Sets: An Essay in Bi-logic* (London: Duckworth).

McLynn, F. (1996) *A Biography: Carl Gustav Jung* (London: Bantam Press).

Meloy, J. R. (1988) *The Psychopathic Mind: Origins, Dynamics and Treatment* (Northvale New Jersey: Jason Aronson Inc).

Meloy, J. R. (1992) *Violent Attachments* (Northvale New Jersey: Jason Aronson Inc).

Meltzer, D. (1966) 'The relation of anal masturbation to projective identification' in B. Spillius (ed.) *Melanie Klein Today, Vol 1, Mainly Theory*, Chapter 5 (London: Routledge).

Meltzer, D. (1968) *The Psycho-Analytical Process* (Strath Tay: Clunie Press).

Meltzer, D. (1973) *Sexual States of Mind* (Strath Tay: Clunie Press).

Meltzer, D. (1986) *The Apprehension of Beauty* (Strath Tay: Clunie Press).

Meltzer, D. (1992) *The Claustrum* (Strath Tay: Clunie Press).

Menninger, K. (1938) *Man against Himself* (New York: Harecourt, Brace and Company).

Menzies, I. E. P. (1961) *The Functioning of Social Systems as a Defence against Anxiety: A Report on a Study of the Nursing Service of a General Hospital.* Tavistock pamphlet no. 3 and in M. Lyth (ed.) (1988), *Containing Anxiety in Institutions: Selected Essays*, Vol. 1 (London: Free Association Books).

Milgram, S. (1974) *Obedience to Authority: An Experimental View* (London: Tavistock Books).

Mizen, R. (2002) 'Love, Hate and Violation', in *Love and Hate – Psychoanalytic Perspectives*, D. Mann (ed.) (London: Routledge).

Money-Kyrle, R. (1978) *Collected Papers of Roger Money-Kyrle* (Strath Tay: Clunie Press).

Morrison, B. (1997) 'On violence and childhood: BAP annual lecture', *British Journal of Psychotherapy*, 14 (4).

Moyer, K. (1976) *The Psychobiology of Aggression* (New York: Harper & Row).

Nietzsche, F. (1961) *Thus Spake Zarathustra* (London: Penguin Books).

Ogden, T. (1986) *The Matrix of the Mind* (New Jersey: Jason Aronson Inc).

Panksepp, J. (1998) *Affective Neuroscience* (Oxford: Oxford University Press).

Panksepp, J. and Watt, D. (2003) Book review 'Looking for Sinoza', by A. Damasio, *Neuro-Psychoanalysis*, 5 (2).

Perelberg, R. (ed.) (1999). *Psychoanalytic Understanding of Violence and Suicide* (London: Routledge).

Piontelli, A. (1989) 'A study on twins before birth', *International Journal of Psychoanalysis*, 16, 413–426.

Piontelli, A. (1992) *From Fetus to Child* (London: Routledge).

Popper, K. (1972) *Conjectures and Refutations* (London: Routledge & Kegan Paul).

Racker, H. (1968) *Transference and Countertransference* (London: Hogarth Press).

Redfearn, J. (1985) *Myself My Many Selves* (London: Academic Press).

Rosenfeld, H. (1971) 'A clinical approach to the psychoanalysis of the life and death instincts: an investigation into the aggressive aspects of narcissism', *International Journal of Psychoanalysis*, 52, 169–178.

Rosenfeld, H. (1982) *Psychotic States* (London: Routledge).

Rosenfeld, H. (1987) *Impasse and Interpretation* (London: Routledge).

Roth, A. and Fonagy, P. (2005) *What Works for Whom?* (New York: Guilford Press).

Rycroft, C. (1967) *A Critical Dictionary of Psychoanalysis* (Harmondsworth: Pelican Books).

Sabini, J. and Silver, M. (1982) *Moralities of Daily Life* (Oxford: Oxford University Press).

Sandler, A. M. (2004) 'Institutional responses to boundary violations', *International Journal of Psychoanalysis*, 85, 27–41.

Sandler, J., Dare, C. and Holder, A. (1973) *The Patient and the Analyst* (London: Allen and Unwin).

Schachter, J. (1999) 'The paradox of suicide: Issues of identity and separateness', in *Psychoanalytic Understanding of Violence and Suicide*, R. Perelberg (ed.) (London: Routledge).

Searles, H. F. (1979) *Countertransference and Related Subjects* (Madison: International Universities Press, Inc).

Segal, H. (1997) *Psychoanalysis. Literature and War* (London: Routledge).

Schore, A. (1994) *Affect Regulation and the Origin of the Self. The Neurobiology of Emotional Development.* (Hilldale, NJ: Lawrence Erlbaum).

Schore, A. (2001) 'Minds in the making: attachment–the self-organizing brain, and developmentally orientated psychoanalytic psychotherapy', *The British Journal of Psychotherapy*, 17, 3, 229–328.

Shakespeare, W. (1606) *Macbeth* (reprinted 1980) (Harmondsworth: Penguin Books).

Siegal, D. J. (1999). *The Developing Mind* (London: The Guilford Press).

Sinason, M. (1993) 'Who is the mad voice inside?', *Psychoanalytic Psychotherapy*, 7, 207–221.

Sinason, V. (1986) 'Secondary mental handicap and its relation to trauma', *Psychoanalytic Psychotherapy*, 2, 131–154.

Solms, M. and Turnbull, O. (2002) *The Brain and the Inner World*. (New York: The Other Press).

Spillius, E. B. (1983) 'Some developments in the work of Melanie Klein', *International Journal of Psychoanalysis*, 64, 321–332.

Steiner, J. (1993) *Psychic Retreats* (London: Routledge).

Stern, D. N. (1985) *The Interpersonal World of the Infant* (New York: Basic Books).'

Stevens, A. and Price, J. (1996) *Evolutionary Psychiatry* (London: Routledge).

Stoller, R. (1975) *Perversion: The Erotic Form of Hatred* (New York: Pantheon Books).

Stoller, R. (1985) *Observing the Erotic Imagination* (New Haven & London: Yale University Press).

Storr, A. (1982) *Human Aggression* (Harmondsworth: Pelican Books).

Symington, N. (1996) 'The origins of rage and aggression', in *Forensic Psychotherapy*, C. Cordess & M. Cox (eds) (London: Jessica Kingsley Publications).

Weldon, E. (1988) *Mother, Madonna, Whore; Idealization and Denigration of Motherhood* (London: Free Association Books).

Wertham, F. (1949) 'Cathathymic crisis', *The show of violence* (NewYork: Doubledry and Company Inc).

Whitman, W. (1998) *The Leaves of Grass*(1855) (Oxford: Oxford Paperbacks).

Wiener, J. (1998) 'Under the volcano', *Journal of Analytical Psychology*, 43 (4).

Williams, G. (1997) *Internal Landscapes and Foreign Bodies* (London: Duckworth).

Winnicott, D. W. (1949) 'Hate in the countertransference', in *Through Paediatrics to Psycho-Analysis* (1984) (London: Hogarth Press).

Winnicott, D. W. (1956a) 'Primary maternal preoccupation', in *Through Paediatrics to Psycho-Analysis* (1984) (London: Hogarth Press).

Winnicott, D. W. (1956b) 'The anti-social tendency', in *Through Paediatrics to Psycho-Analysis* (1984) (London: Hogarth Press).

Winnicott, D. W. (1958) 'The capacity to be alone', in *The Maturational Process and the Facilitating Environment* (1982) (London: Hogarth Press).

Winnicott, D. W. (1962) 'Ego integration in child development', in *The Maturational Process and the Facilitating Environment* (1982) (London: Hogarth Press).

Winnicott, D. W. (1986) *Deprivation and Delinquency* (London: Tavistock Books).

Winnicott, D. W. (1988) *Human Nature* (London: Free Association Books).

Zetzel, E. (1956) 'Current concepts of transference', *International Journal of Psychoanalysis*, 37, 369–376.

Index